INTRODUCTION TO

MODERN PILIPINO LITERATURE

Introduction to Modern

PILIPINO
LITERATURE

Edited by
E. SAN JUAN, JR.
The University of Connecticut

TWAYNE PUBLISHERS, INC.

New York

Library of Congress Catalog Card Number: 72-11001

ISBN 0-8057-3129-6

Printed in the United States of America

ALAY SA REBOLUSYONARYONG MASA NG PILIPINAS

Acknowledgments

I am grateful to Mr. Buenaventura S. Medína, Jr., Mrs. Florlinda Soto-Sarmiento, and Dr. José Villa Panganiban for their kind permission to use their translations, and to the authors of the stories and poems included here for their consent. Professor Teodoro A. Agoncillo of the University of the Philippines kindly allowed me to use his authoritative essay for the introduction to this anthology. My wife Delia Aguilar-San Juan made many improvements in the manuscript; and to her, everyone is indebted.

Dr. José Villa Panganiban translated the following selections: José Corazón de Jesús, "A Tree," "My Country"; Cirio Panganiban, "The Doll." Professor Ben S. Medina, Jr., translated the following: Lope K. Santos, "Before the Grave," Pedro S. Dandan, "The Dog and Her Five Puppies," Genoveva Edroza-Matute, "Twilight Embrace," Liwayway Arceo-Bautista, "Thirsty Is the Arid Land," Professor Florlinda Soto-Sarmiento translated the following: Narciso G. Reyes, "Native Land," Cornelio Reyes, "Blood and Brain," Epifanio G. Matute, "Impong Sela." The rest of the selections were translated by E. San Juan, Jr.

I wish to thank the following persons who helped generously in the preparation of the manuscript: Rogelio Mangahas, Fe Buenaventura, Mila Aguilar, Ricardo Lee, Al Q. Perez, Emmanuel T. Santos, Marra Lanot, José Lacaba, Virgilio Vitug, Lamberto Antonio, Federico Licsi Espino, Jr., Esther Mendoza-Pacheco, Bienvenido Balweg, Reynaldo Bautista, Maria Elena Abesamis, and René Hernández. To them all the authors in this anthology are indebted.

Certain phrases and turns of expression in the translations may seem awkward and unidiomatic in English, though they represent the efforts of the translators to capture the flavor and spirit of the original. However, literal translation in general has been the rule in the interest of greater accuracy—except in certain cases where idioms in Tagalog fail to make sense in a literal English version. In some renderings the passive voice is frequently used to suggest the syntax and the thought process in Tagalog. Owing to such defects and difficulties as are inevitable in this kind of endeavor—and which anyone who has attempted translations fully appreciates—this anthology is being offered as an invitation to the reader to go to the original works for the proper and complete appreciation of their artistry.

The identification of Filipino with Tagalog or Pilipino needs no apology or explanation, especially at this stage of the Philippine revolution and the struggle for national democracy. The contemporary literature in English written by Filipinos being second rate and obsolescent, and the other vernacular literatures being impoverished and quite immature, the choice of Tagalog/Pilipino literature is, I think, justly appropriate for an international English-speaking audience. With this audience in mind, I have included only the classic compositions of the major writers—at least their accessible works. Owing to the total neglect of the arts and literature by the Philippine government, the difficulties of securing the originals have often proved insurmountable. In spite of its shortcomings, however, this anthology is the first of its kind in English, or in any language, in the world which reflects the collective effort of the Filipinos to articulate the nationalist revolutionary spirit at this critical stage of history.

Work on this project was begun in 1960, essentially completed in 1965, and revised in 1967.

E.S.J. Jr.

Storrs, Connecticut

Contents

Acknowledgments   vii

Introduction: The Development of the Tagalog Language   1
    and Literature by Teodoro A. Agoncillo

I FROM IDYLL TO IDEOLOGY:
The Background of Modern
Tagalog Poetry   29

LOPE K. SANTOS   42

    Before the Grave   43
    The Poet   44

JOSÉ CORAZÓN DE JESÚS   45

    The Return   46
    A Tree   47
    My Country   48

CIRIO H. PANGANIBAN   49

    The Doll   49

AMADO V. HERNÁNDEZ   52

    Man I   53
    Man II   55
    Life Sentence   57
    Beyond the Hangman's Rope   58
    The Wolf's Counsel   58

Contents

Bartolina   59
The Seed of an Atis   62
Irony   63
Katipunan   63
Menu   64
A Memorial to My Dog   65
Foundation   66
The Visit   67
To a Child Without New Clothes   70
Skeleton   71
Gallery of Eight Outlaws   71
Life   73
Fiat Lux   74
Queen   75
Who First Tempted Eve: The Louse or the Devil?   76
If Your Tears Have Dried Up, My Native Land   76

ALEJANDRO G. ABADILLA   78

Imbecility   79
Greatness: O Poem   79
I Want to Rest   80
The Heart's Core   81
You Are the Light   82
I, the Law of the Inescapable   83
Palm Trees   83
The Poem   84
Like the Rock Crumbling   85

TEO S. BAYLEN   86

Hungarian Rhapsody   87
The Voice of Things to Come   87
You Are a Nail on My Coffin   88
A Broken Clay Pot   89

MANUEL PRINCIPE BAUTISTA   91

I and the Poem   91

Contents

II FROM NAIVETÉ TO IRONY:
Achievement in the Tagalog Short Story   93

AMADO V. HERNÁNDEZ   103
  A Fly on a Glass of Milk   103

NARCISO G. REYES   113
  Native Land   113

SERAFIN C. GUINIGUNDO   119
  Pulsebeat of the City   119

ALFREDO S. ENRIQUEZ   127
  The Head   127

MACARIO PINEDA   132
  A Wedding in the Big House   132

EPIFANIO G. MATUTE   139
  Impong Sela   139

CORNELIO S. REYES   144
  Blood and Brain
                                                144

PONCIANO B. PERALTA-PINEDA   152
  The Fisherman   152

PEDRO S. DANDAN   159
  The Dog and Her Five Puppies   159

ANDRES CRISTOBAL CRUZ   164
  The Ancient Well   165

BUENAVENTURA S. MEDINA, Jr.   174
    The Cat at My Window   174

GENOVEVA EDROZA-MATUTE   180
    Twilight Embrace   180

TEODORO A. AGONCILLO   185
    The Dawn Is Still Dark   185

BRIGIDO C. BATUNGBAKAL   192
    Light: From the Smoke of Gunshots   192

EDGARDO M. REYES   198
    Decline and Fall of a Town   198

LIWAYWAY ARCEO-BAUTISTA   205
    Thirsty Is the Arid Land   205

APPENDIX I   221

EPIFANIO DE LOS SANTOS CRISTOBAL
Time and the Human Spirit in Philippine Literature

APPENDIX II   219

TEODORO A. AGONCILLO
Balagtás: A Voice in the Wilderness

NOTES   227

GLOSSARY   231

INTRODUCTION TO

MODERN PILIPINO LITERATURE

Introduction

The Development of the Tagalog
Language and Literature

BY TEODORO A. AGONCILLO

I

The horizon of Philippine civilization before the coming of the Spaniards may be termed a lost horizon. This is explained by the dearth of materials on the subject, and the little that we have at present comes from the testimonies of the early Spanish missionaries and chroniclers whose works cannot be checked properly. Hence the difficulty of making an exhaustive survey of Philippine literature before the coming of the Spaniards.

It seems certain, however, that the ancient Filipinos had an indigenous culture that mirrored their social life. They had a language which, belonging to the Malayo-Polynesian family of languages, they developed in accordance with the needs of the new environment. The Malays who migrated to the Philippines found themselves in a different geographical environment and developed the media of communication best suited to express their personal, social, and religious idiosyncrasies. Thus the differentiation in Philippine languages which, though showing some divergencies in their lexicon, exhibit, on the other hand, similar structures.[1] Of the Philippine languages, Tagalog (Pilipino) is, by common consent, the most developed and its written literature the most advanced.

The Jesuit priest, Pedro Chirino, writing at the turn of the seventeenth century, said of Tagalog: "I find in it four qualities of the four great languages of the world—the Hebrew, Greek, Latin, and Spanish. It has the mysticism and difficulties of the Hebrew; the distinctive terms of the Greek not only in the common, but more so in the proper names; the fullness and elegance of Latin; and the civility and courtesy of Spanish."[2]

The early Spanish missionaries who worked among the people to propagate the Catholic religion found the Tagalogs possessed of a

1

syllabary that is possibly of Indian provenance. This syllabary was widely used throughout the Philippines, with some modifications, and consisted of seventeen letters—three vowels and fourteen consonants. The vowels are ᜀ (*a*), ᜁ (*e* or *i*), ᜂ (*o* or *u*); while the consonants are ᜊ (*ba*), ᜃ (*ka*), ᜇ (*da*), ᜄ (*ga*), ᜅ (*nga*), ᜑ (*ha*), ᜎ (*la*), ᜋ (*ma*), ᜈ (*na*), ᜉ (*pa*), ᜐ (*sa*), ᜆ (*ta*), ᜏ (*wa*), and ᜌ (*ya*).

A consonant with a diacritical mark above is pronounced with either an *e* or an *i*, thus: ᜊᜒ (*be* or *bi*). If the diacritical mark is below, the vowel that accompanies it is either *o* or *u* thus: ᜊᜓ (*bo* or *bu*).[3] The early Filipinos wrote from top to bottom, and from to left to right.[4]

Up to the Spanish colonization of the Philippines, the Tagalog language had been influenced, through direct and indirect contact, by Chinese, Arabic, and Sanskrit. Hence the existence in the early Tagalog dictionaries of such Chinese words as *am* (rice broth), *ate* (appellation given to elder sister), *batutay* (pork sausage), *buwisit* (bad luck, misfortune), *hikaw* (earring), such Arabic words as *hukom* (judge), *sulat* (letter), and such Sanskrit words as *basa* (read), *kati* (ten millions), *dusa* (suffer, suffering).

II

The early Spanish missionaries found the Tagalogs with a literature written in the autocthonous syllabary on bark of trees, leaves of plants, and bamboo. The literature consisted of *sabi* (maxims), *sawikaín* (proverbs), *bugtóng* (riddles), *súliranin* and *indulanin* (street songs), *talindáw* (boat songs), *diyuna* (songs of revelry), *kumintáng* (a war song which developed into a love song), *kundiman* (love song), *dalít* and *umbáy* (dirge), *tagumpáy, balikungkong, dupayinin,* and *hiliraw* (war songs), *uyayi* and *helè* (lullabies), *ihiman* (bridal song), *tigpasin* (rowing songs), *tingád* (household songs), and *kutang-kutang* (couplets usually sung by the blind). In most cases the songs were accompanied by dancing, so that the song and the dance, together with the drama, developed almost simultaneously. At other times, the verses were recited. There are no extant examples of these ancient songs and verses, and those that have come down to us had had Spanish influences not only in tone but more so in the versification.

The ancient Tagalogs were quite adept in versification as shown not only in the occasional verses but also in their plays. The latter were written in verse, and maxims and proverbs were employed profusely.

The plays were staged in open spaces or plazas, in the houses of the nobles, and the native temples or places of worship. Staged to the accompaniment of music and the dance, the plays dealt with love, war, legends, the memory of deceased relatives, and the war heroes. The simultaneous development of the stage, the dance, and music led to the differentiation of types. Thus, the dance and music ramified into the *balitaw, balatóng, dalít, hiliraw, kutang-kutang, lulay, indu-lanin, kumintáng, salampati, tagulayláy,* and *bárimbaw,* while the drama, because staged on special occasions, developed into the *pagbati, karagatan, tagayán, pananapatan, sabalán,* and *tibaw.* The last, the *tibaw,* was a play staged on the ninth night following the death of a person. In some remote places of the Tagalog regions, the *tibaw* is still played, though in a modified version and with modern trimmings.

Outside this sketchy, and perhaps inaccurate, knowledge of the distant past nothing definite is known. For when the early Christian fathers stepped on Philippine soil, their religious zeal got the better of them and they proceeded to destroy practically all written records that might, they believed, hinder the propagation of the Catholic faith.[5]

III

The coming of Spaniards did not immediately and radically change either the tempo or the texture of the Tagalog social life. The indigenous floating literature, consisting of legends, myths, maxims, and proverbs, continued to persist, and the early Spanish mission-aries who applied themselves to the study of the Tagalog language recorded these maxims and proverbs in their vocabularies. As the necessity for propagating the Catholic faith grew more intense, the Christian fathers mingled with the Filipinos and ministered to their needs. Such program of activities demanded knowledge of the native languages. It was not at all difficult for them to learn the Tagalog language, for not only were they proficient in linguistics, but they found Tagalog phonetics almost identical with that of Spanish. Father Juan de Quiñones and Father Juan de Plasencia each wrote a grammar and vocabulary of Tagalog which, it may be surmised, were used to advantage by their brethren.[6] In the Manila Synod of 1582, Father Plasencia's *Arte y Vocabulario Tagalo* was approved as a guide because "of the ease by which it permitted an understanding and thorough knowledge of so foreign a language" and because of the "fitness of the terms [in the vocabulary], their efficacy and strength."

The early vocabularies, books of prayers and Christian doctrines were all in manuscript form, for it was not until the last decade of the sixteenth century that a printing press was introduced in Manila. In 1593, the Dominicans put out the first printed book in the Philippines. It was entitled *Doctrina Christiana, en lengua española y tagala.* Printed by xylographic method, the book consisted of prayers in Spanish, with Tagalog translations in roman letters and Tagalog translations in the native syllabary. But printing books by woodblocks was clumsy, and so about 1602 Father Francisco de San Joseph, popularly known as Blancas de San José, introduced printing by typography. Under his direction, Juan de Vera, a Chinese mestizo, printed by movable type the *De los Mysterios del Rosario Nuestra Señora Tagalice.* From then on Tagalog books and pamphlets came off the press regularly as the need for them arose. In 1604, Juan de Vera, now an expert in typography, printed the *Ordinationes Generales Provintiae Sanctissimi Rosarii Philippinarum,* of which the only extant copy so far known *de visu* is now the United States Library of Congress. Father Blancas de San José, who had mastered Tagalog during his stay in Bataan, put out, in 1605 or 1606, his *Memorial de la Vida Christiana en Lengua Tagala,* and in 1610 his *Arte y Reglas de la Lengua Tagala* was printed in Bataan. In the same year, also in Bataan, Tomás Pinpín, popularly called the Prince of Filipino Printers, issued his *Librong Pagaaralan nang manga Tagalog nang uicang Castilla,* a work that was obviously the result of his collaboration with Blancas de San José. Years before the latter left the Philippines (1614), he prepared a Tagalog vocabulary. This work, *Vocabulario de la Lengua Tagala,* was never printed, and the manuscript now lies in the vault of the Bibliothèque Nationale in Paris.

IV

In discussing Tagalog literature under Spain, one should not miss the fact that the friars—the actual leaders of social and community life—brought their influence to bear upon the people and that they fashioned the trend of the Filipino way of thinking. Bearing this in mind, it is not difficult to surmise why Filipino literature during the 333 years of Spanish tutelage was predominantly religious and moral in character and tone. Only in the linguistic works is this tone subdued. The ancient Tagalog proverbs and maxims, even the lullabies and other songs, were impregnated with a religious and moral element. Hundreds of prayer books came off the press, and the people, enchanted by the mysticism of the religious rites and services of the new faith, embraced Catholicism with alacrity. Now their ancient *dalíts* were sung in honor of saints, as in this *dalít* to Saint Augustine:

> *Agusting Amang Marangal*
> *ilao nami't, paraluman,*
>
> (Augustine, the saintly father,
> Our light and guide.)

At the same time, Tagalog was infused, by close contact, with Spanish elements. Thus, the early Tagalog poets, having learned the foreign language, wrote in Tagalog and Spanish verses. They were called *ladinos.* Fernando Bagongbanta wrote octosyllabic verses in Tagalog and Spanish:

> *Salamat nang ualang hanga*
> gracias se den sempiternas,
> *na nagpasilang nang tala*
> al que hizo salir la estrella:
> *macapagpanao nang dilim*
> que destierre las tinieblas
> *sa lahat nang bayan natin*
> de toda nuestra tierra.

And Tomás Pinpín, writing in 1610, wrote verses of five, six, and sometimes, seven syllables:

> *O Ama con Dios*
> O gran Dios mi padre
> *tolongan mo aco*
> quered ayudarme;
> *amponin mo aco*
> sedme favorable;
> *nang mayari ito*
> porque esto se acabe
> *at icao ang purihin*
> y a vos os alaben.

The Spanish missionaries utilized not only the prayer books in propagating the Christian religion but also the stage. The *karagatan* and the *tibaw* were not discouraged since the former, such as it was, dealt with local customs and did not threaten the peace and unity of the people under the aegis of the Cross. In time the *tibaw,* infused with Spanish element, was transformed into the *duplo,* in which the poets extemporized in verses. It was a sort of debate in verse, the male participants of which were called *bellaco* and the women *bellaca*. We shall see how, under the Americans, the *duplo* was transformed into the *balagtasan.*

The first attempt to use the stage as a religious vehicle was made in 1598 when a play, supposed to have been written by one Vicente Puche, was staged in Cebu in honor of its first bishop, Father Pedro de Agurto. Another play on Saint Barbara was staged in Bohol in 1609, and it was this play, so it was claimed, that was responsible for the conversion of the Boholanos to Christianity. Perhaps one of the most potent factors in the rapid spread of Christianity in the Philippines was the introduction of the types of play already laughed out of Europe toward the end of the Middle Ages. They were the religious play known as the *cenáculo* which depicted the passion and death of Christ, the *comedia de capa y espada* or cloak-and-dagger play, and the *moro-moro,* a blood-and-thunder melodrama of combat between the Muslims and the Christians, with the former playing the consistent role of vanquished.

At almost the same time that these plays were being introduced in the Philippines, the Spaniards brought over the type of literature that the inimitable Miguel de Cervantes, through his *Don Quixote de la Mancha,* ridiculed out of existence—the metrical romance. Transplanted in the new soil, the metrical romance branched off into the *awit* and the *corrido.* The former, a heroic-chivalric poem in dodecasyllables, and the latter, a legendary-religious poem in octosyllables, became so popular that the people read practically notning but *awits* and *corridos.* Philippine bibliography records more than a hundred of these metrical romances.

Another type of literature that prevailed during the Spanish occupation was the Passion. Read and sung during the Lenten season, the reading of the Passion symbolized the deep religious sentiment of the Filipinos. To date, there exist several musical variations of the Passion, and the modern life and temper have inspired some innocent souls to sing it rhumba and mambo style—to the horror of the deeply religious. Three Passions have come down to us and are still read during Holy Week. They are the *Pasion ni Jesu Christong P. Natin* (1704), otherwise known as the Aquino de Belen Pasion, after its author, Gaspar Aquino de Belen, a Batangueño printer; the *Mahal Na Pasion* (1814), popularly called the *Pasiong Pilapil,* after the Reverend Dr. Mariano Pilapil, a Filipino cleric who approved the publication of this anonymous work, and *La Pasion de Nuestro*

Señor Jesucristo (1856–58), the so-called *Pasiong de la Merced,* after its author, Aniceto de la Merced.

Novenas, sermons, and moral tracts constituted the other reading fare of the people. A glance at some titles, the majority of which were originally written in Spanish and translated into Tagalog by the Spanish friars and by some Tagalog writers, notably Joaquín Tuason and Pablo Tecson, shows how deeply the friars had conditioned the mentality of the Filipinos. Such tracts as Modesto de Castro's *Urbana at Feliza* (1864); Joaquín Tuason's *Ang manga carangalan ni María* (1878), *Ang Pitong Cabanalan laban sa Pitong Punong Casalanan* (1894), and *Patnubay nang Cabataan* (1892); Father Antonio Florentino Puansen's *Compendio Histórico de la Religión* (1836 or 1837); Father Benito Rivas's *Conceptos Panegiricos del Claus* (1870); Father Pablo Claín's *Ang Infiernong Nabubucsan* (1713) which, in 1871, became *Ang Infiernong Nacabucas;* and many more of similar vein, graced the private libraries of the rich and the well-to-do.

V

So far, most of these types of literature were written or translated into Tagalog by the friars and some Filipino *aficionados.* In examining the written works of the whole period under Spain, one is pained to note how scanty, indeed, are the names of Filipinos who contributed their talent to the development of Tagalog literature. Some, who had a creative urge, contented themselves with writing verses under assumed names or, at best, by appending their initials to their works. Thus, the majority of the *awits* and *corridos* and most of the *comedias* and *moro-moros* remain anonymous to this day. There were, of course, exceptions, and among them were Pedro Suarez Ossorio, Phelipe de Jesús, Vicente García, Juan Dilág, Marcelino Manguiát, Modesto Santiago, Román Ángeles, and most famous of them all, José de la Cruz, popularly called Huséng Sisiw, and Francisco Balagtás.

José de la Cruz (1746–1829) may be regarded as the first Tagalog poet of any consequence. Having learned Spanish and Latin through the tortuous road of self-study, de la Cruz discovered these foreign languages learned, but not the vehicle suited to express his thoughts. Turning to his own language, he wrote occasional poems that, for their melody and simplicity of diction, are matched only by those of his pupil and successor, Francisco Balagtás. De la Cruz lived in an age when poetry was a pastime, when, indeed, any occasion was taken as an excuse for inditing verses, whether the occasion be a christening, a marriage, or a mere invitation to a game. It was not unusual, then, to send out invitations to a party, a marriage, a christening, and the like, in verse form. And in this, de la Cruz was easily the master.

De la Cruz excelled not only in facile verses but also in the *comedia*. In fact, his best poems are often found in the *comedias* he wrote or adapted for presentation to the public on the occasion of a town fiesta. Such plays as *La Guerra Civil de Granada, Hernandez at Galisandra, Reina Encantada o Casamiento por Fuerza, Los dos Virreyes, Príncipe Baldovino, Conde Rodrígo de Villas, Doce Pares de Francia, El Amor y la Envidia, Jason at Media,* and others, some of which, it may be noted, were adaptations from popular *corridos* and *awits,* won the acclamation of the Tagalog public and made the author the foremost writer of his epoch.

De la Cruz was succeeded, after his death, by his talented pupil, Francisco Balagtás (1788–1862). Leaving his native Bigaa, Bulakán, for Manila, he studied at the College of San José and the College of San Juan de Letran where he mastered Spanish and Latin. Between financial depressions—which were frequent—Balagtás wrote verses for the blockheads of his college, and the little he earned thus was spent for his studies. Leaving Tondo about 1836, he settled in Pandakan where he met María Asunción Rivera and promptly fell in love with her. Thrown into prison through the machination of his rival, Balagtás wrote his *Plorante at Laura,* an allegorical *awit* that severely criticized the social evils of his time. The little book was supposedly printed in 1838 by the University of Santo Tomás Press.

Like his predecessor, José de la Cruz, Balagtás wrote many plays written expressly to be staged during town fiestas. About a dozen plays are known to have survived the poet, and among them are *La India Elegante y el Negrito Amante, Orosman at Zafira, Abdal at Miserena, Bavaceto at Dorlisca, Almanzor at Rosalina, Mahomet at Constanza, Don Nuno y Zelinda, Auredato y Astrone,* and *Clara Belmori.* Of these plays, perhaps *Mahomet at Constanza* was the most socially significant, for in writing it Balagtás took the Greek war of independence as a theme to project his idea of freedom at a time when strict censorship precluded the writing of what, according to the Spaniards, was subversive. Balagtás never allowed the presentation of *Mahomet at Constanza* during his lifetime.

VI

It might be suspected that, with the number of *comedias* and *moro-moros* written or adapted to suit local conditions and the taste of the Tagalog public, theaters mushroomed everywhere. This was not the case, however, for though the Filipinos were by nature inclined to theatrical performances, they never seriously undertook the building of genuine theaters. On the contrary, their theaters were nothing but several planks of wood with a roofing of palm or banana leaves.[7]After the last curtain, the planks were removed and carried to another town where the stage presentation was invariably a part of a town fiesta. The Filipino theater, therefore, may be described as a *quita y pone* (withdraw-and-set-up-again) type.

However, attempts had been made to introduce in Manila a semblance of theater. About 1841, the *Primitivo Teatro de Tondo* was built, and probably at about the same time the *Primitivo Teatro de Arroceros* was erected to provide a permanent home for Tagalog plays. Both so-called theaters succumbed, within a few years, to the elements. Another, the *Teatro de Binondo,* was built in 1846, but due to the indifference of the public, its losses at the start of its career led to its early demise. Other theaters were built, such as the *Teatro de Quiapo,* the *Teatro del Príncipe Alfonso,* the *Teatro de Variedades,* the *Teatro Filipino,* and the *Teatro Zorrilla,*[8] but all of them, except the last, did not last long enough to affect the public. Built in 1893 at the corner of what are now Claro M. Recto and Evangelista Streets, the *Teatro Zorrilla* survived for more than thirty years and became, in the middle 1920s, the meeting ground of the two great debaters in verse, José Corazón de Jesús and Florentino T. Collantes.

In some of these theaters, principally in the small ones, the *carrillo,* or shadowgraph, was shown. Supposedly introduced in the Philippines by one Navarro de Peralta,[9] the *carrillo* immediately became popular, and the stage suffered a temporary setback, just as today the legitimate stage is almost nonexistent due to the popularity of the Hollywood-produced moving pictures. The popular *awits* and *corridos* were adapted to the *carrillo,* and *Don Juan Tenorio, Doce Pares de Francia, Ibong Adarna, Siete Infantes de Lara,* and *Don Juan Teñoso* were, through the ingenuity of their producers, seen on the screen.

Most of these theaters were Spanish owned, and all stage troupes were either led by or composed of Spaniards. However, the Filipino partakers in the *comedias* and *moro-moros,* led by Roberto Gabriel, banded together and founded the first Filipino dramatic society—the Compañía Infantil. It had its headquarters in Trozo, and was composed of such popular figures as Ambrosio Gatdulà, Servillano de Vera, Antonio Leysan, Amando Álvarez, Juan F. Bartolomé, Primitiva Tuazón, Adriana Nicolas, Feliza Cleofas, Paulino Casimiro, and others. Another society was founded by Andrés Bonifacio, now a national hero, and soon the Teatro Porvenir was erected in Trozo. This theater was nationalistic and staged Tagalog plays exclusively. The Revolution of 1896 led to the disbandment of the two dramatic societies, some of whose members took to the field to join the "Sons of the People" in their struggle for freedom.

VII

Up to this period, and including that of the revolution, the Tagalog language had been enriched by the adoption of Spanish words and by the literal translation of Spanish phrases and idioms which found acceptance among the people. Handbooks of grammar and books on the Tagalog lexicography were written not only by the Filipinos but also by the Spanish friars. It is to the credit of the friars that instead of suppressing the use of the vernaculars, they in fact encouraged their use and wrote books and pamphlets in Tagalog and other Philippine languages. Aside from Quiñones, Plasencia, and Blancas de San José, other friars like Pedro de San Buenaventura (*Vocabulario de Lengua Tagala,* Pila, 1613), Domingo de los Santos (*Vocabulario de la Lengua Tagala,* Tayabas, 1703), Gaspar de San Agustín (*Compendio del Arte de la Lengua Tagala,* Manila, 1703), Juan de Noceda and Pedro de Sanlucar (*Vocabulario de la Lengua Tagala,* Manila, 1754), Sebastián de Totanes (*Arte de la Lengua Tagala y Manual Tagalog,* Manila, 1745), J. Hevía Campomanes (*Lecciones de Gramática Hispano-Tagala,* Manila, 1872), Toribio Minguella (*Ensayo de Gramatica Hispano-Tagala,* Manila, 1878), Agustín de Coria (*Nueva Gramática Tagalog Teórico Prática,* Manila, 1872), and many others made Tagalog the subject of their intensive studies. Among the Filipinos, Dr. Trinidad H. Pardo de Tavera, José Rizal, and Pedro Serrano Laktáw published studies on Tagalog, Pardo de Tavera published a study of the Sanskrit loanwords in Tagalog (*El Sánscrito en la Lengua Tagala,* Paris, 1887) and another on paleography (*Contribución para el Estudio de los Antiguos Alfabetos Filipinos,* Losana, 1884); José Rizal prepared a study on the Tagalog orthography (*Sobre la Nueva Ortografí de la Lengua Tagala,* Barcelona, 1889) and another on the Tagalog versification (*Die Tagalische Verskunst,* Berlin, 1887); while Pedro Serrano Laktaw prepared a dictionary (*Diccionario Hispano-Tagalog,* Manila, 1889).

The influence of Spanish on the Tagalog language is so profound that today, in spite of the pressure of the American language and culture, Spanish words continue to be adopted into Tagalog. Thus, such words as *sibuyas* (onion), *kabayo* (horse), *bintanà* (window), *mantikà* (lard), *mákina* (machine), *padér* (wall), *silya* (chair), *mesa* (table), *boses* (voice), *beses* (times), and hundreds of others were derived, respectively, from the Spanish *cebolla, caballo, ventana, manteca, máquina, pared, silla, mesa, voz* (plural *voces*), *vez* (plural *veces*), and so on. Not only words were adopted; phrases were translated into Tagalog, such as *dar efecto (bigyáng bisà), al fin (sa wakás), se levanta la sesión (itindíg ang pulog), si se considera (kung áalagataín), más que nunca (higít kailán man), llamar la atención (tawagin ang pansín), por visto (sa malas), aprovechar la ocasión (samantalahin ang pagkakataón), es muy de desear (lubháng kanais-nais), tarde o temprano (malao't mádali),* and a host of others. Even the writing of the Tagalog grammar was, and is still, patterned after the Spanish grammar. Thus, even the official grammar of the Tagalog language, tentatively approved by the Institute of National Language before World War II, is definitely of Spanish vintage—a tropical wine in a Romance bottle.

VIII

In searching for the reason or reasons why Philippine literature developed the worst aspects of medievalism during the rule of Spain, one is inevitably led across the seas to Spain proper. For Spain, at the dawn of the seventeenth century, was no longer the Spain at the height of her intellectual power during the centuries after its conquest by the Moors. She was an intolerant Spain, a Spain where the friars were regnant, a Spain where the masses were ignorant and without freedom of thought, a Spain where corruption in high places was commonplace. The great English historian, Henry Thomas Buckle, said:

The increasing influence of the Spanish Church was the first and most conspicuous consequence of the declining energy of the Spanish government. For, loyalty and superstition being the main ingredients of national character, and both of them being the result of habits of reverence, it was to be expected that . . . what was taken from one ingredient would be given to another. As . . . the Spanish government, during the seventeenth century, did, owing to its extreme imbecility, undoubtedly lose some part of the hold it possessed over the affections of the people, it naturally happened that the Church stepped in, and, occupying the vacant place, received what the crown had forfeited.

* * *

The increasing power of the Spanish Church . . . may be proved by nearly every description of evidence. The convents and churches multiplied with such alarming speed, and their wealth became so prodigious, that even the Cortes, broken and humbled though they were, ventured on a public remonstrance.

* * *

In that country, the Church retained her hold over the highest as well as over the lowest intellects. Such was the pressure of public opinion, that authors of every grade were proud to count themselves members of the ecclesiastical profession, the interests of which they advocated with a zeal worthy of the Dark Ages.

* * *

In such a state of society, anything approaching to a secular or scientific spirit, was, of course, impossible. Everyone believed: no one inquired. . . . Skill and industry worthy of a far better cause, were expended in eulogizing every folly which superstition had invented. The more cruel and preposterous a custom was, the greater the number of persons who wrote in its favour, albeit no one had ventured to assail it. The quantity of Spanish works to prove the necessity of religious persecution is incalculable; and this took place in a country where not one man in a thousand doubted the propriety of burning heretics. As to miracles they were constantly happening, and as constantly being recorded. Saints, too, being in great repute, their biographies were written in profusion, and with an indifference to truth which usually characterize that species of composition.[10]

Buckle then proceeded to cite Spanish documents and scholars to prove the degenerate condition of the country and concluded that since the expulsion of the Moriscos (converted Muslims) in 1609 upon the instigation of the Archbishop of Toledo, Spain had become a backward country. Upward of about a million industrious Spaniards of Muslim descent, who constituted the backbone of Spain, were hounded out of the country with, as Buckle said, "unflinching barbarity." The twilight of Spain dates from this religious persecution.

It is, then, no wonder that when the Spaniards colonized the Philippines, the men of the Sword and the Cross, unable to rise above their level in their own country, transplanted in the colony in the Orient the very conditions then existing in Spain. As in the mother country, the power and wealth of the friars in the Philippines increased scandalously to such an extent that even the highest civil authorities trembled in their boots at the drop of a friar's hat. Education, too, was in the hands of the ecclesiastics, and the social life of any town had its center around the church. All types of literature had to pass the censorship of the Church before they could be granted a license or permit for printing. This *censura previa,* or previous censorship, worked havoc on the intellectual freedom of the writers and was one of the causes of the Filipino intelligentsia's agitation for its abolition. On October 4, 1839, a royal order was issued providing for the establishment of a censors' commission in the Philippines. It was not, however, until October 7, 1856, that a superior decree was promulgated, pursuant to the royal order cited, providing for the establishment of the Permanent Commission of Censors (Comision Permanente de Censura). This commission, as actually established, was composed of four lay members appointed by the governor general, four religious appointed by the archbishop, and a member of the Supreme Court or *Audiencia,* who acted as chairman of the commission.[11]

Under such atmosphere no literature worthy of the name could have been written. The attitude of the friars with respect to the intellectual capacity of the Filipinos created in the latter a sense of inferiority. Thus, Father Miguel Lucio Bustamante, writing his *Si Tandang Basio Macunat* in 1885, expounded his theory, in fiction form, that the Filipinos were fit only to tend carabaos, to pray, and to follow the advice of the friars.

But the latter half of the nineteenth century saw this awakening of the intelligentsia. With the triumph of liberalism in Spain—in fact, in all Europe—liberal ideas began to trickle into the country. This was made easier by the opening of the Suez Canal in 1869, which greatly cut down the distance between Spain and the Philippines. The opening of Philippine ports earlier led to economic progress, and economic progress led to the rise of the Filipino middle class. It was this class that, conscious of its new status in Philippine society, agitated for reforms. This beginning of the movement for reforms resulted, in 1872, in the execution of three Filipino clerics, Burgos, Gomez, and Zamora. The decade that followed this event may be termed a peace of the sword—a peace founded on fear, resentment over the execution of the three priests, and racial conflict. It was made evident to the intelligentsia that it was impossible to initiate reforms in the country without sticking out their necks too far for comfort, and so they secretly sailed to Europe to seek the light that, in their own country, "never was on sea or land."

Of the intellectuals who migrated to Europe, López Jaena, Rizal, M. H. del Pilar, José Ma. Panganiban, Eduardo de Lete, Mariano Ponce, and others became the most popular, not only because of their brilliance, but also because of their spirit of self-sacrifice. The campaigns that these men conducted in behalf of the Philippines may be termed the Propaganda Movement. It began in 1882 when Marcelo H. del Pilar, a lawyer of Bulakán, Bulakán, founded the newspaper *Diariong Tagalog,* a Tagalog-Spanish newspaper that fought for the rights of the Filipinos, and ended in 1896, when del Pilar died penniless in Barcelona and when the revolution unleashed its fury upon the masters. Through the writings of del Pilar, López Jaena, Ponce, de Lete, Panganiban, Antonio Luna, Rizal, and others, the so-called Philippine problem was focused upon the attention of the peninsular Spaniards. The interest of such progressive Spaniards as Morayta and Maura was aroused, and in 1893 the Maura Law was passed providing for municipal reforms in the Philippines. The propagandists, on the other hand, founded, in 1889, their organ *La Solidaridad.* Of these propagandists, two, Rizal and del Pilar, indefatigably defended the Filipinos against the malicious attacks of the friars who, with their newspaper *La Política de España en Filipinas,* wanted to turn back the clock of progress.

In studying the works and character of these two apostles of Philippine progress, one is struck by their opposite temper and techniques. Del Pilar, the elder man, was explosive and aggressive; Rizal was quiet and meditative. The one was a practical politician and a man of action; the other, a thinker and an idealist. Del Pilar wrote in the language of the masses—Tagalog; Rizal wrote in the language of the intelligentsia—Spanish. The one spoke, as it were, from the cockpit; the other spoke from the pulpit. Rizal remained an incurable idealist to the last; del Pilar was a rugged realist who switched his vigorous mind to revolution when he realized that all attempts to initiate reforms proved futile. Rizal could smile through his tears, as when he wrote *Noli Me Tangere* and some of his short pieces like *La Visión de Fray Rodríguez* and *Por Teléfono;* del Pilar could only be contemptuous of the friars, as when he published his *Caingat Cayo* (an answer to the little pamphlet *Caingat Cayó!* by Father

José Rodríguez) and *Dasalan at Toksohan* (a withering satire written as a parody of the catechism).

The writers of *La Solidaridad* influenced the thinking and action, not of the masses, but of the educated and the well-to-do. The latter, however, were diffident, for they belonged to the class that would be intimately affected by any rash action that would, in the final reckoning, upset the status quo. So it remained for Andrés Bonifacio, lowly of origin and occupation, to repudiate the technique of the intelligentsia and to found his revolutionary *Katipunan* with separatist aims. The writings of Bonifacio and his right-hand man, Emilio Jacinto, do not have the polish of the educated propagandists, but they produced a body of works that reflected the needs and aspirations of the masses. They represented in that age a revolt against double-talk, against the "fine writing" that was good to the ear but hardly able to drive the people to take up arms against the oppressors. Bonifacio's *Pag-ibig sa Tinubuang Bayan* (Love of Country), though an inferior poetical piece, was nevertheless an effective weapon that opened the eyes of his countrymen to the necessity of revolt against those responsible for their sufferings. His *Sampung Utos* or Decalogue and his *Ang Dapat Mabatíd nang manga Tagalog* (What the Filipinos Should Know), together with Jacinto's *Liwanag at Dilím* (Light and Darkness), had the effect of strengthening the bonds of unity of the hitherto docile masses and of making them subscribe to the tenets of the revolutionary society. With the secret publication of the *Katipunan's* organ, *Kalayaan,* the number of the society's members swelled tremendously. In August, 1896, the *Katipunan* was still unprepared to wage a full-fledged revolt, but the discovery of its existence and the subsequent arrests and cruelty perpetrated by the Spanish authorities upon the masses drove its members, and the masses with them, to take to the field where they found glory fighting for freedom and the dignity of the individual. The revolution and the coming of the Americans in 1898 sealed the doom of the Spanish empire in the Orient. The Middle Ages in the country were over, and in their fading footsteps there strutted forth a literary movement that represented the temper of the new era.

IX

America's early "days of empire" brought a measure of freedom to the Filipinos. The libel and sedition laws, however, prohibited the Filipinos from making any mention of independence. Within this restricted freedom, the people discussed politics and freely participated in community assemblies where they expressed openly what they thought was good for them. Labor unions, hitherto unknown, mushroomed and clamored for better wages and living conditions. The young writers, now free to buy materials that would not have been allowed to enter the Philippines during the rule of Spain, read avidly the sociological and socialistic works, in Spanish translations, of Grave, Marx, Bakunin, Vandervelde, Fourier, Zola, Spencer, and others. The result was that the Tagalog writers, enjoying more freedom than their *confrères* in Spanish because they wrote in a language unknown to the Americans, succeeded in launching a series of attacks not only against the occupying power but also against the capitalists.

Most potent of the media used by the Tagalog writers was the stage. The *zarzuela,* a musical comedy introduced in the Philippines in 1893, was adopted into Tagalog by Severino Reyes as early as 1902 and became immediately popular, leading to the death of the *comedias* and the *moro-moros.* From then on the nationalistic writers, encouraged by the success of the stage, wrote revolutionary plays intended to be staged. Thus, Juan Abád's *Tanikaláng Ginto* (Golden Chains); Aurelio Tolentino's *Kahapon, Ngayón, at Bukas* (Yesterday, Today, and Tomorrow) and *Luhang Tagalog* (Tagalog Tears); Tomás Remigio's *Malayà* (Free); Juan Matapang Cruz's *Hindi Acó Patáy* (I Am Not Dead); and such other plays as *Sandugóng Panaguinip* (Dream Alliance), a play in Spanish by Pedro A. Paterno and translated into Tagalog by Román Reyes; *Pulóng Pinaglahuan* (Eclipsed Isle); *Tatlóng Pung Salapî* (Fifteen Pesos); and *Kalahì* (Countryman) aroused the nationalistic feelings of the audience, for the plays, symbolically depicting the struggle of the Filipinos for emancipation, vigorously attacked the American occupation of the Philippines.[12] Some of the authors, like Aurelio Tolentino and Juan Abád, were arrested and exposed to the mercy of the courts, for in some instances their plays led to near riots, as when Juan Matapang Cruz's *Hindi Acó Patáy* was staged at the Singalong Theater in 1903. These plays, in the words of the government in its case against Tolentino, were "scurrilous libels . . . which tend to incite and suggest rebellious conspiracies against the United States. . . ."

The imprisonment of Abád and Tolentino, despite the efforts of Manuel L. Quezón, later to become president of the commonwealth, deterred other playwrights from presenting their plays to the public. They contented themselves with staging harmless dramas, such as Román Reyes's *Salamín ng Pag-ibig* (Mirror of Love), Ambrosio

Guzman's *Mga Karaniwang Ugalì* (Common Customs), Román Dimayuga's *Mga Damít ni San Dimas* (St. Dimas's Clothes), Severino Reyes's *Waláng Sugat* (Not Wounded), Manuel Xeres Burgos's *Con la Cruz y Espada* (With Cross and Sword), Patricio Mariano's *Dalawáng Pag-ibig* (Two Loves), Hermógenes Ilagan's *Después de Diós el Dinero* (Money After God), and others.

The period from approximately 1905 to 1930 may be termed the golden age of the *zarzuelas,* for it was during this period that the prolific playwrights produced their best and their most popular works. Patricio Mariano, Severino Reyes, José Ma. Rivera, Pantaleón López, Hermógenes Ilagan, Florentino Ballecer, Precioso Palma, Emiliano Trinidád, and Servando de los Angeles dominated the period. Dramatic societies, such as Compañía de Zarzuela Tagala "Balagtás," Samaháng Ilagan, Gran Compañía de Zarzuela Tagala, and Samaháng Gerónimo, were organized to give impetus to the new drama.[13] At the same time, Filipino music came into its own, for the plays were invariably accompanied by music, and the scores written for the *zarzuelas* by such composers as Gavino Carluén, José Estella, León Ignacio, Simplicio Solís, Juan de S. Hernández, Francisco Buencamino, Bonifacio Abdón, and Calixto Llamas marked, together with some compositions, notably the *kundimans* of Nicanor Abelardo and Francisco Santiago, the apex in the development of Filipino music.

Since 1930, when the "talkies" were introduced from Hollywood, the Tagalog—and for that matter, the Filipino—stage has been in the state of coma. The attempts of Dramatic Philippines[14] during the Japanese occupation to resuscitate the drama and the stage proved successful at first, but after the war, failed miserably. Dramatic Philippines' most successful presentation, *Kuwentong Kutsero,* a radio and stage farce, indicates how the stage could be redeemed. But at this writing,[15] it is doubtful that, with the inroads of the movies, the Dramatic Philippines, the only white hope of Philippine drama and stage, will succeed in its heroic efforts to introduce and keep alive legitimate plays. Today, the Philippine drama is limited to the amateur presentations of college sophomores. A new form of the drama, the radio play, has gone over the airwaves in the form of maudlin song operas.

X

Tagalog prose fiction began when Lope K. Santos, Modesto Santiago, and Valeriano Hernández Peña, writing at the turn of the century, scribbled, respectively, their saccharine novels *Salawahang Pag-ibig* (Fickle Love), *Pagsintáng Naluóy* (Wilted Love), and *Unang Bulaklák* (First Flower). But between 1900, when these novels were written, and 1905, when the labor movement was at its height, Lope K. Santos, now editor of the nationalistic *Muling Pagsilang,* the Tagalog section of *El Renacimiento,* had made a surprising improvement not only in his diction and style but also in his attitude toward society. Influenced first by the socialistic and sociological writings of Marx, Bakunin, Spencer, Zola, and others, and then by the aggressive labor movement headed by Dominador Gomez and Isabelo de los Reyes, Lope K. Santos threw himself into the lap of the awakening labor movement and wrote his novel *Banaag at Sikat* (Rays and Sunrise).[16] The first and only well-written novel in Tagalog, *Banaag at Sikat* is, however, less a novel than a socialistic tract. There are a few chapters that for sheer beauty of exposition and narration might have made the author a genuine artist in words but for his lack of restraint and his overenthusiasm that made his wish father to the thought. Thus, one is bored plowing through pages after pages of long-winded explanations about socialism, the greed and brutality of capitalists, the equality of men, and such catch phrases as would make people today cry "Red"! The characters, in the main, do not talk; they deliver speeches. Incidents are deliberately forced in order to bring about the author's wish. Hence *Banaag at Sikat* remains a tract and belongs to the category of *Uncle Tom's Cabin.*

In studying the Tagalog novels from 1900 to the present, one sees the romantic tendency of the writers. With the exception of Lope K. Santos, who may be called the father of Tagalog Naturalism, the rest are incurably romantic. Iñigo Ed. Regalado *(Madalíng Araw),* Faustino Aguilar *(Pinaglahuan, Busabos ng Palad, Nangalunod sa Katihan,* etc., Valeriano Hernández Peña *(Nene at Neneng, Maginang Mahirap,* etc.), Rosauro Almario *(Nang si Eba ay Likhaín),* José Díaz Ampíl *(Hantik),* Patricio Mariano *(Ang Talà sa Panghulò),* Francisco Laksamana *(Anino ng Kahapon),* Simplicio Flores *(Larawan ng Pag-irog),* Juan L. Arsciwals *(Sakím na Magulang),* Mamerto Hilario *(Pag-ibig at Kamatayan),* and scores of others almost always looked to themselves as heroes and asked the readers to behold them as such. This romantic tradition has gone down to this day, and it is, indeed, difficult to find, except in the short stories, a Naturalist or a Realist. Of the more than a thousand novels written hastily to date, not one, with the probable exception of *Banaag at Sikat,* has any semblance of reality. Love has always been the subject of the novels, and although the subject of love is not bad in itself, the way it is treated by the Tagalog novelists makes it detestable to intelligent readers.

In that literary type which Professor Brander Matthews called the short story, Tagalog is more fortunate. Beginning as mere sketches about 1902, the short story steadily developed through the 1920s and the middle 1930s until, today, it is the most popular reading matter.[17] Such precursors of the short story as Lope K. Santos, Valeriano Hernández Peña, Gonzalo Cue Malay, Rosauro Almario, and Patricio Mariano wrote sketches that laid the pattern for writers of later years to follow. In the two decades that followed 1910, Cirio H. Panganiban, Teodoro E. Gener, Amado V. Hernández, Deogracias A. Rosario, Alberto Cruz, Fausto Galauran, José Esperanza Cruz, Rosalía Aguinaldo, Nieves Baens del Rosario, Vicente G. Cruz, Carmen Herrera, Jovita Martinez, and Hilaria Labog developed the short story along the lines laid for them by their predecessors, namely, that the short story is nothing but an abbreviated novel. It must be admitted that these writers never had the courage to face the facts of life—they were, one and all, escapists and moralists. They were, to use another term, "polite writers," and their age may be called, to use Van Wyck Brooks's phrase, that of the "genteel tradition."

The mid-1930s saw the revolt of the young writers against the Romanticism of their predecessors. The reaction of the new school of writers was sharp and, at times, savage. Gregorio N. García, now traffic judge of Manila, wrote stories that to the romanticists were unpalatable because they portrayed life in its brutal aspects. Brígido C. Batungbakal, Genoveva D. Edroza, Antonio B. L. Rosales, Hernando R. Ocampo, Teótimo S. Buhain, Serafín C. Guinigundo, Macario Pineda, and those who have gone through the college class-rooms started the revolt that shocked the prudes among the writers. Influenced by the writings of Maupassant, O. Henry, Zona Gale, Poe, Saroyan, Hemingway, Anderson, Faulkner, and the Russian Realists the new writers slowly and painfully exerted their influence until today, though still in the minority, they count a decent following, especially in the colleges and universities.

A few anthologies of short stories have been put out as witnesses to the healthy growth of this type of literature. Alejandro G. Abadilla and Clodualdo del Mundo issued in 1935 a collection of short stories, *Mga Kuwentong Gintô*. The stories reflect the romanticism of the early generation of writers. The second anthology, *50 Kuwentong Gintô ng 50 Batikáng Kuwentista*, edited by Pedrito Reyes in 1939, purports to be the authors' best. The Japanese occupation inspired another volume of stories, *Ang 25 Pinakamabuting Maikling Katháng Pilipino ng 1943*, compiled by the editorial staff of the Japanese-directed weekly *Liwaywáy*. This volume sets off its authors from the previous ones by the quality of the stories included and by the attitude of the young writers toward art and life. It is evident that the young writers have developed their technique to a point undreamed of in the preceding epoch.

In 1947, Abadilla persuaded an unsuspecting publisher to put out a collection of the best stories published during the year in all the Tagalog magazines. The result was *Mga Piling Kathâ*, a collection of mediocre stories by some talented writers who have turned to commercial writing for a living. Two years later, in 1949, the present writer made his choice of twenty best stories and clamped them together in a volume called *Ang Maiklíng Kuwentong Tagalog: 1886-1948*. In September, 1952, Genoveva D. Edrosa, probably the best story writer in Tagalog today, privately printed her book of short stories and essays, *Ako'y Isáng Tinig*, with a critical introduction by the present writer.

The short story as a form has come to stay, and the fulminations of the old generation of writers against the Realism and Naturalism of the contemporary practitioners of the art are of no avail. The magazines today, as they have since 1920 or thereabouts, publish more and more stories and fewer and fewer novels. This explains the decline of the novel. But in encouraging the short story, the editors and publishers of the magazines are, however, indiscriminate in their choice of materials: they prefer the saccharine and the maudlin, the mediocre and the fantastic, to the more polished and more significant works. The result is that the short story today, with very few exceptions, has gone back to its age of infancy without having reached its age of maturity. The significant pieces of such contemporary writers as Pablo N. Bautista, Ponciano B. Peralta Pineda, Cezar Francisco, Genevova D. Edroza, Anacleto Ignacio Dizon, Elpidio P. Kapulong, and Pedro Dandan are awaiting the coming of a genuine literary magazine.

Encouragement in this type of literature has come from an entirely unexpected direction. In 1951, the management of *La Tondeña*, a liquor manufacturer owned by Carlos Palanca, Jr., founded the Carlos Palanca Memorial Award for literature (Tagalog and English) and offered P1,000 for the best story, P500 for the second best, and P250 for the third best. The best stories are chosen from among a list of short stories published in the newspapers and magazines from October 1 to September 30 of the following year. For 1951, Miss Genoveva D. Edroza's story *Kuwento ni Mabuti* was awarded the first prize. The defect in this method of choice—at least in the Tagalog section—is that the preliminary choice is left in the hands of incompetent editors whose literary taste is far from flattering. This defect became obvious in 1951 when the editors of the popular Tagalog magazines submitted to the Board of Judges a list of bad stories which any competent editor would not have accepted for publication. The members of the board were stunned at the editors' choice, but they were forced by the rules of the contest to pick the best among the worst submitted by the editors. Of the Tagalog magazines, only the magazine section of the daily *Bagong Buhay* and the college papers publish significant stories.

XI

Filipinos, it has been charged with some truth, are sentimental. This sentimentalism is reflected not alone in their prose works, but more so in their poetry. The Tagalogs, in particular, because they are socially conscious, have made almost any event a cause for sentimental out-burst. The marriage of a daughter, the death of a neighbor, the poverty and helplessness of a blind beggar, the misfortune of a trader, the christening of an infant, the unrequited love of a dear friend—all these are fit subjects for the poetical gifts of the people. Born poets and musicians, they express their feelings in verses and songs. Nowhere in the world is poetry more loved than among the Tagalogs. Illiterate men and women, whose school is experience, burst out declaiming a poem of their creation. One does not have to wander in the outlying hamlets to find and hear them; one has only to stand at one of the corners of a busy thoroughfare—Rizal Avenue, for example—to see and hear for oneself the blind beggar imploring the magnanimity of the passersby in rhymed verse that suits the occasion.

So it is not surprising to find that the Tagalogs have developed their poetry beyond the expectations of even the sophisticated critics of Western background. From 1900 to the present, the number of poems published in the papers would probably reach twenty thousand. The poets at the turn of the century, now free to express their thoughts, gave vent to their fury and attacked, in measured tone, not only the past administration, especially the friars, but also the Americans. A mistake by an overzealous American policeman was taken as an excuse for ridiculing, pilloring, and heckling the offending officer. The daily paper, *Muling Pagsilang,* published poems daily—poems that, because of the new freedom, reflected the social life of the community. Lope K. Santos, Valeriano Hernandez Peña, Iñigo Ed. Regalado, Patricio Mariano, Benigno R. Ramos, Mariano Sequera, Pedro Gatmaitan, Pascual de León, Godofredo Herrera, Francisca Laurel, and Julian C. Balmaseda belonged to that period of Tagalog poetry which was characterized, first, by the "purity" of their diction; second, by their social consciousness; third, by their lack of restraint; fourth, by their lack of imaginative insight; and last, by their messianic delusion. It was during these early attempts at free expression that books of verses were issued—Lope K. Santos's *Puso't Diwà* and *Ang Pangginggera;* Patricio Mariano's *Mga Anàk-Dálitâ;* Iñigo Ed. Regalado's *Bulalakaw ng Paggiliw;* Pedro Gatmaitan's *Tungkos ng Alaala;* Pascual de León's *Mga Buntóng-Hiningá;* Mariano Sequera's *Hustisia ng Diós;* Julian C. Balmaseda's *Sa Bayan ni Plaridel;* Máximo Sevilla's *Tungkos ng mga Tulâ;* Aurelio Tolentino's *Kahapon, Ngayón, at Bukas* (distinguished from his play of the same title) and *Dakilang Asal;* and Angel de los Reyes's *Kristong Magdarayà, Imbíng Kapalaran,* and *Parusa ng Diós.*

What may be termed, for the sake of convenience, the second period of Tagalog poetry under the Americans began, approximately, in 1915 and ended, likewise, in 1935. This period saw the rise of José Corazón de Jesús, the greatest Tagalog lyric poet, Deogracias A. Rosario, Cirio H. Panganiban, Teodoro E. Gener, Amado V. Hernández, Florentino T. Collantes, Basilio Sarmiento, Guillermo Holandez, Alberto Cruz, Ildefonso Santos, Emilio Bunag, Emilio Mar. Antonio, Domingo Raymundo, Aniceto Silvestre, and Jesús Esguerra. They constitute the cream of the Romantics, and their best poems are a mild revolt against the rigid formality of the preceding age. Where Lope K. Santos and his school would stick to the rules of versification—some of them of their own invention—the second generation of poets declared themselves free to experiment on the meter best suited to express themselves. Thus, Cirio H. Panganiban shocked the formalists with the publication of his *Manikà;* José Corazón de Jesús, with *Ang Sawá,* drew the condemnation of the older poets. But while the younger poets were busy experimenting, they forgot their social roots and wrote poems the majority of which were concerned with love and morals. With the exception of José Corazón de Jesús, the most sensitive and most socially conscious of the group, the rest contented themselves with plain homilies, the moon and the stars, and beautiful lasses. Some poems were published in book form during this period: Carlos Gatmaitan's *Ang Dalagang Tagabukid;* Florentino T. Collantes's *Tulisán;* and José Corazón de Jesús's *Dahong Gintô, Mga Itinapon ng Kapalaran, Sa Dakong Silangan,* and *Ang Ilaw ng Kapit-bahay.*

The epoch is well remembered for its *balagtasan* or poetical joust. Conceived in 1924 in memory of Francisco Balagtás, the *balagtasan* was the direct offshoot of the *duplo.* The former laid aside the *bellaco* and the *bellaca,* and were replaced by two or more protagonists. An interesting subject was chosen, and each poet had to defend his side of the question. Thus, when the first *balagtasan* was held on April 6, 1924, Florentino T. Collantes chose the side of *bubuyog* (bee), while José Corazón de Jesús took the side of *paru-paro* (butterfly), both of whom were vying for the fragrant *kampupot* (*Jasminum sambac L.*). The brilliant wit and delivery of the two poets made the *balagtasan* so popular, not only among the masses but also among the intellectuals and the debutantes, that the Ilokanos staged their own version, the *bukanegan* (after the father of Iloko literature, Pedro Bukaneg), the Pampangans their *crissotan* (after their favorite poet, Juan Crisostomo Sotto), and the Filipino collegians their poetical joust in English. After the death of José Corazón de Jesús in 1932, the only poet who could stand up to Collantes, the *balagtasan* has degenerated into a cheap and vulgar sideshow.

To a certain extent, the poetic tradition of the age of Corazón de Jesús has continued to this day. But by the mid-1930s a new generation of poets, schooled in Western culture, shocked both the old and the preceding school of poets by publishing their free verses. The tradition of rhyme and regular meter was, in the minds of the formalists and the academicians, insulted and abused. The young enthusiastic poets were flayed, and what may be loosely termed the "critical debate" was on. The old, old subject of form and content was discussed with such a virulence that in some cases the protagonists went to the courts. The young poets, reacting to the general condemnatory tone of the old, in turn ridiculed their opponents, led by Lope K. Santos and Iñigo Ed. Regalado, and called them not poets but rhymesters, not artists but clumsy craftsmen whose passion was to make a dull grammar out of poetry.

The experiment in free verse, whose high priest was Alejandro G. Abadilla, reached its apex during the Japanese occupation when everybody rushed to the press with his bundle of free verses. This development led even the leaders of the literary revolt to condemn those who, without understanding free verse, least of all poetry, wanted to become poets via the shortest route. The hue and cry over free verse finally died down with the booming guns of the American forces of liberation, and while the young poets today still follow the traditional rules of poetry, they nevertheless have strayed from the beaten path and have thus distinguished themselves by their succinctness, restraints, wider range of imagination, and the use of symbolism. It was also this last period that saw the appearance of Imagistic poems in the magazines. Begun by José Corazón de Jesús, the tendency was developed by Gonzalo K. Flores, Manuel Car. Santiago, Manuel P. Bautista, and Ruben Vega, whose poems are reminiscent of José Corazón de Jesús. They found the language best suited to Imagism, and so they exploited its wealth to express their thoughts and feelings in terms of images.

The Commonwealth Literary Contests, begun in 1940 and continued the following year, inspired the Tagalog poets to bring their works together into volumes. Only one of the many volumes submitted to the contest in poetry was published—Amado V. Hernandez's *Kayumanggi*. In 1949, Alejandro G. Abadilla, after cajoling the poets, published *Parnasong Tagalog,* the first major book of poems ever to come off the press. This anthology represents all schools and tendencies in Tagalog poetry. Significantly, Abadilla, apparently not contented with disposing of Iñigo Ed. Regalado, his counterpart in the "critical debate," wrote a lengthy but muddled introduction to the book in which he laid down, in the manner of a man about to die, his literary testament.

XII

Such is the development of Tagalog literature during the period covering half a century. Simultaneously with this literary development, the language itself underwent changes that have enriched its lexicon and its idioms. The coming of the Americans, who introduced their public school system; broadened the democratic base; intensified the campaign for hygiene and sanitation; built good roads and bridges; developed agriculture, commerce, and industry; and brought over their way of life, have made a lasting impression upon the Filipinos and have influenced their languages, literatures, and mode of life. The new culture, Anglo-Saxon in origin, merged with the indigenous and the Spanish to evolve what is today a heterogeneous culture. The Spanish influence has receded; the impact of the Americans has become so potent that, in spite of political independence, the country has come to look up to the United States as the source of inspiration and manna.

Thus, before the first decade of the Americans in the Philippines was over, the Tagalog writers, having learned a little of the American language, adopted some American words that are now part of the Tagalog lexicon: *bulakból* (from "blackball"), *leging* (from "legging"), *basket, awto* (from "auto"), and a few others, head the long list of words borrowed from the Americans. This new tendency to adopt American words was, however, temporarily nullified by the attempts of such purists as Pedro Serrano Laktaw, Pascual H. Poblete, Valeriano Hernández Peña, Lope K. Santos, and Iñigo Ed. Regalado to purge Tagalog of foreign influences—although unconsiously they were using Sanskrit, Arabic, and Chinese words in their works.

The period, as already intimated, was infused with nationalistic fervor. Independence was a favorite subject of the stage and of whispered conversations, and the writers, no less than the politicians, expressed their nationalistic temper by writing in the "pure" language. Meetings and societies were organized to "develop and enrich our Mother Language" and to find ways and means of making Tagalog the national language of the Filipinos. Manuals and vocabularies were prepared, and outlines of grammar were sold cheap. This interest in the language sprang from a sense of nationalism and from a feeling that the compulsory teaching of the American language in the schools might lead to the ultimate fading out of Tagalog. Even foreigners took an interest in Tagalog and wrote studies of its structure and characteristics. Renward Brandstetter, one of the foremost authorities on Austronesian linguistics, wrote *Tagalen und Madagassen* (1902); Aristide Marre, *Grammaire tagalog, composée sur un nouveau plan (1901);* W. E. W. Mackinlay, *Handbook and Grammar of the Tagalog Language* (1905); Constantino Lendoyro, *The Tagalog Language* (1902); Leonard Bloomfield, *Tagalog Texts with Grammatical Analysis* (3 volumes, 1917); and Frank R. Blake, *A Grammar of the Tagalog Language* (1924), and such articles as "Expressions of Case by the Verb in Tagalog" and "Tagalog Ligature and Analogies in Other Languages."

The climax of the American influence in the Tagalog language and literature commenced in the mid-1930s when the young writers, fresh from college, published stories and articles in which, for the first time, the American idioms were either literally translated or modified to suit their purpose. The reaction against this new tendency was immediate and violent. The "Old Guards," headed by Lope K. Santos, Julian C. Balmaseda, Iñigo Ed. Regalado, and Carlos Ronquillo, rushed to the field bristling with anger and condemned the young writers in no uncertain terms. But theirs were voices in the wilderness. The American influence could not be stopped. The young writers continued writing the way they wanted, and today the voice of protest is no longer heard, though occasionally the remaining members of the "Old Guards" rear their heads as when, in 1951 Iñigo Ed. Regalado, seconded by Lope K. Santos, vehemently wrote that "language does not change." The statement was too absurd to merit a reply from the young writers.

The opposition of the "Old Guards" to the young generation's use of the Tagalog translations of American phrases springs not alone from their notion of "pure" language but also from the fact that, being Spanish educated, they could hardly understand the new phrases which reflect the new society. Such phrases as *"buhat sa sulok ng mga matá"* (out of the corner of one's eyes), *"ang kanyáng buhay ay isáng bukás na aklat"* (his life is an open book), *"sa ibabaw ng lahát"* (above all), *"sa likód ng pangyayaring"* (in spite of the fact that), *"at ngayón ay itó"* (and now this), *"tiník sa tagiliran"* (thorn in his side), *"ilapat ang panulat sa papél"* (put pen on paper), *"ngayón ay masasabi na itó"* (now it can be told), *"sa pagitan ng mga talatà"* (between the lines), *"sa pagitan ng mga hikbí"* (between sobs), *"makita ang magkábiláng mukha ng larawan"* to see both sides of the picture), *"kalangitáng ipinagbawal"* (forbidden glory), *"kumahól ang pistola"* (the pistol barked), *"ipagkanuló ang sarili"* (to betray one's self), and many more are now part of the Tagalog writer's vocabulary. Many English words have been adopted into Tagalog, especially after World War II. The present writer's list contains more than four hundred such words, a few of which are *masinggan* (machine gun), *bakwet* (evacuate), *paks-hol* (foxhole), *armi* (army), *nebi* (navy), *diyíp* (jeep), *basketbol* (basketball), *putbol* (football), *siyatput* (shot put), *boksing* (boxing), *réperi* (referee), *ring* (ring, in boxing), *paul* (foul), *parbol* (foul ball), *nak-aut* (knockout), *ining* (inning), *mindaun* (men down, in baseball), *aut* (out in baseball), besbol or *beisbol* (baseball), *bistík* (beefsteak), *sanwits* (sandwich), *kendi* (candy), *raun* (round, in boxing), *tsasis* (chassis), and so on.

Some young writers, enthusiastic but pathetically wanting in the knowledge of English, have gone so far as to take bodily into Tagalog those American phrases which sound absurd when translated. Some such translations, absurd because too literal, are "*magbukás ng apoy*" (to open fire), "*sumandál laban sa padér*" (lean against the wall), "*hinugasan ni Flora ang mga tuláy*" (typhoon Flora washed away the bridges), "*magbabayad kayó sa pagdalaw sa amin máminsán-minsán*" (it pays to visit us sometime), "*kumuha ng panukat-hukbó*" (to take military measures), "*ihagis ang karitón sa tala*" (hitch the wagon to the stars), "*mapanganib na lumilipad*" (dangerous fly), and so on.

Tagalog today is the basis of the national language, Pilipino.* Its resilience has enabled it to grow by accretion and has thereby not only preserved its structure but has also adopted those elements of the foreign languages which are necessary for its life and growth. Its literature is still in the experimental stage, but given the encouragement it deserves it will, in time, prepare the majority of the people to accept a genuine artist.

* More than 75% of the 38 million Filipinos are able to speak or understand Pilipino, according to the latest figures of the Bureau of Census and Statistics, Manila.

Part I

From Idyll to Ideology: The Background of Modern Tagalog Poetry

In its more than three hundred years of existence, Tagalog (Pilipino) poetry has embraced all the universals and particulars of human experience. Its span is deep and broad in content and manner. From folk rhymes, riddles, and proverbs in verse, to religious hymns, and then to personal lyrics and dramatized projections of insights won from engagement with social and psychological actualities, Tagalog poetry has lived a life of varied confrontations with history and transcendence. One of the earliest foreign observers, Diego Lopéz Povedano, in 1578, rejoiced at the energetic songs of the native communities, the *barangays*. In 1604, Pedro Chirino, the Jesuit grammarian, after examining the Tagalog parts of the *Doctrina Christiana* (1593), testified that he found in the native language the positive qualities of Hebrew, Greek, Latin, and Spanish beautifully combined.

In the *Cronicas* (1738) of Juan Francisco de San Antonio, in Francisco Colin's *Labor evengelica* (1663), and in early accounts, we learn of the Malay's artistic nature. San Antonio writes:

The natives are fond of verses and representations. . . . They are indefatigable where verses are concerned, and they will act them out as they read them. When they write, they heighten their style with so many rhetorical phrases, metaphors, and pictures, that many who think themselves poets would be glad to do as much; and yet this is only in prose. For, when it comes to poesy, he who would understand it must be very learned in their language, even among his own compatriots.

Colin describes his experience thus:

All that we (the missionaries) have been able to learn has been handed down from father to son in tradition, and is preserved in their customs; and in some songs that they retain in their memory and repeat when they go on the sea, sung to the time of their rowing, and in their merrymaking, feasts, and funerals, and even in their work, when many of them work together. In those songs are recounted the fabulous genealogies and vain deeds of their gods.

Thus, early Tagalog poetry is inseparable from the life and death of the people it celebrates.

Before the Spanish conquistadores came, oral tales and epics flourished. The Filipino scholar Trinidad H. Pardo de Tavera, desiring to illuminate the nature of pre-Spanish Tagalog literature, made a study of Sanskrit loanwords in Tagalog, thus clarifying the provenience of certain Tagalog concepts. He notes the Sanskrit borrowings in Tagalog: "Las palabras que los Tagalog han adoptado son aquellas que significan actos intelectuales, operaciones morales, pasiones, supersticiones, nombres de deidades, de planetas, de numerales de una cifra elevada. . . . El Tagalog podia expresar conceptos mas elevados, ideas abstractos sin emplear circunlocuciones."

A Tagalog epic, the *Kumintang,* survives today in a few war dances and songs played in ancient times on the *kulintang,* a bamboo musical tom-tom with strings raised up from its own surface fibers. The epic as a whole describes the martial exploits of three sons of King Anka Widyaya of the Royal House of Madjapahit in the fourteenth century, when the Philippine Islands were recognized as northern bastions of the Malayan empire. Here is a free translation of a *kumintang* made in 1859 by the renowned English traveler Sir John Bowring in his book *A Visit to the Philippine Islands:*

> To know is to remember thee:
>   And yet in grief I rove,
> Because thou will not fathom me,
>   Nor feel how much I love.
> All traitors are stars on high—
>   For broken hopes I grieve;
> I cannot live—I fain would die:
>   It is misery to live.
> Sweet bird! yet flutter o'er my way,
>   And chant thy victim's doom;
> Be thine, be thine the funeral lay
>   That consecrate my tomb.

Sentiment and introspection, in general, tend to loosen the form of these verses. But the attention to concrete details clearly exhibits the kind of poetic sensibility at work on a common predicament. Stars, birds, love and so on—these elements prevail in almost all personal forms of literary self-expression.

Reminiscent of an archaic past are the familiar incantations used by the pagan priests as ritual prayers or recitative formulas. They are largely characterized by repetition, mimetic plasticity, syntactic grace, and a music of mysterious insinuation. Wordplay in poetry, based on the changing meaning of a word as it is pronounced in different ways, predominates in gnomic stanzas that evince the religious sense of the early inhabitants whom the Spaniards called *Indios:*

> Dito ang sala ay magdaan,
> Tungkol salâ na sinoman.
> Salá kaya tinibayan.
> Maging salá, napilian.

In spite of its dependence on the genius of the original, a literal translation can suggest the complex thought processes involved in the original, which only *explication de texte* can fully demonstrate:

> Here the error may pass,
> Whoever erroneous be,
> By weaving was strengthened,
> And filtered for elimination.

After careful research and examination of the grammars and *vocabularios* of the seventeenth and eighteenth centuries, Epifanio de los Santos, the first Filipino literary critic, enumerates some categories of poems that existed then: *soliranin* (rowing song), *talindaw* (boat song), *diona* (nuptial or courtship song), *uyayi* (lullaby), *dalit* (hymn), *kumintang* (war song), *sambotani* (victory song), *kundiman* (love song), and others. Here is a sample of a rowing song with its stubborn folk wisdom:

> Come on, let's row, spare not self,
> all hardships, learn to suffer,
> far be any place, if we want to reach it,
> beats any place near to which we don't travel.

Here is an excerpt of a *tikam,* or battle hymn:

> All our ancestors
> Dared the frightful thunder,
> Never ceased in the fight;
> Their lives are in wager,
> And their energy
> So that we, their sons,
> May live without thunderstorms.

These—our fields and all
Our lives, homes—
They vowed to wrest it
And tear it from our hands—
Shall we who are alive
Act as though dead?

Sir James G. Frazer, in *The Golden Bough,* cites poetic formulas used in ceremonies of primitive cults in the legendary age of the Philippines up to the fourteenth century. Given the temper of the Filipino sensibility, unaffected by the puerile sophistication of the Castilian decadent, it was not difficult for the Spanish missionaries to transform Tagalog poetry into effective mediating vehicles of Christian revelation.

Before the first *pasion,* or versified hymn of Christ's life, was written by Gaspar Aquino de Belén in 1704, the orientation of Tagalog poetry had by then radically altered from what was once a deep elemental concern with nature and nature's miracles to invocations and hymns to a supranatural divinity. Translation of the catechism had of course been initiated by the *Doctrina Christiana Tagala Española* in the late sixteenth century. Other books of the same nature followed, among which was Tomás Pinpín's *Librong pag-aaralan nang manga Tagalog ng uicang Castilla* in 1910. Pinpín, the first printer, wrote verses in which lines in Tagalog and Spanish alternated.

A contemporary of Pinpín, Fernando Bagongbanta ranks as one of the first pioneering Filipino poets of the Spanish regime. Because of the vogue of interweaving Spanish and Tagalog verses, the term *ladino,* which applies to natives who knew both languages, came to designate the works of Pinpín, Bagongbanta, and their successors. Here is a passage from Bagongbanta's poetry:

> Salamat nang walang hangga
> *gracias se den sempiternas,*
> nagpasilang nang tala
> *al que salir la estrella;*
> macapagpanao ng dilim
> *que destierrose las tinieblas*
> sa lahat nang bayan natin
> *de todo nuestra tierra*

An approximate translation is this: "Eternal thanks are offered/ to the One who made the stars,/who drove away the darkness/ from all our land."

Another versifier of this epoch is Pedro Suarez Ossorio, whose poetic invocation may be found in *Explicación de la Doctrina Lengua Tagala* (1627) by Father Alonso de Santa Ana. It is not without significance that Tagalog poetry acquired self-consciousness and an ontology through association with the propaganda of the Catholic church.

Of this group, Phelipe de Jesús is generally agreed to be the only gifted artist with an intuitive sense for analogy and sensuous evocation worked out in the language. Witness this short poem of his included in Father Antonio de Borja's *Barlaan and Josaphat* (1708):

> Ybong camunti sa pugad
> sa inang inaalagad
> ay dili macalipad
> hanga sa di magcapacpac.
>
> Loob ninyong masilacbo
> parang ningas alipato
> sa alapaap ang tongo
> ay bago hamac na abo.

Here is a literal translation:

> Birdling in the nest
> Reared by mother bird
> Cannot fly
> Until its wings sprout.
>
> Intense emotions
> Are like flying embers
> Floating high into the clouds
> Though really of humble dust.

Notice how the octosyllabic lines of the poem, the monorhyme and stanza form all convey an intricate theme through a subtle process of imaginative syllogism.

The poem quoted above unquestionably derives from the indigenous poetic form called *tanaga*. The *tanaga* is a Tagalog poem made up of a stanza of four rhyming lines with seven syllables to each line. Usually it develops an allegorical mode of presenting diverse material, *topoi* drawn from maxims, homilies, homespun philosophy, and so on. In its concentration and in the esthetic theory behind its highly equivocal perception of reality, the *tanaga* resembles the Malay *pantun* and the Japanese *haiku*. The symbolic complexity of the *tanaga* may be gleaned from this specimen taken from the first authoritative *Vocabulario de la Lengua Tagala* (1754) of Fathers Pedro San Lucar and Juan de Noceda:

> Lonsar na sa bacoor
> yayamang pa sa bondoc
> baquit mararagosgos
> ualang cocong icamot.

A free English translation runs thus:

> He is already on high land
> But he wants to ascend the mountain,
> He will only slide down
> For he has no claws.

Exploiting the *sawikain* or idiomatic molds of the language, Tagalog poetry achieved emotional intensity and compression by the middle of the eighteenth century. The *dalit,* or snatches of verse, showed economy and refinement, a handling of the resources of language so skilled that the Spanish rhetoricians, though partial to their own medieval learning, all unanimously acknowledged the maturity of Tagalog poetics even before they had completely understood its prosody. One can cite here Father Gaspar de San Agustin, among others, who wrote *Compendio del Arte de la Lengua Tagala* (1703); and Father Francisco Bencuchillo, who wrote *Arte Poetico Tagalo* (circa 1750). As a rule, many of the literary-minded clergy discoursed on Tagalog poetry along lines laid down by classical grammarians. However, their studies were limited to the description of traditional prosody, supplemented with comparisons to Latin, Spanish, and Tagalog rhetorics. If the spelling of words and their meanings have changed since then, the poems quoted by these priests exhibit measure, caesura, and rhyming scheme which up to now still determine on the surface the formal properties of Tagalog poetry and which pedants and peasant alike still regard as primary requisites that any composition which claims to be a poem must needs fulfill.

On the whole, Tagalog versification manifests an elegant simplicity which is deceptively easy to imitate. A line of conventional verse is organized by syllabic counts; verses therefore usually have six, eight, twelve, sixteen, or eighteen syllables, the count depending on the rightness of a pause after a phrase or any normal duration of utterance. Melody and cadence are determined by intonation patterns as well as by the play of consonants and vowels, Tagalog metrics being largely a question of assonance and alliteration. In other words, the placing of the caesura varies according to the division of a long line; there are customary line measures and stanzaic patterns that the apprentice follows.

The rhyming system of early Tagalog poetry is based on simple assonance of end syllables. Recently, however, the system has been refined to produce twelve kinds of rhymes. Briefly put, the vowels *a, e* (*i*) and *o* (*u*) distinguish six classes of words as ending either with a glottal stop or with a liquid vowel sound. Now the association of these vowel sounds with two groups of phonemes, namely, *B, K, D, G, P, T, S* and *L, M, N, Ng, W, R, Y,* result in six kinds of end rhymes. Consequently, there are twelve possible rhyming schemes in modern Tagalog poetry.

For our present purposes, it would be cumbersome and unnecessary to go further into the minutiae of Tagalog prosody. The elements of meter and rhyme have been indicated fully enough so that some notion of how Tagalog poetry is formally integrated may be conveyed to English-speaking readers. I should mention here the fact that Dr. José Rizal, the Filipino national hero, displayed his resourcefulness by delivering a lecture in German on Tagalog poetics, *Tagalische Verskunst,* before the Ethnographic Society of Berlin in April, 1887, which he later translated into Spanish. Rizal's *Arte Metrica del Tagalog* summarizes in a few pages all that the Spanish grammarians have discovered about the formal characteristics of Tagalog poetry. But between the 1896 revolution against Spain and these evangelists lies a long stretch of intellectual activity which, if concealed in isolated and withdrawn minds, finally disclosed its climax in the allegorical romance-epic, *Plorante et Laura,* and the propaganda movement that ensued.

From 1700 to 1872, a variety of poetic forms—*dalit, bugtongs,* verses for the *duplos* and *karagatan*—flourished side by side with the *pasion* and the exuberant prose of the preachers. Of the many *pasions,* or versified lives of Christ, those of Dr. Mariano Pilapil (1814) and Father Aniceto de la Mercéd (1856) still excite some critical interest. While the *pasion* is composed of octosyllabic five-line stanzas in monorhyme and therefore falls into the class of *corridos* (literally, events retold), the *awit* (song)—the other poetic form that dominated the eighteenth and nineteenth centuries—has twelve-syllable lines, four lines to a stanza with varying rhyme schemes. The *awits* usually dealt with either folklore motifs or wholly fantastic incidents. Fancy, not the operation of the imagination, prevailed in the *awit* and *corrido*. The two forms are considered to be similar, except in their manner of delivery: *the awit* is sung or chanted, while the *corrido* is merely read. Both forms are alike in that they use a loose narrative plot whose texture and rhetorical pattern afford lyric density and resonance. Meditative moods and rich connotativeness characterize the transition from direct report of episodes and the concrete allusions to manifold realms of human activity, as illustrated for instance by the masterpiece *Plorante at Laura* (1838) by Francisco Baltazar, otherwise known as Balagtás.

Plorante at Laura, regarded by consensus as the *locus classicus* of Tagalog poetry in its golden age, adheres to the narrative structure of the *corridos* like *Ang Ibong Adarna,* or *Bernardo del Carpio,* this last being attributed to Balagtás's versatile tutor José de la Cruz. *Florante,* however, is written in dodecasyllabic lines. Furthermore, its intrinsic epic design distinguishes it from the metrical tales. The beginning *in medias res,* the infernal landscape, the protagonist who is a figure both of heroism and pathos, the flashbacks, the layers of allusions to actual conditions of the times, and so forth—all these features converge in the complex handling of language to produce a work comparable, I think, to Dante's *Divine Comedy* if not in scope, at least in artistic method. Like the Italian's four-dimensional world, Balagtás's imagined theater of action develops the literal, moral, allegorical, and anagogical meanings of his theme in a way which is up to now still unexplored. I should like to point out here the technique of scenic montage, among other techniques, that Balagtás used and which is hinted at by the full title, *Pinagdaanang Buhay ni Florante at ni Laura sa Cahariang Alvania Quinuha sa madlang cuadro historico o pinturang. . . .* Retrospection and pictorial elaboration of the story are at once announced as the technique of rendering the lovers' past lives. I should also mention here Balagtás's use of intricate devices of foreshortening, closeup angle, panorama, summary, and scene—in fact, all the novelistic devices possible in order to render the drama of feeling and thought as forcefully immediate as today's news. The issues of Balagtás's time, of course, had particular references to persons and events then. But on the whole they epitomized the fundamental contraditions in a dialectical manner: man's relations with his fellow men, with nature, with society, and with his gods.

Censorship in direct and indirect form is responsible for the stagnation and monolithic nature of the reading matter—*novenas,* hymns, hagiology of all sorts—throughout the Spanish rule. Since the Comision Permanente de Censura forbade works critical of the milieu, Balagtas and his contemporaries, including the authors of the *zarzuelas, moro-moros* and other dramatic pieces, ingeniously chose the guise of allegorical or parabolic fable which was designed to amuse, and at the same time to instruct, the readers. But the Filipinos, after a while, were amused to the point of bitter self-mockery and instructed to the point of armed revolt. One prelude to revolt is the ironic *commedia* of Balagtás, *La India Elegante y El Negrito Amante.* At the height of conflict, Marcelo H. del Pilar, editor of the *La Solidaridad,* the liberal newspaper of Filipino intellectuals in Madrid, burlesqued the Paternoster and ridiculed ecclesiastical conduct. Soon the twelve-syllable line of the *awit* was mobilized for national solidarity when Andres Bonifacio wrote his spirited hymn for Mother Philippines, *Katapusang Hibik ng Pilipinas sa Inang España* (circa 1890).

Other propagandists and agitators—Rizal, Antonio Luna, Hermenegildo Flores, Pascual Poblete, Lopez Jaena, Mariano Ponce, and others—explored the possibility of Tagalog for polemical ends. Such cultivation of the language for eloquent persuasion, impassioned appeal, and rhapsodic odes to ideals and principles, led eventually to an awareness of identity through a common tongue. When Spanish forces succumbed to Filipino might, the first Philippine Republic proclaimed Tagalog as the language of the new nation. Immediately there followed the renaissance of Tagalog literature, particularly in the field of the novel, in the first two decades of the twentieth century.

At the beginning of the modern era and the end of Spanish domination in the Philippines, Tagalog poetry expanded its compressed intuitions into a medium varied in scope and generalized in implication so as to be able to handle abstractions and to successfully render the crisis of beliefs and orientations that gripped the country. The Filipino sensibility was suddenly initiated into a transvaluation of values and of ideologies, which compelled self-scrutiny and reshaping of the linguistic medium. Continuity of literary tradition, however, affirmed itself in many ways. Through the turbulent years of the revolution, the indefatigable scholar Pedro Serrano Laktaw labored to complete his monumental *Diccionario Tagalog-Hispano,* published in 1914. Meanwhile, the aristocrat Pedro Paterno adopted a nostalgic stance in his researches into *La Antigua Civilización Tagalog* (1892) and other monographs.

A manifestation of the historical sense that the Filipino consciousness slowly cultivated and sharpened through the years of the American occupation may be found in the literary histories and criticisms of

Tagalog writers sponsored by the Institute of National Language. Julian Cruz Balmaséda, who later became a director of the institute, wrote in 1938 a historical survey of Tagalog poetry entitled *Ang Tatlong Panahon ng Tulang Tagalog*. This survey proposed three main periods in the history of Tagalog poetry: (1) the period of the *dalit,* from Legazpi's time or even earlier, to the 1896 revolution, (2) the period of "reformation"—I do not know what Balmaséda means by "reformation" in this context—comprising the decades before and after the revolution, and (3) the period of "propagation," from 1899 to 1938. These divisions are, to be sure, artificial means of giving order since its only logic is that of chronology. Obviously they do not clarify changes in taste and shifts in idiom and sensibility. They do not elucidate the nuances of reorientation, the disparity of attitudes among poets of different periods, the interaction between convention and revolt in all the genres or poetic modes.

In its orthodox and wrongheaded dogmatism, Iñigo Ed. Regalado's essay on Tagalog poetry, *Ang Panulaang Tagalog* (1947), is a negative example, repeating old platitudes and indiscriminately praising the commonplace works of the generation who matured in the years between 1900 and 1920. Compared with Regalado's essay, Balmaséda's has a suggestive, congenial openness to novelty and variety which informs and inspires. The literary discourses of Lope K. Santos also possess the same virtues.

Any division into periods or epoch, such as Romantic and Neoclassic, etc., is apt to mislead us into conceiving profound disruptions of technique and substance when, in fact, there is a definite tendency in Tagalog poetry to cling to past performances. This observation applies specifically to the output of the generation that lived through the revolution only to be surprised or jolted by the pragmatic, outward-looking efficiency of the American bureaucrat. Among the poets whose work still draws occasional interest are Patricio Mariano, Valeriano Hernández Peña, Lope K. Santos, Aurelio Tolentino, Julian C. Balmaséda, Pedro Gatmaitan, Florentino Collantes, Teodoro Gener, Cirio H. Panganiban, Benigno Ramos and José Corazón de Jesús. The two outstanding poets of this group are Lope K. Santos, the "father" of the Tagalog *Balarila* (grammar) and José Corazon de Jesus, better known as Huseng Batute, who is considered the Byronic hero of Tagalog literature.

The poems of Santos, like "Pagtatapat" or "Pagbabalatkayo," exemplify nothing new in method or outlook; they are, however, remarkable for their finesse, their lovely consistency of tone, and their sure melody which are so finely adjusted to such familiar motifs as love and death. Santos's volumes of poetry signify a culmination of the formalist trend toward clarity, order, and quiet sensibleness. Only when we come to the publicly declaimed elegies and odes of José Corazón de Jesús does Tagalog poetry reach a consciousness of craft and power never before attained. Corazón de Jesús's style, as represented by dramatic monologues like "Ang Pagbabalik" (1924), illustrates the triumph of objective situation as a kind of concrete correlative to psychological tension and a means of reconciliation. The poet uses the lyric monologue, the poetic persona, mainly to acquire the psychic distance needed to be able to manipulate through the linguistic artifact the emotional responses of his listeners.

It is true that Corazón de Jesús did not invent remarkably new prosodic arrangements. He did not contrive radical innovations such as those which his contemporary Cirio H. Panganiban, for instance, did in "Three O'Clock in the Morning," and in other poems in *Salamisim* (1955). In short, Corazón de Jesús did not "modernize" Tagalog poetics. With a fixation on a mythical past, a past embodying an ideal of primitive purity, obsessed with dream-visions, Corazón de Jesús worked on common susceptibilities of his audience, heightening macabre detail, amplifying melodrama and building epic narratives by accumulation of incidents, personages, accidents, enlivened here and there by taut nervous diction and melodic grace of phrasing. Perhaps the archaism, the backward-looking sensibility of the Tagalog poet, arises from the fact that Tagalog verbs have no proper past tense, that the tense of the Tagalog verb is oriented to the axis of the present. Hence, the confusion of past with present, the perpetuation of the past in the contemporaneous. Why it does not work the other way, imposing the present process and flux on the past, is a problem for further analysis.

Endeavoring then to sustain the life of the past, Corazón de Jesús had to compose long and perhaps long-winded poems; *e.g., Ang Sawá,* a *corrido* of 344 lines; or *Sa Dakong Silangan,* an *awit* of 443 stanzas with dodecasyllabic quatrains. These tremendous efforts to revive the old metrical romances, if a mistake and a failure, are nevertheless useful clues, betraying the ruling passion of the poet to conceive an imaginative cosmos of great magnitude which would be complete in itself. Perhaps the energy called for by the *balagtasan* (the public debates in verse held in honor of Balagtás), drove the poet irresistibly to a frenzy of creation. In his brief life from 1896 to 1932, Corazón de Jesús turned out a staggering volume of verse unequaled in its massiveness, its unity, and its masterly handling of symbols, metaphor, wit, and cultural overtones of the language. Corazón de Jesús had in a great measure the feeling for, and sensation of, the beauty of mere utterance.

Among those who participated in the yearly *balagtasan* in which Corazón de Jesús reigned supreme, is Amado V. Hernández. Hernández, on the basis of the honors and recognition he has received, was (before his death in 1970) the dean of Tagalog letters, succeeding Lope K. Santos in this role. If Hernández's work focuses attention on the poem's commitment to social actualities, elevating a historical-dialectical-materialist view of literature as a weapon in the conflict of ideas, Alejandro Abadilla's art by contrast asserts laissez faire in art—with a new twist, though, derived from the whimsical and cthonic faculties of a maker.

Abadilla's art steadily and vigorously magnifies the self, the *ako,* as a microcosm functioning in an esthetic framework. He treats personal sensibility as the organon of knowledge, dictating image, rhythm, and controlling theme in a poem. The "I" becomes a central concept from which all organic unity and tension springs, from which all hope of integration and wholeness arises. Teo Baylen's poems, on the other hand, seek a mediating center, a subsuming archetype, by which material and spiritual dimensions may be fused on the face of the constant threat of man's total annihilation by nuclear war. These three poets, though they differ from one another in subject and approach, resemble one another in their virtuosity and the amount of expressive power they can wield. And though they have written purely in Tagalog before, these three poets are now employing a language which uses Tagalog as a base and which, as the evolving language of the Republic, can justly be called Pilipino. The confluence of vernaculars, together with the residues and borrowings from English and Spanish, gives birth to the common language, Pilipino.

Among the noteworthy poets included in the new edition of Abadilla's anthology *Parnasong Tagalog* (1965) are Manuel Car. Santiago, Manuel Principe Bautista and Celestino Vega, all of whom now overshadow their predecessors born at about the turn of the century: Basilio Sarmiento, Rufino Alejandro, Nemesio Caravana, José Esperanza Cruz, José Domingo Karasig, Ildefonso Santos, Emiliano Mar. Antonio, Fernando Monleon, and others. In the years after World War II, led by Abadilla's rebellion against conventions of thought and feeling, against all restricting rules which are after all contingent and relative to a temporary frame of reference, the young generation—those born in the 1920s and 1930s—has continuously indulged in daring experimentation and in fertile invention of new structures to bring forth revealing experiences. The young poets today seek to penetrate history and society, apprehending mythic shapes, harnessing all the qualities of language for the articulation of insights and intuitions that would resolve all tragic doubt, anxiety, and alienation; their poems strive to establish again the communion between man and his world. That is the hope, the goal of all poetics: to make the world a home for man.

Tragic, comic, satiric, burlesque, parodic, dialectical, surrealistic, projective and so forth—all these qualities and impulses modern Pilipino poetry attempts to develop, always aiming to fuse the demands of artistic integrity with the exigencies of life in a young Republic convulsed by the pains of growth, initiation, and radical discovery.

Lope K. Santos

(1879-1965)

Lope K. Santos is generally recognized as the first great Tagalog artist whose novel, *Banaag at Sikat* (Gleam and Sunrise, 1906), a realistic epic of the class struggle in Philippine society, firmly placed the native literary tradition right in the international mainstream of progressive and democratic art.

Born in Pasig, Rizal, on September 25, 1879, Santos quickly learned his father's trade as a printer. He studied at the Higher Normal School for Teachers and then finished at the Colegio Filipino. He studied law at the Academia de la Jurisprudencia and the Escuela de Derecho de Manila, receiving his Bachelor of Arts in 1912.

During the 1896 revolution against Spain, Santos joined the rebel forces. He performed brilliant journalistic work afterward in various newspapers like *Ang Kaliwanagan, Muling Pagsilang, Ang Mithi,* and many others. He served as governor of Rizal province (1910–13) and Nueva Vizcaya province (1918–20), and then as a senator from the twelfth district of the Philippines. Later he headed the Academy of the Tagalog Language and the Institute of National Language.

It was Lope K. Santos who organized in 1903 one of the first militant labor groups in the country, the Union del Trabajo de Filipinas, after the dissolution of the first labor federation founded by Isabelo de los Reyes, the Union Obrera Democratica. While he was leading the workers in the city and attacking the feudal landlords in the countryside, Santos composed his masterpiece, *Banaag at Sikat* (1903–6).

Unlike the analytic style and wide-ranging grasp of complex social forces shown in his fiction, Santo's poems adhere to conventional norms in meter and rhyme, in technique and substance. His mistaken ideas regarding the permanence of poetic forms and the unchanging nature of language are reflected in the hackneyed idiom and worn-out formulas and tropes of his poems in his volumes: *Puso at Diwa* (3 volumes, 1913), *Sino ka? . . . Ako'y Si. . . .* (1946), *Mga Hamak na*

Dakila (1950), and *Ang Diwa ng mga Salawikain* (1953). His researches in linguistics, among them the valuable *Balarila* or Grammar of the National Language, are too numerous to list here.

For all their deceptive simplicity, Santos' poems reveal an intense narrative vitality infusing the allegorical cast of his perceptions. In this lies the unquestioned merit of his poetic art. Santos' writings as a whole illustrate the continuity in Tagalog literature of a realistic, critical but warm understanding of human problems and of the socio-historical contradictions in each man's life. In this lies the enduring value of his works.

BEFORE THE GRAVE

At the foot of the cross
With eyes shut prostrate is she,
holding a handkerchief to wipe away the tears that flow down her cheeks;
flowers all fragrant thrown upon the stone,
are made fresh again, watered by dew-serving tears;
through the cold of stone deeply are wedged
the myriad sighs!

    Listening to find
    if there is response to the pulsating breast;
    in the bosom of the earth with someone conversing, listening
    to the answer to what the closed lips mutter;
    as though waiting for a soul to descend from heaven,
    and with the interred corpse of Love
    again to blend.

    What love could be
    the cause of her quiet prayer?
    Father? Mother? Child? Or husband seized from her company
    and lap that was a nest of love and cradle of quaint affection?
    Whose corpse is it under the slab of stone,
    with whom she speaks so fervently
    as though also alive?

    Not the Father, not the Mother!
    And not a Child, nor the Husband!
    All these have not died and are still alive.

The dead that she visits there secretly often
has been buried without a chance of being together with her:
dead was this Love which could be sin
if recognized with her!

Whom she secretly loved
in the eyes of men forbidden, a sin . . .
Heart was united with the Heart of one by parents forced,
when with somebody wed now came the well-suited Heart,
and from this Heart she had welcomed a seed of the plant of love
which when at last it was thriving
the offering Heart died! . . .

THE POET

I am a poet fed well by visions,
Rich in desires but wanting in silver;
The universe I've almost in my grip,
But the hand's will is beyond my own control.

Truly mankind is good and evil—
I witness and foresee this truth fixedly;
But I am blind and poor in knowledge
Amid the daily subterfuge of one's own life.

I endure the grind of the daylight hours
With mind well-fed but with stomach hollow;
In the time of my life time is not gold;
Rather, time is poison to my honor.

What is it to me if all of what has been
Created in the light completely vanish?
If what survive are the spirit and the pen . . .
How fortunate I am among the lucky ones!

José Corazón de Jesús

(1896–1932)

The most acclaimed lyricist and bardic performer of his generation, José Corazón de Jesús, better known as "Huseng Batute," probably deserves the honor next to Balagtás of having proved Tagalog a most powerful and inexhaustible medium for conveying the full gamut of human emotions, from the whimsical and banal to the tragic and sublime.

Born in Santa Maria, Bulacan, on November 22, 1896, de Jesús finished a Bachelor of Arts course and earned a law degree before he became known as a writer through his satiric commentary on current events in verse, "Buhay Maynila" (Life in Manila), in the daily *Taliba*. Beating his numerous opponents in the poetic joust called *balagtasan* (after Balagtás), de Jesús became the undefeated "King of Balagtasan" in the 1930s. His romantic sensibility induced him to take up lessons in painting, singing, and acting on stage and in films. A penchant for the theatrical and histrionic motivates the poignantly rhapsodic pathos, the elegiac and pastoral naïveté of his many poems in the following books: *Mga Dahong Ginto, Gloria, Mga Itinapon ng Kapalaran, Sa Dakong Silangan,* and *Ilaw sa Kapitbahay.*

The best of de Jesús' poems are collected in *Mga Tulang Ginto* (1958). Essentially a poet of melancholy love, de Jesús never departed from the conventional metrical and rhyme schemes, idioms, and imagery, of Tagalog poetry stemming from Balagtás. But within the limits of this tradition, he was able to execute skillful modulations of tone—witty, allusive, colloquial, plain, comic, sophisticated—which refined and expanded the language. De Jesús succeeded in mediating between the poet's temperament and the social realities of his time.

One can suggest that de Jesús' private meditations in his bittersweet reflective poems are also public arguments, movingly rhetorical in the best sense of the term. Responsive equally to the expectations of his audience and to the demands of his integrating vision, de Jesús easily became the unsurpassed people's poet of his time.

THE RETURN

Scarcely had I kissed her forehead,
tears rushed down my eyes;
a white handkerchief was fluttering
when I left her beside the ladder! . . .
In such sorrow of separation
I grieved as much as she all in grief.

When I passed through the gate
she shouted to me, "Come back at once,"
and I answered, "Yes, it won't be long . . . !"
I smiled, my tears descending!
and I set out on my way, pursued the trail,
with my halved heart, one half left there.

The sun has sunk, the darkness widely scattered,
and the moon wanted to shine;
it was past angelus when I arrived
at the distant land I hoped to reach;
owls in the nipa hut and black birds
greeted me at my coming!

On the door of the house there I knocked,
I was welcomed with glad hearts;
I ate a little, slept in sorrow,
with my heart that no longer wants to beat;
myself uttering: heart that will snap,
cease when I am truly asleep!

When morning came darkness fell,
the sun peeped through with dazzling eyes,
I began to do what I had to do:
I plowed, harrowed and sowed;
when December came, the crops on the hillside clearing
I reaped as a gift I will bring to my love.

And I returned home bringing all I could,
clusters of fruits and a sack of rice;
flowers on the edge of the path
I gathered as an offering to my love,

when I left her she was weeping,
Now perhaps she will rejoice!

And I sped on, almost running!
Near our place there was music even,
our house resounded in festive merriment,
and the guests milled in confusion!
"Thank God!" escaped from my lips,
"They know I was coming!"

But, O fate! when the door opened,
my eyes shut tight on what I beheld!
four candles stood there in vigil
watching around my beloved who is now a corpse,
her face smiling, her face that—when I kissed her—
seemed to say: "Farewell! Farewell!"

A TREE

Viewed from a distant vantage
I appear as a cross with arms outstretched;
As I stayed on my knees long enduring,
It seems that I am kissing God's feet.

Like an organ in a church,
Praying amid extreme sorrows,
Is the candle flame of my life
Keeping vigil upon my tomb.

At my feet is a spring
That sobs all day and all night;
Upon my branches lie
The nests of love-birds.

By the sparkling of that spring
You'd think of flowing tears bubbling;
And the Moon that seems to be praying
Greets me with a pale smile.

The bells tolling the vespers
Hint to me their wailing;
Birds on my branches are covered with leaves,
The spring at my feet has tears welling.

But look at my fate,
Dried-up, dying alone comforting myself.
I became the cross of withered love,
And a watcher of tombs in the darkness.

All is ended! Night is a mantle of mourning
That I use to cover my face!
A fallen piece of wood am I, and prostrate
Neither bird nor people find any pleasure.

And to think that in the days past
A tree I was of luxuriant and leafy growth;
Now my branches are crosses over graves,
My leaves made into wreaths on tombs!

MY COUNTRY

Filipinas, my country,
Land of gold and of flowers.
To her hand, love
Gave beauty and splendor,
And to her tenderness and fairness
Aliens were attracted.
My country! Captured you were,
Victim of sufferings.

A bird who is free to fly away,
Put it in a cage, it will cry—
Worse if it be a country full of splendor.

If a bird freely flying
When caged would cry,
A country of splendor would
Desire more to escape thraldom.
Filipinas that I love so much,
You are a nest of tears and pain,
My dream is to see you fully free.

Cirio H. Panganiban

(1896–1955)

A versatile man, Cirio Panganiban was not only a poet but also a noted fiction writer, dramatist, grammarian, teacher of language and literature, and a lawyer. His single volume of poetry, *Salamisim* (Reverie, 1955), which contains the well-known pieces "Manika" and "Three O'Clock in the Morning," was edited after his death by Teodoro E. Gener.

Literary historians attribute to Panganiban the singular accomplishment of having ushered in the technical maturity of the Tagalog short story form with his "Bunga ng Kasalanan," published in *Taliba* in 1920. His play *Veronidia,* presented at the Zorilla Theater in 1927 with José Corazón de Jesús and Atang de la Rama as star performers, is considered to have renewed the dramatic impulse among Tagalog writers in that period.

Born in Bukawe, Bulakan, on August 21, 1895, Panganiban spent most of his life in Manila as a college teacher and later as director of the Institute of National Language. He has long been considered as one of the more resourceful poets in his handling of new metrical patterns, distinguishing himself from his more tradition-bound contemporaries in the writer's group known as *Ilaw at Panitik* (Light and Literature) such as Deogracias A. Rosario and Teodoro Gener. Panganiban's poetry may be conceived as a link between José Corazón de Jesús with his bardic style and Alejandro Abadilla with his introspective self-dramatizations.

THE DOLL

You? . . .
You seem to be mysterious!
My dear mother tells me
You are her old doll.

I don't know if
What mother said is true ...
She said that when she was a child she had
A beautiful doll with eyes that shone.
Its winking, its smiling was like
Your smiling and your winking that gave pleasure.
The hair, mother said, was curly, the cheeks were red, the chin
    was pointed.
She looked like a "chinita" whose eyes disappeared
    when laughing.

I was told
By my darling mother
That what she wanted was to kiss once again
Her most beloved doll.
Like an old love
Returning
To my mother's heart, she recalled
The innocent days of happiness;
She remembered that when we were yet young and unknowing
Her darlings who were part of the heart and
    picture of life
Were once small dolls on her lap;
But that we grew up in her care;
Nobody cradles anymore in my mother's empty arms.
Now she looks for the doll of her youth
    (her old doll
Of curly hair, red cheeks, pointed chin,
Looking like a "chinita" whose eyes disappear
    when laughing.)

What I would like, my beloved,
Inasmuch as you look like her doll that died long ago
Its winking, its smiling are like
Your smiling and your winking that give pleasure—
Is to have my mother kiss you, jewel of my life,
So you may know that I love you, my only muse,
And will love you until the grave.
But you?
You seem to be mysterious!
If you may be called a doll,

You are perhaps the doll of my sufferings.
If you look like
My mother's old doll,
I feel that perhaps you are her real doll,
And that because you were neglected
When my darling mother grew up to womanhood,
Now what you do is to inflict vengeance
And I am the victim of your vengefulness, although I am innocent
Even when you know that you are my only love,
Though I call to you, you seem not to hear me;
Though I ask you for just one fleeting glance,
You close your eyes that are the light of my life;
When you sing about all your dreams,
If I listen to your song, you lock even your lips;
Even if I pour into your heart my love a thousandfold,
You tighten your heavenly chest just to make me suffer.

Doll! Doll!
You seem to be mysterious!
Your blood is alive and quite fresh,
Your flesh is wrapped in gossamer,
You hair is curly, your cheeks are red, your chin pointed,
You look like a "chinita" whose eyes disappear
    when laughing. . . .
But you are so beautiful and so admirable,
You are a human doll who refuses to talk;
In your silence you are a sphinx perhaps . . .
Closed are your eyes . . .
Speechless your tongue . . .
Marble your heart . . .

Amado V. Hernández

(1903-70)

Considered today by Filipino intellectuals and the broad majority of Filipinos as the foremost revolutionary artist of his time, Amado V. Hernández spent sixty-seven years of his life organizing the masses and struggling with them for freedom, social justice, and national democracy.

Born in Tondo, Manila, on September 13, 1903, Hernández studied fine arts at the University of the Philippines after which he plunged into journalistic work. He began his literary career in the 1920s, serving as editor of the city Tagalog daily *Mabuhay* from 1934 to 1941. In 1939 he won the Philippine Commonwealth Award for a historical epic, *Pilipinas;* in 1940 his collection of poems, *Kayumanggi,* won the same award. During the Japanese occupation (1942–45), Hernández participated in guerrilla activities as an intelligence officer for the underground resistance.

After the war, Hernández engaged in politics, becoming councilor of Manila in 1945–46 and in 1948–51. He also organized the Philippines Newspaper Guild, a pioneering union. It was during his incumbency as national president from 1947 to 1951 of the Congress of Labor Organizations (CLO), the largest and most militant labor federation in the Philippines, that he was framed by the fascist state for alleged complicity in the Huk rebellion of that time. Released from prison by the Supreme Court in July, 1956, and finally acquitted of all charges against him in 1964, Hernández once more flung himself energetically into the cultural and political life of the nation. He edited a fighting newspaper, *Makabayan* (1956–58).

Hernández's experience in prison bore fruit in the tremendous revolutionary fervor of his masterpieces: the novels *Luha ng Buwaya* (1963), *Mga Ibong Mandaragit* (1969); *Isang Dipang Langit* (1962), a collection of his poems; the epic *Bayang Malaya* (1969); and numerous award-winning plays, novels, short stories, and essays. In 1958 the National Press Club gave Hernández a certificate of merit for more

than twenty-five years of distinguished service to Philippine journalism.
For his volume of poems, *Isang Dipang Langit,* Hernández received
the Republic Cultural Heritage Award. In 1966 he won the NPC-Esso
Award (first prize) in journalism for distinguished writing in Pilipino.
A book of Hernández's poems in English translation entitled *Rice
Grains,* ed. E. San Juan, Jr., was published by International Publishers,
New York, in 1966.

A recipient of thirty-three major literary awards as writer and journalist, Hernández was a distinguished member of the International
War Crimes Tribunal organized by the philosopher Bertrand Russell
to investigate U.S. crimes in Vietnam. Before he died on March 24,
1970, he was a leading protagonist in mass rallies and protest demon-
strations then raging against imperialism, feudalism, and bureaucrat-
capitalism—the prime oppressors of the Filipino people. Hernández
is now generally honored as the symbol of the Filipino people's
revolutionary struggle against oppression and exploitation, for social
justice and national democracy.

"A Fly on a Glass of Milk" ("Langaw Sa Isang Basong Gatas")
was written just after Hernández's release from prison in 1956 and is
included in a posthumous collection of his writings, *Panata Sa
Kalayaan ni Ka Amado,* ed. Andres C. Cruz, Manila, 1970.

MAN I

A worldful of mystery and miracle is this earth,
man has chosen to realize mankind;
though he does not yet know
Where he came from, nor where he is going to,
he inquires
already into time and space, exploring the moon,
desiring to clarify: what? why? how?

Decision and thought collide
as to what is man, whence did he come:
God created
every living organism, the Bible teaches;
the Scientist
takes exception: "Man's ancestor is the ape."
How muddy the fountain and the lake.

From one root stemmed
faith and learning;
though kins
sprang and flourished beneath a single roof,
each acted with his own impetus and desire, wish and usage;
will it be science? or religion?

In times when consciousness was still young
man worshiped many things—
wind and fire,
mountain and sea, sky and sun;
when learning grew ripe
proud daring flared
until man challenged God.
The mind's flight and reach competed with the
speed of thunder, lightning's velocity,
the profoundest
secrets of life he tried to plumb;
he mined
the enigmas of earth as deep as the sky,
desiring to change the earth.

But in the thousand years that have passed
man still possesses the jungle's urge,
the tower of Babel
soaring through its groundwork
has been kneaded well below;

Cannibalism descended and roamed the city,
the wily strong devoured the weak.
Man to man and country to country
is now Abel to Cain, iron to rust;
every bullet
is manufactured for ends of violence:
to crush skulls!
Gold buys iron and life,
gold and life are now bound by steel.

Each man divided the lot and got his share:
here's poverty, there's wealth;
on each side of the fence

there's the white race, there the black,
and even God
is dragged to the conflict
allied—it seems—with whoever is winning.

What shall one do with strength, wealth, wisdom?
What is the use of victories and trophies?
How can man's answer be correct—
answer to the question
why the heart is a nest of vipers of evil intent?
What is the value of progress?

It is not on the big, the rich, the armed,
the pedantry of pedagogues,
that the triumph of ideals and purposes and dreams rest;
the purity of spring
will not come from muddy pools;
the angel drops with burnt wings.

A circle without beginning or end,
mankind has revolved in the long centuries;
facing a mirror
he believes someone ominous is reflected there
to be vanquished
but it's only his own futile shadow;
how often does he smash his own head.

But the thousand years gone are not mere bubbles,
man will walk forward, erect;
granted that he found himself
aware on a barren branch,
in the end he will enjoy
the power and wisdom of civilization:
what was once a monkey has become a god.

MAN II

Man:
born according to the law
of life
and nature:

like plants,
fish, animals, snakes, birds;
lives according to the law
proposed by himself.

He created conventions and creeds,
myths,
and the materials, necessities and tools
of gods
Whom he worshiped with absolute trust;
but man's love and worship,
his faith
are all like fragrance easily diffused—
like spark, scent, bubble;
he destroys
and levels old altars;
even Paradise he would refuse
in order to search for an oasis in the desert.

Though bereft of a lion's strength, of iron's,
he has electricity in his blood and diamonds in his brain,
he quickly tamed all power:
he became a king of every living creature,
a lord of this earth.

Now he perseveres, exploring the whole world
yet never attempts to know himself;
he covets the reign over other planets
though he can not discipline himself;
forcibly he tries to alter the world
though he cannot alter himself.

Sometimes he's a beggar as destitute as a worm,
an empty stomach that crawls;
sometimes a criminal ugly as hate
and Satan with horns and tail;
sometimes a sage, poet, prophet;
Socrates, Homer, Moses, and Buddha;
once he performed miracles in art—
Wagner and Beethoven, Da Vinci, Michelangelo:
warrior, or martyr, or saint:

Caesar, Napoleon, Rizal, Galileo;
once he was a man who became God
and God who was once Christ!

History is a noble monument
of the life of every hero,
history is a never-ending bridge
of the past and present and future,
history is man
and man is history . . .

And if God so chooses to go down
in another time,
he will give a sign to the rebel
whose shadow looms equal to God:

"I witnessed all your deeds,
greater than mine on the earth's surface were they.
you have discovered and created much more,
you have demolished and killed much more;
the world is yours, it's your responsibility now,
but suppress your ambition
to steal and wrest heaven from your God!"

LIFE SENTENCE

Perpetual chains for the crime of murder,
but for the "big shot": eight months after,
the suffering's done and "Pardon"
is even offered by Car Number 1.

How many thousand prisoners are rotting
in their kennels, hardened by their afflictions;
so many cry—"O God, God!"
without any warning, riot breaks out
engulfing the cells in flames!

BEYOND THE HANGMAN'S ROPE

Guarded and bound was he when they pushed him
toward the last rampart protecting the gallows;
and though his face was pale, he stood proudly—
he who was once the terror of revolt.

Thirteen strides toward the stone arcade,
and each trod a knock on the coffin!
when the hangman shut his dark office,
the graveyard's mouth creaked and tightened.

Without warning the tolling of bronze bells
pierced and chilled the crowd,
all the convicts were shrouded in black
as the Law snapped the "traitor's" breath.

A handful of charcoal is all that survives;
a handful prayed, others struck on steel—
that's the end. Whether he be hero
or bandit—a question awaiting reply.

Muntinlupa
1952

THE WOLF'S COUNSEL

Into the jungle entered two friends
        to shoot game in the bush;
after a while, not far from them,
        they sighted a wolf on the run.

One rifleman sped at once,
        climbed a tree as swift as a monkey,
and the other, left alone, crouched on the ground;
        feigned death, forgetting his gun.

The wolf approached and calmly nosed about;
        he, breathless, crumpled up;

it seemed that the wolf whispered something,
    then left and was nevermore seen.

From the tree slipped down the frightened monkey,
    and eagerly asked the resurrected one:
"What did the wolf leave as counsel?"
    "That I should flee from cowards!"

Fort McKinley
1955

BARTOLINA

I. *Bartolina*

My life has been spent this way for many days now:
from the world removed and my only world
the four walls of this stone fortress . . .
in cold season, ice; in summer, an oven.

I cannot breathe the fresh wind,
only air thick with poisonous gas;
darkness pursues me night and day,
lines on my forehead are thick as footmarks.

Night and day join in this conspiracy,
a totality suffused with gloom;
my guard is a mute whose gaze
seems a hurled ax-blade on your face.

The blood-red soil and blue sky
are not seen by the man in a coffin,
nobody answers my call
except my voice sprung from its own grave.

But I do not want to surrender even for a moment
to fear, despair, or treachery:
God hears every word of my prayer
and His love is my sole companion.

My memory is there for every second,
impossible to bind and incarcerate;
the fragrance of roses is my message,
the kiss of stars my profound kiss.

Following the night is the joyful dawn—
is there any road that does not arrive at its end?
behold the gloom—at the eyelid's fluttering,
a heaven of stars radiates in splendor.

After the storm a certain calm;
faith shall retreat, poised, to the mountain;
so long as we are near God
every shouldered cross is a ladder to beatitude.

II. *Faith*

I saw the sun
rise blood-stained,
every new morning is a new life
which brings to man his day's fortune.

I heard the wind's bliss
and caress, singing
in the fields, brook, and garden,
singing freedom up to my prison cell.

For your sake, dearest,
who is my sole happiness,
the burden of my cross I do not feel—
your love exceeds the whole world's punishment.

Ah! while on earth
there's life and love;
while heart and faith are still free,
a thousand prisons will not conquer me.

III. *Dejection*

Bleak, rainy,
the wind's spite frightens,
threatening with the assault of typhoon.

Bleak, cold,
dreary ocean is the atmosphere
whose only light is the lightning's blow.

A time of deprivation
when the mother weeps over the corpse of her child,
and the maddened earth laughs and cries.

All seethes,
the breeze blows with a spray of blood
and terror's the only king—terror of bullets!

The curse of heaven
slammed down on the man who has remained obstinate,
he has returned from the hospital to war.

All desolation,
grief and pain has escaped my care:
in this prison I am buried alive.

IV. *Illumination*

In my captivity I witnessed a bird
        singing on the twig of a tree;
completely free, while my freedom is denied—
        twit, twit, mocking my imprisonment.

The wind knocks on the barred windows
        of my cell and despises me;
it brings the scorn of arrogant society
        for me a victim who'll never be free.

From afar I saw my bereaved love
        waving disconsolate, unable to come near;
dumbly crying from extreme sorrow,
        my tearful kiss conveyed by somber groans.

Bird and wind liberated, my suffering beloved;
        the mind's freedom, the heart's, cannot be bound
like the light of exultant dawn
        and the clamor of the people avenging.

V. *Victory*

The torch of my hope alternately dims and brightens,
    there are nights that seem endless,
but the torch will sustain continually the life of light;
    even if my voice fades out in hardship
the gift of a past dream will still resound;
in my prison the old pen never grows dull,
each letter yields the echo of bullets and the cut
    of a blade.

There are debates in which, defeated or victorious,
    one gains glory;
    the prison is not the epilogue;
there are struggles in which, though defeated, the
    protagonist still triumphs
    so that darkness may be overpowered;
if my poem to freedom, right, and justice
will reach the heart of the people who also have been
    long imprisoned,
thanks, even though my reward is execution.

THE SEED OF AN ATIS

Once a young woman picked up the seed
    of an *atis*. When she came home
she told her mother what she thought about it—
    the seed should be planted and tended.

"And when the seed grows and bears fruit,
    the fruit I shall take to the market;
with the sales," she said smiling,
    "I shall use to buy earrings and rings."

The mother, angered, assailed the daughter;
    pinching the girl's groin:
"Let your own jewels be loaned to someone,
    lightning from me will kill you!"

Fort McKinley
1955

IRONY

The impoverished hut shivers with cold—
under its roof not a bit of coal:
the father, though a miner, has lost what he found
when he mined abundant carbon in the earth.

Hungry is the whole family without rice,
their enormous debt still piles up for weeks;
the farmer twists in hunger
though the harvest fills the overflowing granary.

KATIPUNAN

There is a woman shriveled by grief
with blindfolded eyes, hands bound;
by token of her flowing tears and her groans
it seems that God has completely forsaken her.

She has been imprisoned for a long time now;
a luckless maid violated,
stripped of wealth, deprived of grace,
her freedom irretrievably lost.

Before, she was Maria Clara of miraculous charm:
now she is a mad frightened Sisa;
while she suffers the torture inflicted by all,
friars and soldiers rape her.

She calls amidst the darkness of the night,
praying to be redeemed from pain . . .
"O my children," is her continual cry;
"Where are you, Basilio, and you, Crispin?"

In prison she perceives around her
the exaltation of all evil;
Burgos, Gomez, Zamora were killed
because they stood up for native honor.

Suddenly the pitiful woman bursts into song
as though not the slightest hope remained,
and her sigh in the last moment
pierces the deaf heart and dumb conscience.

In the dark a shadow approaches,
pries open the prison with a sword . . .
"Who are you?" exclaims the prisoner;
"Andres Bonifacio!" is his quick reply.

Revolt! Water yesterday that was silky
booms in cyclone, bringing flood;
with a spark bonfires kindle
throughout a tumultuous blaze.

Will the country languish forever
in tyranny and still beg pardon?
a tiny ant can also slay,
a tiny nail can become a blade!

A thousand children of this battered country
gather together for vengeance,
the edge of a bolo in the dark of the night
signals independence for all.

The country is a volcano exploding
when Taal rumbles and Mayon ignites;
Balintawak, Kawit, and all of Luzon
wakes up a Bernardo Carpio in uprising.

Many died in the funeral night:
Rizal, Bonifacio, Mabini, Del Pilar . . .
So that this race will live forever
greeted by the unfolding rays of dawn.

MENU

Once in Escolta, in a select restaurant,
A poet and a banker dined together;
Each drank a glass of Martini
Staring at the ubiquitous menu.

By chance they suddenly inhaled
The fragrance of Beauty who strutted in . . .
The poet remarked: "Ah, that's the wine
You cannot drink with a thousand gulps!"

The banker retorted: "Own for yourself
Her loveliness; leave for me
Her jewelry that makes me squint cross-eyed."
The Beauty glanced when they burst laughing.

A MEMORIAL TO MY DOG

I wept and wept
over my dead dog;
Mother said: "Stop your crying,
I'll look for one better than that dog."

A dog is like a man
in intelligence;
for how many years were we companions together,
playmate and guardian in my childhood days.

Wilted gardens
are Aprils unnumbered;
my mother was snatched by the grave
and my happiness, by fellow men.

Countless frustrations
have taught me
the heart can easily find gold
but hardly its golden counterpart.

My mind wakes up
to a new enlightenment:
every Eve seems to nurture a pet snake,
Every Christ seems to jostle with a Judas.

Ah, where is it now,
the flock of birds
when I was a flourishing leafy tree
and not a cross supine on a coffin?

My friends
of prosperous times,
days of victory, comfort, honor, revelry,
flowers, stars . . . all faded, gone.

Often it is said
that my old dog,
among my friends that went unnumbered,
stands out alone and without an heir.

Muntinlupa
November, 1954

FOUNDATION

A handful of beggars
sprung from nowhere,
a crowd of muscles and sons of sorrow,
united by purpose—
to build their own life with the help of the Creator.

Ax and sharp steel
did not triumph,
the hardened earth softened under the pick-blows;
within half a year
the thorny hill became a thriving cultivated field!

Cooperating in all
difficult work,
sharing harvests and the good that all receive;
each hut keeps rice
and a bolo behind the wide open door.

All are moved
by exemplary custom,
as sweet as water that springs from the mountain;
but for those without honor,
as hard as the mountain is the outstretched hand.

A handful of the poor
from the earth rose up,
a crowd of muscles and sons of the poor;
they form the power of Labor—
Ah, they are the foundation of this noble land.

THE VISIT

In that two-square-meter cell
of a prison so huge that the crow's flight cannot measure it,
a monstrous jaw of Satan,
he exists in solitude, exiled from the world.
As though the world turned over topsy-turvy,
hurled him out into another continent;
even then, his mind and sensibility
        sharpened:
he has counted
all the chains of the hours,
time is a black handkerchief on the tears of midnight;
rough and ugly the gaping wound
of all the landscapes, shadows and suspicions
inside and outside
of a prison cell, accepted or denied
        by his consciousness—
the rude iron mat, the steel bars,
all around are ramparts of cold hard stone,
the little window seems shut
        though it's open
because every stolen glance is blocked at once
by a curtain of wire;
a tin plate and a cracked glass,
old bread for which cockroach and mildew compete,
a bucket of water where maggots sow disease;
a thin spider,
a net woven to shroud him; stub of a pencil
fatigued by writing,
three sheets of paper, half a book
with faded letters and torn-off binding;
a hazy light which in the gloom seems
        the eye of a blind man,

a piece of sky: a sail tempest-tossed in the sea of clouds,
a piece of ground: yawning grave of the unfortunate,
old wooden cross supine
    from burdensome hardship . . .
and this is his only world:
    night without tomorrow
in an absence of freedom that cannot be understood . . .
My God! My God!—my imploring call,
but even God has fled from his wreckage.

Those were the moments: not meaningful signs
but composing a shroud that then obscured time and number,
a coil of rope that hours and days cannot unwind;
he will wake in the cell that is his tomb,
the whole afternoon counted
by the steps of the guard;
the prisoner's ration cannot be tasted
because his spirit hungers for freedom, the world, life;
when darkness spreads, an ashy coffin is his bed,
the grief of night as long as his sorrow within;
ask the wind, address the moon:
where is my loved one, where? . . .
When will be my liberation, when?
The wind's response is a jeering laughter
and the moon rips off the melancholy air
with the stare of its exquisite eyes!

But what the tongue and the mind mumble
continually are the days . . . Grains
of prayer repeated since Monday
to Saturday are six knots of a thousand afflictions,
every movement detached is a thorn,
and whatever flower it bears is a gash in the breast;
but
how indolent the day—the boy sent on an errand
    has never returned!
how the night drags on—hardly can one roll the iron mat!

Finally arrived
the Sunday which is the cause of all his impatience
the seventh mark of
the blunt pencil,

day of good fortune, day of happiness—
ah, an eagerly awaited chance!
he would be visited by the graceful sharer of his heart,
devoted embrace and faithful kiss . . .
And he celebrated, cast off grief,
quickly prepared himself in some sort of order,
his meal a gulp of water;
overwhelmed by this day he whistles, hums, sings,
while waiting for his only joy in bondage.

Hour of visitation . . .
Breath reined in apprehension;
waited, hoped,
hoped, waited,
how this afternoon already seemed over . . .
suddenly resounded
throughout the row the guard's voice. . . .

Ah, then he read the roll call . . .
he listened!
"Umali . . . Pasumbal . .
"Lumanog . . . Dakanday . . .
"Baking . . . Nava . . . Brusal. . . ."
Then "Quick! Hep, hep, hep! Two files
and no noise!"

Like a flock of beasts released from the cage,
the prisoners raced to the door.
In tedious laughter the hours passed,
the call—none yet . . . how late, how slow!
Was he not forgotten by the guard?
Burning feverishly, anxiously,
without warning the known voice resounded;
"Delacruz . . . Palmehar . . .
"Balerio . . . Adelan . . ."
His name again unuttered!
An hour . . . two . . . and he perceived
the cheerful company of prisoners from the visiting room,
visiting time is over.
The sun's face darkened at once
until finally

the golden threads were knotted and the black strands let loose;
he was choked with despair,
hope turned into chagrin
until the palms touched
the cheeks on which bitter tears streamed. . . .
When the old bell tolled
the hour, he noticed that it was night
    with heavy mournfulness,
and only then he believed in the heart thus wrecked:
No Visitor!
Absent the visitation!
O how cruel a truth to a prisoner impoverished by fate . . .
And he knew that prison
can kill
because those loved ones who are free can so easily forget!

Cell House, Muntinlupa
June, 1952

TO A CHILD WITHOUT NEW CLOTHES

Impoverished boy! Do not grieve
if you do not have pretty clothes,
do not sulk even for a moment
before the arrogance of those wearing new clothes;
be intensely yourself and be good
despite the vanity around you.

Though small you have nothing to be ashamed of
in being called son of the poor;
Was Jesus not born lowly
in a crude manger unswaddled,
without silver spoon, with silken coverlet,
and those who visited him were all in rags?

Let them laugh and frolic,
spendthrift in drunken revelry;
the prettiest clothes fade fast
and gaiety also has an end;
the boy used to harships will be
a sturdy oak amid prostrate vines.

Clothes are fragile, fragile too is life;
fashionable attire will soon be worn out,
so do not be sad if you have no gifts
for you are like tiny Jesus;
you also have a day of exaltation
bearing all afflictions in your innocence.

SKELETON

Ugly lips of a body whose life
has drained away—all men
are like that when they die:
in the cold earth all are skeletons.

Dry driftwood scattered here and there,
one cannot even trace in it
the beauty of the flowers it once bore;
like a woman withered by pain.

A rag so filthy that one could scarcely
notice its outline in a dark nook—
earlier it was the Virgin's dress
that the worshiper caressed and kissed.

All things grow old and crumble
inevitably—the strong, beautiful, noble—
in the long run, you man,
shall be devoured by hungry earth.

Around us everything gives token
of our fate drawn in our palms;
strength, grace, robust arms
suddenly become an ugly skeleton.

GALLERY OF EIGHT OUTLAWS

With hissing fangs of a Viper's mouth
The stonehouse swallowed,
Gulped seven luckless men . . .
Who are they?

I realized, in asking myself the history
Of these men become outlaws,
How their fates transcend devouring time.

The First Outlaw

A father kicked out of his work
Because the buying and selling went crippled;
With his sick wife stretched out
Like a corpse, one night, he stole a sack of rice.

The Second Outlaw

Meek worker sweating out his perpetual afflictions;
How humble, though his weekly wage
Seemed good for the hogs . . . When the fated day
Of recompense arrived, the payment's withheld:
Enraged he could not stop himself
From using the ax.

The Third Outlaw

A poor farmer whose narrow field lay
In perpetual order, fertile, on which
Rain and sun's warmth shed their blessings
For the rice to burgeon and ripen—
But when the harvest came, someone else reaped!
Others ravished the pregnant stalks . . .
And so he slaughtered those evil hearts.

The Fourth Outlaw

Elect citizen with aspirations, his energy
Flowering in movements that stake the country's fate;
Once he was involved in an election
For a worthy office, but how luckless!
When he was cheated he chose the office of killer.

The Fifth Outlaw

A brain most subtle, overflowing with wisdom;
To common minds his strategy of reasoning
Always appeared tangential;

In God he reposed no faith, so naturally
Prison's good for him—dangerous gadfly!

The Sixth Outlaw

A woman graceful in gesture and shape
Bearing all virtues of a native muse
In her remote natural home; sincere in love
Yet suddenly deceived by her clever suitor—
Tagalog honor, when blemished, needs blood
To wash it pure.

The Seventh Outlaw

Spokesman of this impoverished nation,
All rottenness of bureaucrats he dried out in the sun
Defending justice, freedom, the insulted
And injured; but on a luckless day
Every citizen has the jail for haven.

The Eighth Outlaw

And the guilty one who excels all, the mastermind
Of all these "acts of law," gives no answer
For the sins that surround and besiege us . . .

Here is Society
Who created all laws which beget only
Violence and cruelty:
"Prison's the sole property of the common man!"

LIFE

There was once a woman so beautiful and charming
who gained all that she desired;
but when once her lover forgot her,
poison became her last farewell.

There was once a man, wise and renowned,
that even the sly he could reach;
but when his fame all suddenly declined
bullets snapped the thread of his life.

There was once a beggar as poor as a rat
who couldn't even beg for charred rice in the pot;
holding fast like a lizard to his misery
he drags wormlike his threadbare skeleton.

There was once an old man who moved like a tortoise
unable to carry the burden of his years,
yet every time he prayed to his dear Creator
he whispered hunger for a longer life.

How ironical is life in this world:
a butterfly succumbs to sweetness
yet in the graveyard, on the stone one stands,
flowers the sickly impoverished weed.

There are lives exposed to one another
and though great hardly nourish a single seed;
there are lives that recall a canary,
so sweet the songs at each momentary stroke.

It is a question difficult to resolve;
out of nothing, things will end in nothing.
There are people who, though breathing, are dead
while others are murdered by those they buried.

The commonplace life is that of tiny shrimps
struggling with noble spirit;
man argues that even a dog's poor life
exceeds in worth the value of a dead king.

Man is born with ease in this world,
with leisure the weed also flourishes;
yet my grandfather always dinned to my ears:
"Child, strive hard to attain *virtù*."

FIAT LUX

Mystery

A fable whose answer bears a shroud of superstition,
dark horizon of a room that bears a key

amid black nothingness, apples in Paradise
not yet eaten—each trivial thing is there
before truth is finally recognized.

Miracle

Even day seems dark to eyes that are shut;
lightning, once a god, is now the servant of all;
man has conquered the birds in upward flight;
the Present is a book we can read
in which the world and time are inscribed.

Stars

If the earth is a grain of sand amidst the galaxies,
from here, if one looks, man appears a husked grain—
if he is even seen at all; so why then
does your pride exceed the measure of the world?

Man

The scale of a star is a thousand times that of earth
but since the star has no life its magnitude is meaningless;
I am the being of this world who has given shape
and conscious life to everything;
I discovered the stars, I created God!

QUEEN

Her gallant courtier promised
    to make her a queen
of the true celestial kingdom
    of marriage.

The "Miss" became a "Mrs."
    and she was a queen
but the heavenly realm could not be found . . .
    in a squatter's hovel.

WHO FIRST TEMPTED EVE:
THE LOUSE OR THE DEVIL?

Eve, before
the Devil loomed
to tempt her,
was picking lice in her hair
in paradise.

IF YOUR TEARS HAVE DRIED UP, MY NATIVE LAND

Weep, my native land. With strong-breathing sorrow cry out
Your pitiful fate, land that's almost beyond pity:
The flag that symbolizes your integral being is shrouded by a
   foreign flag,
Even the language you've inherited is bastardized by another tongue;
This day resurrects the day when once your freedom was wrested
   from you,
On the thirteenth of August, American invaders raped Manila.*

Weep, while they celebrate with brutish futile vanity;
By the underdogs' graves the running dogs of imperialism amuse
   themselves.
You resemble Juli, sold to redeem a debt and thus enslaved;
You resemble Sisa, crazed by suffering;
Lacking the strength to defend herself, lacking the courage to fight;
Wailing when beaten to death, wailing when robbed!

Cry out the thousand-and-one torments that afflict you,
Ills that torture your body but nourish the foreigner's:
All your wealth plundered, all your resources pillaged,
All your freedoms ended, vanished, gone!
Gaze on your estranged land, imperialist armies watch over it;
Gaze on your alienated sea, the exploiter's ships roam freely there.

(*On August 13, 1898, after a "mock battle," Manila was surrendered by the
Spanish colonizers already defeated by Filipino revolutionary forces to the American
imperialist invaders.)

Weep if in your heart all aspiration has faded,
If the sun in your sky is always the sun of cold twilight,
If the waves of your seas no longer thunder against the shores,
If the volcano in your breast no longer rumbles,
If no one mourns for you in the night of awakening,
Cry out and whimper, for your independence is indeed buried.

But a day will dawn when your tears will dry up completely,
A day will come when tears will no longer gush forth from your
  swollen eyes
But fire, fire that's the color of blood will burst out and rage
While your blood seethes and boils like molten steel!
You'll shout with noble defiance amid the fires of a million torches
And the old chains you'll snap with bullets!

Alejandro G. Abadilla

(1905-69)

Born in Rosario, Cavite, on March 10, 1905, Abadilla belongs to the generation of Amado V. Hernández which spearheaded the resurgence of Tagalog literature in the late 1930s and early 1940s. But unlike the socialist Hernández and others like Benigno Ramos and Teodoro Agoncillo, Abadilla chose a liberal-individualist stance.

Upto the end of his life, Abadilla espoused a bohemian and somewhat elitist theory of artistic vocation which led him inevitably to the abysmal depths of mysticism, pseudo-Jungian analysis, and oracular pronouncements verging on nonsense. Whatever his grave failings, Abadilla is credited with having introduced "free verse," more precisely a Coleridgean adjustment of content and form, into the Tagalog poetic tradition. His speculations about poetic form invoke the self—the complex of feelings, moods, visions which he conceives of as the "I"—as the fundamental justification for inventing new metrical forms, stanzaic patterns, surrealistic imagery, and various expressionistic experiments.

Highly subjective and spuriously metaphysical, Abadilla's poems often lapse into melodramatic and sentimental excess. However, his later "erotic" explorations may have introduced into the poetic tradition a new field for thematic probing—even at the sacrifice of the neoclassic ideal of "good sense."

Abadilla began his career as a critic of poetry and the short story in 1932, with his popular column "Talaang Bughaw" ("Blue List") in the Tagalog daily *Mabuhay*. After World War II, he continued this occupation in various newspapers while working as college teacher of literature, insurance salesman, magazine editor, and journalist at separate times. Abadilla contributed immensely to the important task of anthologizing works printed in the newspapers. Among his own books are: *Ako ang Daigdig* (1955), *Tanagabadilla* (1964), and *Piniling Mga Tula ni AGA* (1965). He also edited the avant-garde monthly *Panitikan* (1962–67).

In 1968 Abadilla was awarded the Republic Cultural Heritage Award in Literature. A year after his death in 1969, the capital city of Manila gave him the posthumous honor "Patnubay ng Kalinangan" for his literary achievement.

IMBECILITY

Death is not life
(It cannot be)
So to die is for you not to have lived truly.
So to live is for you not to have died truly.

Alive is life
If the awareness of death
Is alive.

Dead is life
If the awareness of death
Has no life.

So to die is not to have lived truly,
So to live is not to have died truly.

GREATNESS: O POEM

Heat,
Blaze,
And the conflagration of feelings. . . .

Color of desire,
Seizure
Of the craving
To be wed to her,
The rose in the heart's beat,
The greenness in the landscape of the mind,
The soul's holiness beyond measure.

Heat
And the color of feelings,
Blaze

And seizure of wanting
To experience the honey in the hive of life.

Earthly
Sensations directed to the sky,
Praying on folded knees
Wanting to be united,
And staggering before
The godhood of the soul reposing
In the creature's self.

I WANT TO REST

Brightness,
yes, you bear illuminations in your eyes,
and your blood is a poem scorching my soul
but
I still wish to remain
in darkness.

It's true
you are a priceless treasure in my life
and I do not wish to be removed from your loveliness;
but
I do not know why in the darkness of this fate
I lie down despairing.

With you
when you play music I want to join
and rejoice, dancing to your crazy rhythm,
but
why am I always a slave
of my adored darkness?

Celebrate?
but I do not wish to rejoice anymore—
existence on this earth is a mystery that perplexes;
so now
to my withered life you become everything—
I do not want to rejoice

Because
I am prepared for one mission:
to rest, to sleep, to lie down in the lap of death!
because
only in this way can I prove
I have lived.

THE HEART'S CORE

The heart, the breeding ground
Of a knowledge without disguise—
Whisper of mind-life
In the fated obeisance, supine,
Of the reasoning mind.

The blood that runs
In the veins is the trill of the life
Without end in its rebellion
Against death.

The paganism in you
Is the naked beauty of life
(Despite the trappings of thought's *isms*)
Exposing its own center:
Revolt against idiocy:

You are sufficient in your self,
O heart's core of hearts:
Because civilization that wants to lead you forth
Are eyes that (though wide open)
Lack vision.

His youthfulness
In front of your decrepitude
Is the bitter history of what exists
In the destiny of moths
Rushing impetuously into your flame.

YOU ARE THE LIGHT

You are the light,
is what you said;
You, I answer then:
darkness am I.

You are the brightness,
but I don't need you to see who I am.
You are the light,
eyes glaring starkly are your eyes
electric spark of a puzzled and puzzling gaze
at my appearance:
darkness am I.

Go, mirror
your graceful light,
you will witness yourself bared and baring.
You are the brightness,
eyes glaring starkly are your eyes—
eyes that cannot stare out my eyes.

I observe your noble posture:
dazzling are the trappings round your flesh,
you are the muse
of stupid shallow spirits.

I see you
but you cannot see me,
their eyes and your eyes
in my heart,
in that mystery and darkness
which none will ever penetrate.

You are the brightness,
is what you said;
You, I answer then:
darkness am I.

I, THE LAW OF THE INESCAPABLE

The absence
of those who have been yours,
death that's absent from your consciousness . . .
 you who are not you
 you who are not a slave
 of others you now claim to possess.

Hold and embrace
with all your courage
that pure conscience of your own soul,
 he will proclaim you
 in your servitude
 life's challenge to death—

I in you
who are the shroud of mystery
do not wish to discover myself in solitude. . . .
 Not you but I
 am born now so that tomorrow
 I could glimpse your wretched soul.

You who have none
of those desires
in my deepest self—you are a wasted candle
of the night's long vigil
at the foot of my symbol—
I, the law of the inescapable.

PALM TREES

Strung in a file
On both shores . . .

By this long river
They watch,
God's warriors.

Diminutive palm trees,
Go and ascend from the deeps,

Come in to my poor hut:
My soul overflowing with anguish
You will feel through the leak in the roof.

THE POEM

Of me
You ask
What a poem is . . .
But
Would my whisper or my weak voice
Be able to stir your slumbering spirit?
Of me
Therefore
Ask again what a poem is.

The wind
You don't perceive
But feel:
Ah, that is the poem—
The beauty that shuns to be recognized
By your too critical eyes;
In life
Beauty
Is that passion yet to be experienced!

A poem
Is like a woman
To you, man—
How strong!
Despite her muteness, not uttering any command,
You are a slave and she is your god.
Ah, because
She is the soul that
In her purity never argues nor reasons.

Observe,
The night is dark
And utterly obscure . . .
But night is beauty for the poetic spirit

Tottering with its burden of grief:
Because
For him
Evil or good is no longer gold.

Of me
You ask
What a poem is . . .
Ah, that is any spirit of dumb beauty
Dressed by feelings of chaste color,
Because in life
It is the deep holy prayer in the heart.

LIKE THE ROCK CRUMBLING

Like the rock crumbling
In the long drawn-out night,
Dawn comes—
I wake in you with feelings wounded. . . .

Now, observe, you
Will not be able to return to your origin
In greed's summit
Which you call your own victory. . . .

Like the rock crumbling
In the long drawn-out night—
When I awoke that morning
To my smarting eyes was revealed
The naked form
Of truth without disguise.

Teo S. Baylen

(1904–   )

Born of poor parents in Noveleta, Cavite, on January 24, 1904, Baylen finished high school and immediately began working as an elementary school teacher from 1922 to 1927. He also participated in dramatic performances and other theatrical work before Wold War II. In 1930 he was recognized as the "King of Balagtasan" in Cavite. Baylen studied music, enabling him not only to write lyrics for musical compositions but also to conduct church choirs.

Baylen has served as preacher in the United Evangelical Churches while working as an accounting clerk for the United States Navy from which he retired recently with a monthly pension. Aside from his literary activities, Baylen also served as secretary to the City Council of Cavite for many years.

Baylen has received the highest prize in literature in the country, the Republic Cultural Heritage Award for 1962–63. He has been chosen by the Institute of National Language as Poet of the Year for 1962 and for 1964. Baylen has published his work in two volumes, *Tinig ng Darating* (1963) and *Pinsel at Pamansing* (1967).

Most of Baylen's poems deal with religious and apocalyptic themes, often in a highly rhetorical manner and loaded with mythical or biblical allusions. His tendency to allegorize even contemporary subjects from real life like the horrors of nuclear war, oppression of the people, politics, and so on, reveal his underlying sentimental and moralizing impulse—a major source of his weakness. For his sustained musical rhythms and elaborate pastoral imagery, Baylen seems unrivaled by any of the older generation of Tagalog writers.

HUNGARIAN RHAPSODY

Free?
    Prosperous?
        Peaceful?
We are also free inside the cage,
Free with minds chained;
Prosperous the flowing blood,
Self-sufficient in the refuse of the greedy;
Peaceful with saints as weapons,
Peaceful and persecuted!

    (The chameleons are lucky,
    well fed like Judas
    Though the silver is bloody!)

Free to weep in the gutter,
Free with a life not yours;
The tables abundant with fear,
Prosperous and gaunt;
Peaceful the door at gunpoint,
Calm? . . . Ah, yes, in the pit!
    (But the rage of the dark
    In the anguished night
    Is a signal of a dazzling dawn,

Peaceful!
    Prosperous!
        Free!)

THE VOICE OF THINGS TO COME

Let your imagination journey there
In the bloody paths of our century;
You will meet the figure of a time
Approaching with a load of questions:

—Is this the land I am going to claim,
A place inhabited by fire and sharp steel?
Is this the inheritance I shall plow,
A heap of bones and gaping graves?

Is this the world dragged from somewhere
By the wheel of your devious Progress?
Is this the fruit of your Art and Science?
Is this the civilization you bequeathed?

—Is that the meadow, that the mountain
I will find already charcoal and stump?
Is that the end of God's purpose
When the first man received the christening grace?

Are those the fields that had conserved
Nothing but the skulls of brothers, kins?
Sterilized by your venomous bullets,
Where no grass will spread roots?

—Bare bodies, hunger, minds crippled,
Faiths betrayed and hopes wrecked;
Is this the inheritance I shall enjoy,
Relics of your planting, your vows?

O mankind of this century
Whom children hence will reproach;
Tomorrow how will you answer
The charge of generations following you?

YOU ARE A NAIL ON MY COFFIN

You are a fruit that has ripened on a sap-filled tree.
You are a gold wine cup on the palm of my table
Overflowing with the honey of my adoration.

But you are also the torrent that eloped and fled
From the sweet spring in which you woke up
So that you have grown salty in the mire at the foothill!

Now in my heart you are a dagger violently struck,
In my head a fiber of the grief that's raveled;
On my forehead a rent, in my breath a knot,
And on my coffin a sharp nail!

You snapped the stick that I should hold
And wield to murder my exemplary life!
(Forgive me, Swan of Bulacan!)

Yes, still unripe I did not shake you
Because my heart would be the first to rot from ripeness!

Now . . . society is a judge before me.

A BROKEN CLAY POT

An old man at the hillside
Once molded a clay pot
To keep miracles there—
When you put to trial the excellent work,
Excelling all the fruits of the spirit,
You were chagrined upon seeing how fragile
The earthen vault you have sweated for.

Your hatred flamed!
And in a flood you let drift
The chest you have shaped, now broken!
This creation of the mind floated somewhere
When the flood ebbed and light shone again.
But you repented. And your grief
Cast its rainbow and pity glimmered.

You fashioned once more . . . .

It was a china-clay jar of diamonds
Which did not crack in the ordeal at the forge;
And you triumphed! O Sage, you! . . .
This is your true, authentic creation.
Now what then, in that fate that flooded,
Of the clay pot driven somewhere?

O maker of clay pots:

Now that this jar of diamonds has realized
        What the earthen pot could not do,
And now that you have a pattern of lofty quality
        Seek and make whole
Your first fragile artifice; perhaps,
        The refuse of the flood may then be fulfilled.

Manuel Principe Bautista

(1919–)

Noted for his delicate and sensitive renditions of *haiku* lyrics, Bautista ranks among the more innovative modernist writers in Pilipino today.

Born in Manila on June 20, 1919, he began writing when he was only sixteen years old. He produced in English and Tagalog not only poems but also radio plays, dramas, short stories, essays, and other journalistic writing. In 1937 he served as a member in the board of judges of the literary organization *Ilaw ng Bayan* (Light of the Country). He also worked as assistant editor of the monthly *Kayumanggi* after World War II. His poem "Akin Man Ang Lungkot" was chosen as one of the best poems published in 1947 by the Institute of National Language, Manila.

Husband to the well-known writer Liwayway A. Arceo, Bautista is at present division head at the Philippine National Bank.

Bautista's poetic achievement is meager but distinguished in the handling of idiom, imagery, symbolic structure, and tone. He deserves to be read more intensely and sympathetically.

I AND THE POEM

I could not grasp our tryst:
No fixed hour . . . no appointed day.
Once at the fountainhead . . . or else, downstream;
And when we meet, there's no response at all.

Always I yearn for the promises
That though muttered the heart knows;
(In quiet it grows more beautiful—
The elected tryst of our liaison!)

And there are moments when there's sulking
And greetings are withheld, as though irked;
From my offers she secretly escapes
Like an outlaw that flees captivity.

That is usually our way: one dream
That once is formed and once destroyed;
But at the encounter, the hour of tryst,
Now and tomorrow become noble, sublime.

PART II

Of all the genres in contemporary Philippine literature, the short story written in Tagalog since the beginning of the twentieth century may be said to render the form and texture of the Filipino experience more successfully than any other literary type in any other language in the Republic. In the transcription of life with concrete exactness, with fidelity to the complex implications of any idea or insight thus imaged in fiction, the Tagalog writer excels supremely. Why this is so, the reason for such an achievement, inheres in two factors. First, there is the nature of the short story form; second, there is the milieu in which the creative act was brought to perfection.

For the Tagalog writer, the act of writing implies a responsibility to both self and the world. Apprehending the permanent essentials that transcend the facts of everyday life, yet always conscious that all ideals inhabit the contingent world of time and space—"the rag-and-bone shop of the heart"—the writer strives to conceive and contain that unique form of experience which is his spiritual and material life. I believe that only from a grasp of the dialectic between the artist and his age can we illumine the significance of literature for our time.

Like its counterparts in the West, the short story in Tagalog arose from folktales, yarns about fairies and supernatural beings, romances, cycles of beast fables, and other narratives of adventure which functioned as the vehicle of the popular imagination. Examples range from the pre-Homeric sagas to the Egyptian chronicles in hieroglyph. One will observe to what great extent themes or motifs of Philippine legends that have survived from archaic times before the coming of Magellan and the Spanish *conquistadores,* before the sixteenth century, show basic affinities with the "matter of India"—the ramifications of the *Ramayana* and the *Mahabharata.* The germ of such legends may be any suggestive word, jest, or gesture. Characteristically, the heroic figures of the Indo-Malayan civilization of which the Philippines then formed a part acted as protagonists in highly stylized exploits.

It is difficult to describe precisely the routes of communication between cultures—that is, why folklore motifs recur universally—without perhaps intruding a theory of literary archetypes such as Northrop Frye has proposed. I should mention here the fact that the hypothesis of Malayan cultural unity by common descent, which the noted anthropologist H. Otley Beyer has formulated, is still under question despite the results of excavations and comparative research. Folklorists have pointed out the correspondence of patterns between the feats of Suwan (the Juan Tamad of antiquity) and the other heroes of stories popular in Asia Minor and the Mediterranean world. But what survives now of these stories are anecdotes which have lost their quality of being "news." Vivid happenings have metamorphosed into set tales (French *contes,* for example), something told or recounted. They have become stereotypes of fancy.

The rigid formulas of the tall tale, the ingenious twist of satiric humor, and the persistent harping on subjects of sex and death, which pervade Filipino folk narratives, have sustained up to now their powerful appeal among the *bakya* crowd, the masses. This appeal is due perhaps to the simplicity of plot and the memorable earthy language in which behavior and talk are conveyed. Many of the stories in Carlos Bulosan's best-selling *The Laughter of My Father* are subtle recastings of Philippine folk tales.

When the Spanish missionaries came and found a flourishing oral tradition among the natives—for the Filipino communities then enjoyed a highly developed culture and art of their own—they had only to reorient such tales, introduce biblical themes and motives, for them to serve as *exempla* of Christian truths and virtues. Consequently, most popular tales acquired a moralistic tone.

From the publication of the *Doctrina Christiana* in 1593 up to the revolution against Spain in 1896, the passion for catechism and indoctrination prevailed. Pleasure, *dulce,* subserved *utile,* the evangelical duty. Since those who wrote and managed the printing of books were priests, the country was quickly flooded with *novenas,* lives of saints, homilies, and other religious cant. The Tagalog *pasion* recounted in octosyllabic verse the life of Christ in a vivid sequence of scenes heavily interwoven with *arals* or lessons. This tendency still runs strong. The didactic habit can be seen operating indirectly in many stories, like a wraith of the past driving the engine of artistic form. This habit is almost an exorcism of the indulgence in a pleasurable act, the act of self-expression.

Lope K. Santos, the "grand old man" of Tagalog letters, had long ago deplored the mechanical goodyism of the reading material which some historians, in desperate nostalgia, proudly claim as the origin of Philippine literature. Because the Spanish missionaries destroyed the pagan literature of the early Malays, the only material for any historical account of Philippine literature is that produced by priests and their factotums.

For three centuries, a superegoistic impulse seems to have seized and dominated the mind and the heart of every Filipino until, the dark unconscious revolting, intellectuals like José Rizal, M. H. del Pilar, and the propagandists of the nineteenth century who had sat under Voltaire and Swift, turned the Philippine "paradise" topsy-turvy. Sanctimonious piety gave way to *pietas,* the will to collective destiny. But the *platicas* or sermons of the past were not all absolutely worthless, for they refined the idiom toward sensuous particularity, toward a wider and deeper range of metaphoric combinations. Setting aside *Barlaan and Josaphát* (1709), which is a mere translation, one finds in Modesto de Castro's *Urbana at Felísa* (1856) a classic style, smooth, flexible, richly connotative, lucid yet musical in the order of its sentences. Padre de Castro had schooled himself in the rhetoric of the pulpit.

The epistolary form of *Urbana at Felísa* labored under the excess of peroration, further burdened with incidents wholly subordinated to character portrayal done in bold typifying strokes. But the virtue of the work is its own vice. Its major concern imposes a rigid structure of dogmas about social mores. And the topics elaborated upon—love, courtship, marriage, family ties—were deprived of their inherent resistance and variety. The argument is thus vulnerable to changes of customs and outlook. Nonetheless, something positive has been accomplished here. Padre de Castro's work clearly illustrates how Tagalog prose has gained a character obsessed with manners, ethics, sincerity, as evidenced by its vocabulary and its figurative turns of expression. It has become obsessed with what Henry James calls "the thick web of experience" spun by the constant tension and ambiguities of human relationships.

The context of society in almost all of the thousands of Tagalog stories written since 1900, including the *dagli,* betrays its control in both the process of plot development and the delineation of personages. The *dagli,* literally "immediacy," was the first short story in Tagalog. But actually it was a personal or familiar essay, with mood and atmosphere of setting predominant over observed situation and dramatized events. The *dagli* resembles the English character sketch, the *vignette,* or the isolated episodes of the *Pickwick Papers.*

The masters of the *dagli,* like Lope K. Santos, Valeriano Hernández Peña, Faustino Aguilar, Patricio Mariano, and Rosauro Almario, frequently laid stress on entertainment value rather than on "the shock of recognition." One is hard put to ascertain whether they cherished worthier purposes such as those declared by Washington Irving in emphasizing atmosphere and scene, the pictorial representation of life, in his sketches. Their awareness of an audience, however, saved them from decadent preciosity and from the narrow cultivation of the occult and the supernatural.

Until the 1920s, the emergent short story in the form of the *dagli* submitted to the condition of its appearance in the newspapers as an amusement piece. It assumed its primitive novelty as "news" only when it subdued the author's temperament to the demands of plot, dialogue, and the interest of objective creation. But that was rarely the case. The pioneers of what Santos calls *kakana,* later the *kuwento* (after the Spanish word *cuento*), such as Deogracias Rosario, Arsenio R. Afan, Buenaventura G. Medina, Teofilo Sauco, Cirio Panganiban, José Esperanza Cruz, and others, attempted to explore the impact of elemental passions on human conduct. Love, jealousy, treachery, revenge, grief—the primary emotions that social problems provoked into tense play often manipulated the course of dramatic encounters. Thus, abstractions were sometimes credibly fleshed. Ultimately the sketch turned out to be a melodramatic allegory of a platitude, often a tableau of pathos, in which accident or simple fortune determines the complication and resolution of the story.

In the first anthology of short stories in Tagalog, *Mga Kuwentong Ginto* (1935), the writers' feeling for, and grasp of, words manifest themselves as the foreground of the creative activity. Verisimilitude, if at all, was a minor requirement. The love for words, the curious fondling of words, often led to sentimentalism in which the circumstances depicted do not at all justify the surplusage of feelings so warmly discoursed upon. Exuberance, the dominance of the lyric essence of the short story, gets out of hand; the discriminating reader justifiably asks, why so much fuss for that trivial cause, that petty reason? Sometimes the flaws arise from too disproportionate a reliance on the presumed intensity of effect of a given situation. This disparity of content and manner produces an incongruous effect. For instance, Rosalia L. Aguinaldo's "Ay, Ay!" in which a girl, because of misplaced prudence, forfeits the love of a young man and dies disconsolate, presents a basically humorous situation as a spectacle to trigger off our sympathy. Likewise, Deogracias A. Rosario's "Ako'y Mayroong Isang Ibon," considered a model of maturity and a point of departure for the modern short story, suffers from a too willing surrender to the emotional charge of language. What comes out is not fiction but straight confession. Lacking any detachment, adopting an introspective tone, it fails to project a plausible analysis of character by directly describing in essayistic fashion the attitudes and thoughts of the narrator.

Esthetic detachment and a regard for the potentialities of the medium can be acquired only after a prior awareness of self and the free exercise of sensibility. But these attributes most Filipino writers, subject to the strict rituals of religion and social conduct, had not as yet attained, oddly enough, for after all, the elements of the short story form had long since germinated, grown, blossomed on native soil—although during the Spanish regime it had assumed the guise of parable. When the American colonial careerists arrived, a radical disruption of frameworks and myths occurred; pragmatic outwardness overshadowed the indulgence in angelic/diabolic fantasies. To sublimate the daemonic rage of the irrational, the *dagli* served most efficiently. But the times demanded something more rounded and complex.

The public school system set up by the American civil administrators sped up secularization. It restored to the things of this world their organic outlines and the integrity of their sensory existence. The activities of everyday life became "news" to be put into words, to be fully articulated, and then retold. Gradually the magazines appeared: *Ang Kaliwanagan, Muling Pagsilang, Buhay Pilipinas, Liwayway.* Recently, the *Free Press sa Wikang Pilipino* began to patronize short fiction as viable art form.

In spite of the shift in ideology and the vicissitudes of taste, the predicaments of life still proved intractable to the artists of the language. One must bear in mind the burden of English, the new language of bureaucracy, to be reckoned with. If the polemical burlesques of the propagandists failed to completely purge the Filipino of his habit to romanticize his situation, they at least succeeded in transvaluing the formula of liturgical escapism. Rizal's imagination tended to subsume an idealized, pastoral world in the *mythos* of irony and parody. But still the value of art depended upon the rapport between author and audience, the characters of the story in question being simply an instrument. Only in the 1930s, after the experimentation with the techniques of flat figures in clever though flimsy plots, did the presence of the protagonists in the literary work become the center of specific gravity, the element that matters. Only then was the short story form given a life of its own.

The direct or indirect influence of Irving, Poe, O. Henry, and European writers on early Tagalog fiction has yet to be examined in detail. Whether the theories and practice of American and European artists really affected the evolution of the Tagalog short story much more than the social and cultural changes in the country is still conjectural. A great deal remains to be analyzed and evaluated in this field. But it is a fact that historical forces have compelled the writers to attend to their material with intuitive thoroughness, loving respect, and a more disciplined craft. Evidence for this "progress" may be seen in Matute's "Impong Sela." Here the accuracy of detail illustrated in the clash between tradition-bound affections and practical reason testifies to that respect for, and understanding of, the nature of the material which alone can disclose the conflicts and ironies of life.

Throughout the entire decade before the outbreak of World War II, the country struggled to make independence a cultural and economic reality. Tagalog fiction in general, however, had refused to reflect the inner tremors of doubt and defiance until it became futile wish fulfillment. The Sakdalista rebelion in 1935, preceded by the Tayug uprising and other sporadic revolts throughout the islands, signaled a need for a new breakthrough in the arts, in literature. Equality among races has been the worn-out "thesis" of many pieces like "Ang Beterano" by Lazaro Francisco, in which an American woman recognizes her error in despising the whole nation because of her personal grudge against a Filipino who, she discovers, has sacrificed both arms fighting side by side with her father in World War I. What a beautiful but facile turnabout! Such easy resolution, in retrospect, seems a kind of cheating. The plot strikes me as a contrived switching of black to white, thus vitiating the fine disposition of incidents. Other stories, like Severino Reyes's "Isang Punglo sa Noo ni Rizal" and Iñigo Ed. Regalado's "Ang Dalaginding," among others, display crudeness and superficiality.

At moments of crisis, however, the order of time in the psyche differs from the order of time in the world of routine. Filipino critics, insensitive to the revolutions in taste and criteria of judgment, have forsworn their privilege of illuminating the function of literature in periods of change. For instance, Dr. Fausto J. Galauran, in a lecture on *The Tagalog Short Story* (*Ang Maiikling Kathang Tagalog,* August, 1938), exhorts practitioners of fiction to adhere strictly to the unities of time, place, and action. Unforgivably he mistakes "unity of action" for "unity of plot." Reputed scholars like Eufronio Alip and Julian Cruz Balmaséda are not at all interested in serious questions of style and meaning. And Rufino Alejandro's comments in *Pag-aaral ng Panitikan* are hopelessly jejune.

With the publication of *Ang 25 Pinakamabuting Maikling Kathang Pilipino ng 1943,* the short story in Tagalog may be said to have come of age. Under pressure of choice and commitment, the writers were compelled to exercise cunning and subtlety in harnessing naturalistic means for symbolic ends. Compared with the potboilers produced by elders like Nemesio Caravana, Susana de Guzmán, Remigio Mat. Castro, Teodoro Virrey, and others, the *maikling katha* (literally, short composition) of 1943, in general, shows competence and virtuosity in the handling of rhetorical devices, point of view, stream-of-consciousness technique, and other "tricks of the trade" to attain a preconceived unity and singleness of effect. The Tagalog writers evinced the mastery and "possession" of the form of fiction in both its epic and lyric possibilities. A renaissance had in effect begun.

The most distinguished achievement of writers like Brigido Batungbakal, Macario Píneda, and Serafín Guinigundo lies in the beautiful control of tone, the masked voice, of the story. The matter-of-fact reportorial voice in Guinigundo's "Pulsebeat of the City," the innocent knowingness of the central intelligence in Narciso Reyes's "Native Land," the cinematic telescoping of impressions in Cornelio Reyes's "Blood and Brain"—all these solutions to the specific problems implicit in the material testify to the extent the short story has advanced in depth and complexity since the *dagli.* As the imagination affirms its reconciling power, reality becomes not too painful to gaze upon. From Matute's moving portrayal of Impong Sela to Sikat's "Tata Selo," the initiation into the discovery of evil-good fusion in life intensifies into tragic clarity.

Although the Tagalog writers have finally taught themselves the effective management of the formal properties of fiction, they have not abandoned the "surview," the commanding import, which thematic value provides. For fiction is an interpretation of life through action. And by "action" is meant the paradigm, the analogy which comprehends ritual and myth. Plastic restraint and the most economical mode of revelation may be perceived in the stories of Genoveva Edroza-Matute, Mariano C. Pascual, Pablo Glorioso, Hernando R. Ocampo, Ben Medina, Jr., and others. While Batungbakal's art (see his unpublished collection *Walang Hanggan ang Pangarap,* the only Commonwealth Award winner in Tagalog fiction) evokes a subdued excitement in its celebration of memory and nature, the stories of Dandan, Agoncillo, Anacleto Dizon, Mabini Rey Centeno, embody a sharply edged, realistic form of social criticism which has always been the paraphrasable substance of the Tagalog short story from its earliest beginnings as folktale and witty, comic descriptions of "a slice of life."

Faithful to its tradition, the Tagalog short story has not forgotten the hovering, enigmatic presence of the supranatural. I would like to mention here Pablo N. Bautista and Elpidio Kapulong who, among the postwar generation, have ventured into the realms of the grotesque and arabesque. Treating neurosis, magic, and superstition as valid subject matters of fiction, they have expanded the field for psychological probing. Alfredo Enriquez, with superb detachment, has claimed the macabre and the brutal as his own province. A new development is signified by Peralta Pineda's "The Fisherman," which employs the method of the German *novelle* with flashbacks and interior monologue. Actualities qualify opinion, judgment, and subjective response in Agoncillo's "The Dawn Is Still Dark" and Hernández's "A Fly on a Glass of Milk."

Accompanying the writer's cultivation of talent is the growth of concern with society. That the commitment to the imperatives of social consciousness engages almost all Tagalog writers like the urging of conscience is a fact which a mere glance at any of the stories will easily verify. Even those pieces with a domestic intimate stage betray an impulse for weighing values with experience, speculation with data. Consider, for instance, the youthful disillusion poetically recorded in epiphanic moments in Arceo-Bautista's "Thirsty Is the Arid Land." Medina's "The Cat at My Window," with nervous objective correlative, yields an image of society as strongly colored as the bitter ironies of Batungbakal's "Light from the Smoke of Gunshots" and its timely use of the Hukbalahap rebellion as background, as counterpoint of continuity to the indecisions of the hero-victim's self.

Obviously the Tagalog writers have wrestled with the problems of art and life in its manifold interconnections. If they have not fully succeeded in contriving answers, they have at least fixed their eye steadily on "the object as it is." As artists they have fulfilled their responsibility to themselves. Electing human action in word and deed, as the paramount target of imitation and symbolic definition, they have mirrored the time of history and the time of transcendence in the most moving artifice.

What, at this point, may be said to be the distinct contribution of the Tagalog short story to the art of fiction as a whole? I believe that this can be seen in the invention and deployment of the "choric voice," the third protagonist with its energy of judgment and its consistent hold of the enveloping landscape of time and space of the drama. It is here that the artist's responsibility to society meets a fulfillment proper to the *métier*. For this single quality, the Tagalog short story can be said to stand out in world literature.

Let the reader consider, for example, the fabric of community interests and its unifying virtue in Cruz's "The Ancient Well" and in Macario Pineda's "A Wedding in the Big House." Cruz's all-knowing narrator comprehends both time past and time future in an epic sweep of vision suggested by particular details of dialogue, setting, and summary. On the other hand, Pineda's angle of insight registers both the seen and the unseen. His outpost of observation is a young man with a naïveté informed by selfless exposure to the discords of experience and the concord of ceremony. In spite of the difference between the omniscient and the first-person-plural-participant point of view, both share the quality of opposing to individual acts the superstructure of loyalties which dictate such patterns of solidarity that make life, the life of men on earth together, possible. Literary artifice now seeks to establish the norms of decorum. Authority in fiction now rests on inclusiveness of vision. Such a humanistic intent functions as a motivation for the selective, form-inducing genius of the fabulist. Given such qualities, the Tagalog short story acquires classic poise.

After the first half of the century, what other fields for exploration lie open to Tagalog fiction writers? One can cite here the example of Edgardo M. Reyes's "Decline and Fall of a Town." The original title of the story, "Lugmok na ang Nayon" ("Prostrate Is the Town"), attributed to the narrator, lends a deceptive note of finality to the remarks of the cynical adolescent. But the youthful awareness, disaffected by the wretched surroundings and impoverished circumstances of the peasants, is unable to conceal or distort the miraculous burst of life and generosity, that animal vitality and gusto without which civilizations decay bursting in a gesture of selfless total giving— this gesture resurrects the paralyzed spirit and reveals the ugly truth and the painful beauty, the shrieking pathos, of the common life in the Philippines today. Here the form of the Filipino experience emerges in the tactful modulation of voice and the ambience of the surrounding objects, the perceptive integration of private notions and public response, and above all in the effortless joining of lyric meditation and its constant weighing of values, with objective report of the almost immortal dignity and aliveness of the worker-farmer's life. In the end, a quiet harmony of structure prevails.

Today, with more than 75 percent of thirty-eight million Filipinos able to speak or understand Pilipino (the official language based on Tagalog), the task and "office" of the Filipino fiction writer has magnified from a simple act of holding the mirror up to nature to the versatile projection of ideal forms. I have in mind such forms of theoretic possibilities born of the clash between the imagination and the external world which offer alternatives of action to men. The challenge invokes both the steadiness of convention and the need for novelty, for creative change.

As democratic processes of government descend from abstract theory to actual politics, as predatory feudalism and capitalism yield to the radical protests of a public mindful of the landlord's exploitation of his tenants and the factory owner's exploitation of his workers; as the masses consistently fight to implement social justice, and as the writers grow intelligent and flexible enough to conceive and respect differences in ways of life and thinking, in the variety of individual personalities in one progressive community; as art becomes no longer the property of the wealthy few but the possession of all the citizens and thus becomes in truth a cooperative endeavor, the short story in Pilipino (Tagalog), like all other literary genres, will find itself elevated to the rank of a major force in renewing the strength and sustaining the hope of the young Republic, in providing an image of its future life.

Amado V. Hernández*

(1903–70)

A Fly on a Glass of Milk

It was as though Bandong witnessed a miracle.

One morning two trucks and one bulldozer rumbled thunderously, arriving at his place. The first truck transported a group of laborers, and the other the tools and materials they would use. The foreman busied himself fingering a blueprint.

Before noon struck the workers had already erected a shack of wood planks and scrap iron. There they kept their tools and materials.

When the next day dawned the workers began clearing the place of wild grass; fire quickly crawled over the expanse of thirty hectares of farmland.

Bandong vigilantly observed what was happening from the back of his house. A peasant who had wakened to the task of tilling the soil, Bandong was a healthy strong man. It was his daily occupation to plow the fields, build dikes, split wood, tend plants, and fetch water. Despite his fifty years he seemed to be in the springtime of youth in feeling. In clearing the rice paddies of weeds, he did not resort to burning them; instead he uprooted the grass and shrubbery, cutting them one by one. But those workers who were clearing what was once a wide wilderness had left it to the flames to devour even the natural fertilizing growth of the soil. Possibly that soil would never again be used for growing crops.

On the third day Bandong saw the bulldozer starting to move. It quickly leveled and compressed the upturned soil. During that afternoon trucks came loaded with crushed rocks which were deposited on the flattened ground. On this stretch the bulldozer again rolled.

Soon the workers laid out the necessary roads after they had buried the pipes that would conduct the water. To every margin of the road they built a shallow cemented canal.

---

* For biographical data, see p. 52.

Barely had a week passed when Bandong witnessed the posts of the houses already stuck into the ground. Simultaneously with these structures they put up electric posts at every corner; they also planted in rows an arm's-length height of acacia and banaba on the roadside.

Two dozen houses shaped like bungalows were first constructed. Day by day the once bare field was being enclosed in a separate fenced area which comprised two thousand square meters or more, a size enough to give room to a big garden of flowering plants, to a spacious garage and a residence for the servants, together with a medium-sized swimming pool. Bandong had somehow gathered the information that the twenty-four houses, when completed, would finally be followed by others.

The houses were not yet wholly finished when on each yard soft garden soil was dumped; a few trees that would provide shade were planted, with roses and other shrubs which upon blossoming would perfume and beautify the entire surrounding.

Bandong got acquainted with some workers in that subdivision. They were the first to approach him at the time when the water pipes had not yet been installed. They inquired where they could fetch water. Bandong offered his help.

In the succeeding days the workers requested that they be included in Bandong's cooking—they were ready to pay whatever expenses might be incurred in providing for their meals. So from then on, even when morning was still dark, Bandong's wife Ana was already on her way to the market of the nearby town which was four kilometers away; she would buy viands and other foodstuffs for *merienda* enough to feed twenty to twenty-five persons. At that time the daily number of workers employed in the building of the houses in that subdivision had reached the total of sixty. More than half had brought their own lunch; others cooked their own. Those who became customers of Bandong and his wife were the first ones who arrived with the bulldozer.

Bandong therefore learned early what was happening to the former large grasslands of Don Felipe. He learned that the land had been bought by a corporation of merchants and government officials. The houses being built there would be occupied by members of the corporation who all belonged to the moneyed class.

"The fellow I saw here the other day was a Chinese," remarked Bandong to the worker he was talking with.

"They claim they make up a small United Nations, mix-mix," explained the worker. "There's an American, a Chinese, a Jew, a mestizo, a Filipino."

"Ah, I even saw a Bombay."

"Yes, there is one. The only condition is—money. He who has a definite income of thirty thousand pesos every year, and has a bank account of half a million, can be counted in."

"And so those people are the ones called 'big shots,' isn't that so?" eagerly responded Bandong.

"Correct. Their boss seems to be the millionaire Don Lamberto Ladron. He has resided for a long time in America and grew wealthy during the Prohibition period. He's an expert in concocting illegal whiskey. He returned after the war, already an American citizen. According to reports, he now has the biggest capital acquired from smuggling."

"That goes without saying."

"And now that he has wealth, he can be *delicado* in taste. He can buy friends and neighbors. That is why those who have nothing, the 'small fries,' cannot live in this subdivision. . . ."

"It seems that this guy Lamberto's not too good a man," ventured the peasant.

"What do you mean?" the worker countered.

"If what you said about his riches is true, then his life is not really without blemish."

"And who on this earth has a spotless life, ha?" intruded the worker. "He's a millionaire, isn't that enough? Isn't it that outside and inside our government there are thousands who commit shameless crimes simply to acquire millions?"

"But I am their neighbor, whether they like it or not," Bandong reminded him.

"Possibly, but you're outside the wall," added the worker. "Is this lot yours?"

"Surely," Bandong's voice emphasized with pride. "I was born here. My father inherited it from my ancestors, and I inherited it from my father. Long ago this place was a jungle. They cleared it, cleaned it, put fertilizer in the soil, and planted on it. My grandfathers were Katipuneros, companions of Andrés Bonifacio."

Bandong confessed that he did not lament the fact of the subdivision. He hoped indeed that that district would afterward prosper with cheerful solidarity. In any case Bandong and his family were not given to frolic and gaiety. They had three children: the eldest was in town studying, the second helped the father, and the youngest, their daughter, assisted the mother in daily chores. Their only joy was to live a quiet and untroubled life. For his reading pleasure Bandong owned some books, *Florante, The Twelve Peers,* and

other romances; and old copies of *Noli Me Tangere* and *El Filibusterismo*. Cabesang Tales was his idol.

"We don't even go to the movies," said Bandong as affirmation
of the peace in their home. "It will be sickness needing dire remedy
the day I go to Manila."

The private yard of Bandong measured to one hectare. In front
of it stood an old hut of bamboo and nipa. The rain may pour and
the sun's heat beat on the roofs for so many years, still the house
would stand as erect as ever. Bandong preferred dwelling in it
instead of in a new bungalow. His family was happy amidst their
poverty.

At the farthest end of the backyard stood six mango trees that
bore thick fruits every summer season; there were also some guava
trees, some *chicos* and *atis*. Bandong harvested vegetables nearby.
On one side of his yard he tended a few pigs and some chickens.
These constituted the source of subsistence for the couple and their
children.

All the bungalows in that subdivision were finished at the same
time. Immediately they were painted with different colors, according
to the wishes of their individual owners. Each yard was enclosed by
a steel railing; a wire netting served as a fence. Quickly telephone
lines sprang up connected to every house; from every roof sprouted a
television antenna.

All these activities were performed within five or six months.
What was once before fallow land on which grass and thick shrubs
flourished and where enormous clods of earth turned into muddy lakes
during rain, with shrill frogs croaking all round, now had become a
small city of enviable houses, of lights and flowers, of real prosperity
and comfort. And all these were a miracle of money. Bandong often
rubbed his eyes to verify whether that astounding miracle done by
men was not just a fancied landscape, an illusion.

The day of settling in the houses arrived. Every moving family
owned property loaded in several trucks. Pianos, refrigerators,
televisions, hi-fi-radio combinations, dressers and equipment
for the kitchen and the dining room, beds, sofas, divans, adjuncts
of furniture for the whole house, terrace and garden, enormous
mirrors, exquisite lamps, electric ranges, luxurious dining tables,
desks, expensive works of famous painters, porcelain pots, files of
books, thick cushions, saints inhabiting crystal cages, rubber
sprinklers, lawnmowers, children's toys, and a million other sundry
things that Bandong and his family had seen there only for the

first time. They stared at every family who moved into the new deluxe bungalows.

"They even surpass the newly opened bazaar of a rich trader," blurted Bandong. "Where are they going to deposit all that property?" he mumbled to himself while musing on the fact that their property for the last twenty years consisted of a few plates, a shallow laundry tub, two jars for storing water, one flat iron, one pick, one hoe, one spade, one saw, an ax, and two bolos.

At the front of the road entering the subdivision Bandong saw a stone arch erected on which was written: *Royal Lanes* (Private). Bandong didn't understand what the sign meant, but his son who was going to school explained it to him.

"That is a place exclusive to those who live inside; it's forbidden for outsiders to intrude."

Quickly the father grasped the child's interpretation.

Also at the mouth of that road was a station for guards, special policemen. Three watchmen with badges on their chests and revolvers on their waists alternated day and night. Everyone who entered and who were not residents were questioned, particularly if they came on foot or in jitneys.

When Bandong first glimpsed the special policeman, he thought that he was arrogant and ill-tempered.

"It appears that he should be the one to be guarded," Bandong mused.

Meanwhile the workers finished their jobs. One day those whose meals they cooked bade goodbye to Bandong and his wife. They properly paid their accounts. Their wholesale contract was over; they would never come back to that place. Thanks, Mang Bandong. Thanks, Aling Ana.

That night Ana piled up her earnings from feeding the workers for the past few months. She had saved five hundred pesos. She counted the money in front of Bandong.

"It is only now that we have saved so much, ha Bandong?" Ana cheerfully noted. "Tonying will no longer be so needy when school-days come." Tonying was their only son, who went to school in the *municipio*.

"Let us see, now that we have this little sum," and Ana confessed calmly her plans, "we might be able to have a faucet installed. Surely we can connect it to the subdivision and pay that charge."

Bandong seemed surprised, but he did not interrupt the wife's proposal.

"So, consider that," added the woman, "it's hard labor to be fetching water always from the nearby stream."

"But I do not complain of getting water," Bandong spoke.

"And where do I wash clothes but in that stream?" Ana reminded him. "How far that place is, though. And when rainy season comes, you cannot drink the water anymore."

"Eh, and what do you want to happen now?" Bandong asked frankly.

"It may be possible to have pipes connected with those over there," the woman suggested, jokingly, referring to the houses of the rich. "Surely this five hundred pesos won't be spent entirely for that."

"Let us not have a faucet if all your hard-won earnings will only be wasted on that," Bandong's smile hardly broke out in his lips.

"Oh you . . ." Ana snapped.

Bandong went to the administrator of *Royal Lanes* (Private). It was not easy for him to go through the guard's house. They questioned him to the point of irritation, and finally the guard had to telephone the office of the administrator. When the guard heard the "Okay" signal, only then did he allow the peasant to enter the place.

The administrator posed in a merry mood before Bandong.

"I was really intending to go to your house," opened the administrator before Bandong had mentioned his purpose. The administrator said his name was Peña.

"I had wanted to talk to you a long time ago," added Mr. Peña.

"My nipa hut is open to you any time," Bandong offered; but when he heard the reason why Mr. Peña wanted to talk to him, he thought of revoking his invitation.

"Have you been staying here long?" the man inquired.

"A thousand years since my ancestor settled on this place," retorted Bandong.

"Can I ask if the yard you occupy is yours?"

"Definitely; no doubt at all," firmly answered the peasant.

"And so you have a Torrens title?"

Bandong was stunned, but nevertheless he replied in a composed manner.

"Why do you ask?" he said.

"Mang Bandong," Peña uttered in clear tones," the corporation wants to purchase your land."

"Quickly the peasant answered that his land is not for sale; but Mr. Peña continued as though he heard nothing.

"They will purchase it if you have a title," continued the administrator. "But if you don't have any, then you're just a squatter."

"Squatter," Bandong shook in anger because Peña even accentuated his utterance of "squatter." Peña glanced at Bandong's hands and arms.

"Do not be angry, Mang Bandong," slowly spoke the administrator. "I do not mean any malice. I'm just trying to explain a legal point.

"Law! What law?" burst the farmer; now on his forehead dark fury wrinkled.

"What I refer to as law is that if you are a squatter you may be forced to abandon your place," explained Peña.

"Before that happens, water and oil will have to mix first," Bandong insinuated, his politeness exhausted.

"But if this case can be resolved in an orderly fashion," pursued the administrator, "it is certain that they will give you help in transferring to another location."

Bandong forced himself to remain serene. It came to his mind that his going there was in obedience to his wife's desire—aside from his having no wish to start breaking skulls. After loosening the knot of his breath, he was able to ask despite the wrath raging within him: "Why do they want me to leave my land, to leave this place where I became a human being?"

"Because they established a dream project here that is without comparison in the Philippines. They want the beauty of *Royal Lanes* to be a reality inside and outside its walls. Your hut is out of place and destroys the landscape."

Bandong could not restrain himself in his seat; he bolted upon hearing such humiliation and scorn of his home.

"Sir," he said enraged, the tendons of his neck bulging, "I am leaving now . . ."

"Mang Bandong," Peña tried to check him. "What I came here for, Mr. Peña," Bandong struggled to speak when he recalled that he had not yet revealed his object in going to the subdivision, "the cause of my visit here concerns our intention to improve our place. We thought of having a faucet and electricity connected to our house if . . ."

"Impossible!" abruptly Peña cut Bandong's sentence.

"If that is so, then assume that I have said nothing," and the farmer lurched to the door.

"Wait," Peña shouted. "It is good also for you to know that they have complained of the offensive smell spread out by your roaming pigs, and the noise of your chickens."

"How extremely sensitive they are," remarked Bandong.

"Here in *Royal Lanes* those animals are forbidden," Peña said.

"Nothing is allowed here except cats, expensive dogs, canaries, and goldfish."

"Animals that cannot be eaten," Bandong astonishingly remarked. "But the people here eat chicken and pork, don't they?"

"Yes, they eat but they don't raise them," said Peña. "Trees that bear fruits like mangoes are also forbidden."

"Why?" Bandong asked, thinking of his six mango trees.

"Because when they bloom and bear fruit, they attract swarms of flies in the daytime and mosquitoes at night.

"Don't they eat mangoes?"

"They do not lack ripe mangoes in their refrigerators."

Bandong's eyes shut; his mind experienced a shock of recognition. In the few minutes that he had conversed with the servile administrator of the "dream project" conceived by extraordinary creatures Bandong learned things he had never dreamt of before. Things which would never spring up in his untutored brain and entertained by his naïve character.

Nursing sore disappointment in the end, Bandong summed up the exchange, exercising full self-restraint in asking Peña: "If I leave this place, what will they do to my land?"

"They will wreck your hut and hew down the mango trees. From the corporation's viewpoint, the proximity of your yard to *Royal Lanes* is like a fly that has alighted on a glass of milk."

Quickly Bandong left without a word of parting. When he reached home and told Ana of the result of his visit, it seemed that there was a fishbone stuck up and pricking his throat. The woman listened attentively to the man's words and hardly spoke. She scarcely muttered, but her inner self seemed to be constantly punctured by the needle which she was then using to darn their clothes.

"We have never harbored hatred against our neighbors," whispered Ana as though her words were soaked in tears. "God will not ignore our plight."

One fair glorious day *Royal Lanes* (Private) cheerfully woke up. The arch that stood at the approach to the entrance was decked with banners of the United Nations; lanterns hung swaying at the windows and thresholds of the bungalows. The reason for these showy embellishments was the inauguration of the luxurious chapel; the distinguished guest would be the president of the Republic and the papal nuncio.

The only house without a prepared feast was that of Bandong's outside the fence of *Royal Lanes*. Though the farmer had not expected a guest, suddenly somebody called from outside. The man announced himself as the agent of the provincial treasurer. There was a summons for Bandong to appear before the said official as soon as possible.

"What could be the reason, sir?" he asked with a note of surprise.

In the past half of this century, that was the only time he was called by the provincial treasurer.

"Do you have a Torrens title for this land?" asked the agent.

Bandong could not recall where his Torrens title was; the truth was that he could not really ascertain whether or not he had such a document. The only thing he was certain of was that the land belonged to his grandfather. When his grandfather died, the land passed on to his father who in turn passed it on to him.

"Do you pay taxes for this land?" the agent queried once more. In years the agent seemed to be only a son of Bandong, but he would not use the polite form of "you" in addressing the old farmer.

Bandong explained that he had not been delinquent in paying taxes until the last two years when his children and wife got sick, when the storm damaged the flowers of the mango trees, when the chickens caught a disastrous pest.

"So then the government will have to confiscate this land," the agent hurled this reply on Bandong.

The threat voiced by the agent sounded like the blast of a revolver to Bandong's ears. He tried to connect everything that had happened to him lately. And the suspicions formed in the heart and mind of the peasant that what he was being summoned for by the provincial treasurer had something to do with what the administrator of *Royal Lanes* (Private) had told him previously.

While the inhabitants of the "dream project" in that subdivision boisterously celebrated, Bandong was slowly leafing through the pages of a section in Rizal's *El Filibusterismo,* through that episode which related how Cabesang Tales was driven to become an outlaw. Cabesang Tales was his idol. Bandong's voice grew loud spontaneously in reading the following passage:

"Cabesang Tales believed that the managing priest was joking, but when he pointed to one of the servants who would get the land the Chief grew pale; his ears hummed, a reddish cloud obscured his eyesight, and he saw his wife and his skeleton-thin daughter, pale and groaning with the ceaseless attack of fever. He seemed to behold the dense jungle that became a rich rice field. He saw himself ploughing beneath a sun scorching his skin while that priest rambled leisurely in his carriage and the servant to whom he would give the land followed his master like an ignoble slave. Tales decided not to yield the land."

Bandong continued reading up to the point when Cabesang Tales stole Simoun's revolver, exchanging it for the priceless relic of Maria Clara, leaving a note declaring: "I need this weapon for I am going to join the bandits."

Upon folding the book Bandong approached Ana who was then building a bonfire in the yard, asking her:

"Where did you keep my bolos?"

"What for?" the woman lifted her gaze and searched the husband's countenance.

"I will hone them so as to make them sharp."

While Bandong was looking for the whetstone on which to sharpen the two bolos that he kept in a box beneath the house, from a distance echoed the peal of bells which signaled the climax of the celebration inaugurating the chapel of *Royal Lanes* (Private).

Narciso G. Reyes

(1914-   )

Born in Tondo, Manila, on February 2, 1914, Reyes received his A.B. (1935) from the University of Santo Tomas where he taught English from 1935 to 1937. Then he joined the National Language Faculty of the Ateneo de Manila (1939–41). His journalistic experience includes: associate editor, *Philippines Commonweal* (1935–41); associate editor, *Manila Post* (1945–47); and member of the editorial staff, *Evening News* (1947–48).

Reyes began service in the government as member of the Philippine Mission to the United Nations (1948–54) and then moved on to several important official positions, among them: director, Philippine Information Agency (1954–56); minister-counselor, Philippine Embassy, Bangkok (1956–57); ambassador to Burma (August, 1958–March, 1962); and then ambassador to Indonesia (March, 1962).

Reyes began writing in English in 1932 when his "I, the Father" was adjudged by José Garcia Villa as the best short story of the year.

"Native Land" ("Tinubuang Lupa"), first published in *Ang 25 Pinakamabuting Maikling Kathang Pilipino ng 1943,* was unanimously selected by a national committee of Tagalog writers as the best piece of that year in terms of formal qualities and thematic significance for the times.

In a letter to the editor dated September 21, 1965, Ambassador Reyes writes: "I have not yet encountered a satisfactory translation of *Tinubuang Lupa.* This is no reflection on the ability of the translators. It is simply that the story depends so much on the unique qualities and genius of the Tagalog language that it is bound to suffer in translation."

Native Land

The train moved out of the station amidst much noise and confusion. Newsboys shouted their wares: Miss, Miss, *Mabuhay! Mabuhay*

Extra! Mister, *Heraaaaald! Foto News,* Mister! Snatches of goodbyes and last minute messages. Don't you forget, Sindo, you get off at Sta. Isabel; watch out for your station. Temyong, don't you ever let go of that bag, pickpockets are everywhere, be careful. Regards to Ka Uweng, Sela, and tell them we'll go home for Holy Week. Happy trip, Mrs. Enriquez. Give me a smile, Ben, I won't be gone long, I'll write every day. Thank goodness that pest of a Turo has left at last; now we'll have peace in the house. Just extend my best wishes. Goodbye. Goodbye. Till next time. The sudden and sharp snort of the engine. Then the screech of the cars hooked to one another. A long blast and the doubtful chug-chug of the pistons. The train sprang to life and moved slowly. H-s-s-s-sss. Chug-chug-chug. . . .

Danding left behind the dimness of the Tutuban Station as the untrammeled air and the brightness of the morning enveloped him.

His Tia Juana breathed deeply and said, "Thank goodness we're on our way at last. It was very noisy and so warm in the station." His Tio Goryo was looking beyond the window at the houses and gardens along the tracks.

The movement of the engine was now fast and rhythmical, like the beating of a healthy heart. The din of their departure was gradually lifted from Danding like a mist, and into his mind crept the purpose of their trip to Malawig. His Tia Juana was saying something again.

"The man who had died is your *Tata* Inong, nephew of your *Lola* Asyang, and is also my and your father's cousin. He was a good man."

Danding grew sad although he had never seen the relative who had died. The mention of his father bared a hidden portion of his heart and brought his feelings closer to the unknown dead. He remembered that his father was born and brought up in Malawig. He turned to his Tia Juana and asked about the barrio: whether it was prosperous or poor, whether it was near the town or out of the way. And while his good aunt was ransacking her memory, a pleasant image of the place took shape in Danding's mind, and in his heart dawned an unusual eagerness.

At first glance Malawig was no different from any other barrio in Central Luzon. A narrow and crooked road, coated with thick and yellow dust. Bamboo clumps, mango, coconut, and acacia trees. Nipa houses, most of which were very old, and walls and roofs burnt from too long exposures to the sun. In between the nipa houses was an occasional wooden house or two, big and unpainted; or a store, hardly recognizable from a distance. Here and there, between the thin rows of houses, could be seen the beautiful and beneficent countryside.

And above everything else, the cloudless sky was wreathed in smiles, full of the glory of the morning.

"Nothing is beautiful here except the sky," jokingly said the *kutsero* of the calesa they had hired. Danding fought against the disappointment that had welled up in his heart.

"It is not so," he replied softly, then added to himself: "In barrios like this one were born and brought up men like Del Pilar and other martyrs of the race; in their fields precipitated the heroism of the Revolution." This thought consoled him and gave a new face to the surroundings.

He had so many relatives. *Tia* Juana did the endless introductions. This is your *Lolo* Tasyo and this is your *Lola* Ines. Your cousins Juan, Celing, Maria, and Asyas. Your *Nana* Bito. Your *Tata* Enting. Bow and smile here, handkissing there. Relatives close and distant, real and adopted, old and young. It seemed as if all the people in the house, from the ones at the foot of the stairs to those in the rooms, were Danding's relatives. "It's good that my nose is naturally flat," he thought. "Otherwise, it would have been worn down to a stub by now."

Because they were the only ones who arrived from Manila, all the attention of the people was focused on them. Greetings buzzed forth. Everybody inquired about Danding's sick father, and his mother, who was now the sole support of the family. Danding glanced at his *Tia* Juana who was trying to catch and answer the more particular questions. She was already indifferent to her nephew's sensitiveness, and she knew that the misfortune of his father was an unhealing wound in his heart. But she could not understand the replies of Danding, who now seemed to be more communicative, at least with his relatives, whom he had just met.

A thin *sawali* wall was all that divided the living room from the inmost recess of the house wherein the dead lay in state. The people, paying their respects to the dead and to the bereaved family, kept streaming in and out of the entrance which was decorated on both sides with white curtains caught by black ribbons. But when Danding entered the room something within him changed.

The noise from the outside seemed to have ceased all of a sudden and the silence of death touched his heart. Slowly he approached the coffin and gazed at the face of the dead man. He saw a fair and pleasant visage that showed honesty and courage in every line. Danding traced in the breadth of the forehead, in the eyes which were not completely closed and in the shape of the nose, a slight resemblance to his father. He was moved to sudden sadness and sympathy.

"You haven't greeted your *Nana* Marya yet," his *Tia* Juana softly reminded him. "And your cousin Bining," she added in a whisper.

Danding kissed the hand of the widow of the dead man. Afterward he sat down beside Bining, but he could not say anything to her. His heart was somehow full. After a few moments he reached for an album from the table nearby, opened it, and then reflected on the mysterious and powerful role of blood in joining people together.

After lunch, Danding went downstairs and walked to the rice field at the back of the house. The harvest season was over, the sheafs of *palay* were gathered in a neat stack. The bare earth which smoldered from the heat of the sun was already cleared. Danding sat down beneath a bamboo clump and looked around him.

At his left, not far away, was his *Lolo* Tasyo who was at that time splitting several bamboo poles. The keen blade of the old man's bolo glinted like a jewel in the sun. Danding got up and approached the old man. *Lolo* Tasyo was the first one to speak.

"You are like your father," he said.

"Why, sir?"

"Because you are restless in the midst of many people; you prefer to be by yourself."

"There are moments when one must be alone."

"He also talked that way, young in years but possessed of a mature mind."

"Did you witness his youth, sir?"

"Witness!" Lolo Tasyo laughed. "This boy! It was I who buried your father's *inunan*. I made him his first toy. He was orphaned early by his father."

Lolo Tasyo stood suddenly and pointed his bolo toward the boundary of the rice field.

"There he often flew his kite when he was still a child. At the other side of the field he fell from his *carabao* when once he went to plow with me. He was hurt that time, I thought he would not stop crying."

The old man turned his head and looked up the mango tree behind him. "I made your father climb up this tree and hide among its branches one afternoon, during the heat of the revolution, when it was rumored that some Spaniards who had run berserk were coming this way. And over there, where you had been sitting just a few moments ago, he wrote his first poem—dedicated to the beauty of one of the maidens he had met in town. Your father had a naughty streak in him."

Danding smiled. "Was that girl the reason why he went to Manila?"

"Yes," *Lolo* Tasyo paused for a while, as if he were recalling to mind what had happened. "They were caught beside a palay stack."

"Caught, sir?"

"Yes—under the light of a few flickering stars."

There were many things which Danding wanted to ask the old man, but he remembered the dead and the people in the house; they might be looking for him. Gradually he cut off the conversation, leaving old *Lolo* Tasyo to his memories.

"What did you see in the field?" teased one of his newly discovered cousins.

"The sun," said Danding as he closed his eyes which had not yet adjusted themselves to the twilight that seemed to shroud the house.

The cemetery was situated beside the church; this reminded Danding of God's promise to Adam and his children, and the sad and painful parting between them which only death could end completely. He also remembered that in the small graveyard forever slept the dust of his forebears the poor remnants of the *Katipunan,* of the hopes, love, sorrow, and joy, the noble dreams and the frustrations which were his heritage from his family. His tread was light on the soft earth; he tried not to step on even the meanest plant.

The grave was ready. There was nothing more to be done except the lowering of the casket and the covering of the hole afterward. But at the last moment the lid of the coffin opposite the face of the dead man was opened again, so that the orphans could take their last look at the deceased. The silence was ruffled; suppressed sobs and mute cries, more heartrending than loud outbursts, reigned for several minutes. Danding clamped his jaws together, but in spite of his restraint on his emotions, he felt tears clustering around his eyes. For a moment his sight became blurred. An intense grief and a vague feeling that he was also undergoing another kind of death flooded his heart. Feeling uneasy and disturbed by the tightness in his breast, Danding slowly left the cemetery and returned to the house.

He wanted to be alone, but when he saw that some people still remained in the house he slipped away toward the field. The sun was already going down, and the wind was becoming chilly. The gray arm of dusk threatened the sky. Danding stopped beside a bamboo clump and wiped away the perspiration on his face and neck.

The serenity of the field was like a mother's hand that caressed Danding's hot brow. He breathed deeply, sat down on the ground and closed his eyes. Slowly he straightened his legs and pressed his palms against the earth. He raised his head, letting the gentle breeze play on his feverish face.

How cold and sweet-smelling was the breeze.

Gradually his sadness and anxiety left him; his tired body began to feel relaxed. His heart felt light on the piece of land which nurtured his father.

The wind was blowing harder and harder, bringing with it the scent of the earth and the *palay* stack. Danding remembered the stories of his *Lolo* Tasyo about his father, and he smiled to himself. The flying of the kites in the fields, the fall from the *carabao*. Hiding from the Spaniards, composing poems. The girl beside the palay stack—all these became fresh in his mind. Danding laughed softly and made himself more comfortable on the ground. Like a tree whose roots were deeply bedded, he felt a kinship with the field which once was watered by tears and rang with the laughter of his father.

At that moment Danding seemed to hold within his grasp the secret of love for the native land. Now he understood why banishment to a foreign country was a heavy punishment; why the sons who were separated from their families by distance braved typhoons and floods just to reach their homeland; why Rizal and Bonifacio, unflinchingly and without question, gave up their lives.

Beyond the courageous words, the unusual sacrifices and the death of heroes, Danding caught a glimpse of the piece of land upon which had stood their homes, the source of their livelihood, a sharer of their secrets and keeper of their heritage. . . .

From the direction of the house he heard voices; his name was being called. He got up slowly. Night had fallen, and the darkness had spread everywhere. The moonless sky was dusky. But Danding could still discern the bamboo tops which had seen his father composing his first poem, and the few twinkling stars which had witnessed his first love.

Serafin C. Guinigundo

(1913–   )

Born in Mandili, San Miguel, Bulacan on January 5, 1913, Guinigundo attended the public elementary school in his province and the high school branch of National University in 1932. He received a Bachelor of Science and Commerce from Far Eastern University (1935), Bachelor of Laws (1947), and Master of Laws (1950) from Manila University. He served as councilor of San Miguel (1937–42) and member of the provincial board of Bulacan (1952–55, 1959).

Guinigundo was president of the literary group Panitikan or *Literature* (organized by Abadilla, Agoncillo, and others) from 1948 to 1959. He was also president of the *Kalipunang Pangbansa ng mga Manunulat* or National Organization of Writers (1949–53), president of *Kawika* (Language Association) (1965 to the present) and president of the Nacionalista Party Lawyers of Bulacan (1953–65).

Guinigundo has served as member of the board of judges for the short story contest sponsored by the Palanca Memorial Awards in the years 1952–53, 1955–56, and 1964–65. Among his distinguished short stories may be cited the following: "Gatas," "At Patuloy ang mga Anino," "Bahagyang Tag-araw sa Isang Tahanan," "Sir Ingkong Gaton at ang Kanyang Kalakian," "Kabukiran," and others. His novels include *Krus na Ilaw, Mga Hinirang, Anak ng Lupa, Kariktang Walang Maliw, PKM, Bughaw ang aking Paligid.*

"Pulsebeat of the City" ("Nagmamadali ang Maynila") captures the atmosphere of Manila during the Japanese occupation with a fidelity unmatched by any other story dealing with the same subject. It is considered one of the twenty-five best stories of 1943.

Pulsebeat of the City

"Gold . . . Gold . . . Would you have gold with you, sirs? Gentlemen . . . Ladies . . . Gold . . ." was the offer-invitation of a woman wearing

119

a *kimona,* her skirt dragging at the heels, sweeping the thick dust of the gutters.

"Perhaps you have gold with you, sirs?" shouted the woman again.

"If I have gold why should I sell it? Isn't gold more precious than money?" retorted one man who was talking to his companion.

The throng of people that filled Azcarraga, Rizal Avenue, and Escolta were buyers without capital (the majority of them) and vendors of things they didn't have, besides the fact that they didn't own the property they were selling. Their occupation was to list down on a piece of paper the goods which they had heard were for sale. They conducted lightning-swift deals. The dealers and buyers immediately concurred with one another. The place of appointment was agreed upon before a table on which one can observe steaming cups of coffee mixed with roasted corn; the coffee made pale the color of coconut-diluted milk. If they were lucky they would collect thousands; if disappointed they would have nothing but hunger all day.

During the process of transaction the voices never ceased nor softened. A look, a price proposed. Another glance. A peep. Haggling. Gaze on a ring, a necklace, an earring and bracelet.

"How many ply do the tires have?" someone inquired.

"What? Is it in running condition? Maybe not. We'll be embarrassed," another wanted to make sure.

"*Abá!* I'm telling you . . . guaranteed. You'll not be embarrassed," responded the person being asked.

"*Hoy, tsiko,* your lot, someone has offered a price. What, how much is my share? Do we have them now? Maybe none? Prepare the papers. Tomorrow's the payment. Make certain of our agreement, *ha*? Even though not in writing. . . . You're responsible?"

"I'm responsible, boy. You know how fast we operate. You'll not be affected. We're clutching the bird tight."

Others were prudent, cautious: they used a lens to scrutinize diamond chips. They turned away from broken jewelry, the carbon type, the one with cracks; they would lose money if they unwisely closed a deal. For every person with a scrutinizing lens there were others shifting around, waiting to inspect, appraise and haggle for a ring, an earring, a bracelet. The people ignored the heat of the sun. Everyone refused to leave the mass haggling for real estate, houses, steel, nails, trucks, launches, horses, typewriter machines and other merchandise. They went to eat and, after eating, quickly returned. They came back to talk, haggle, and examine the goods. The days were

spent in such wasteful business. People could only hope for a tomorrow that would perhaps be a lucky day.

"*Balut . . . balut . . . baluuut . . . baluuuut!*"

"*Puto . . . puto . . . puto . . . puto. . . .*"

Those were the disturbers of sleeping people, of those whose knees
wobbled.

"Just an hour, neighbor, okay? I'll just show it to my buyer. He
will like this. Cash right now. I'll leave these to you; they're valuable."

"Never mind. Take them. Would you break your promise? Anyway
I know you. Just hurry. My friend promised the owner that it would
only take an hour. So if you're going to bring it with you, go ahead.
But return at once. I'll wait for you. I won't leave this place. Before
twelve o'clock."

The person to whom the ring was handed rushed off impulsively,
anxiously. He penetrated the thick multitude. Knocked off or knock-
ing others, he went on. He paved a way amid the crowd with his arms,
making a path for himself, squeezing his thin body among sweating
pedestrians. His time allotment for the ring was short—an hour.

The man who shot off in desperate frenzy, speeding in a race against
time, was Maciong. He numbered among those who bought without
capital except his saliva and sold without anything on hand except a
list. He counted among the agents of the street market whose profit on
his list exceeded what his pockets received; for his pockets, indeed,
were always filled with frustrated hopes and dreams.

Maciong, who served as the foe in argument and the support of his
wife Luisita, cherished the belief that success in life depends on a little
agility of mind which he called *abilidad*. This business cunning of
Maciong was his promise to Luisita. He could prove this with his
quotations in tires of varied sizes; with the options he had on trucks,
autos, houses, real estate, and many other merchandise. Those were
the things he hoped he could convert into hard cash. He confided his
resources only to his trustworthy friends. Others might grab the opportunity if he revealed his prospects to them. His dreams would
simply be aborted. Luisita would again scold him.

Maciong was at last able to pass through the dense mass of people
in the street.

"Teng . . . teng . . . teng . . . teng . . ." was the signal of the thun-
dering monster—the trolley overflowing with passengers who could
not get in, a trolley that resembled a *carabao* unable to swallow the
chewed hay in his overstuffed mouth.

Maciong clutched and clung to the handle of the door, hanging onto it for some time.

"Please enter . . . come inside . . . here inside where there's enough room. Get in . . . get in . . ." the conductor ordered.

Maciong ignored the conductor's haste. He did not see that the conductor had seen him grabbing someone else's ticket as passengers got off. Maciong's going farther into the vehicle was not concealed from the conductor, either. Maciong did not pay attention to the loud clicking of the conductor's puncher.

"Chief . . . your ticket," the conductor demanded from Maciong.

"Here," Maciong replied, handing the ticket which was still warm from the hand of the charitable passenger from whom he took it.

"Didn't you just get in?"

"I had gotten in a long time ago. I just transferred seats."

"Where did you get in?"

"In a streetcar. Where else?"

Those around could not keep from laughing; the conductor flushed.

"At what district of Manila did you board the streetcar?" explained the conductor in precise detail, trying to recover from his embarrassment.

"You've asked me that already," Maciong retorted. "And now you're asking me again. What do I know? Look at the ticket. You've punched it there. Don't you know how to read?

The passengers around, observing the hearty and heated exchanges, shook with laughter.

The conductor stared with furious anger at Maciong's disheveled hair. He mentally measured Maciong's arms, surveyed his height, and when his critical eyes alighted on Maciong's gnarled ears, which were like *sitsaron* from Bocaue, he pretended to go to the door of the trolley so that the passengers could enter and exit.

It was almost thirty minutes after eleven o'clock in the morning. A half hour more was left of the alloted time given to him to sell the ring. Maciong was sure of the profit which he was already counting on his palm; his palm had not smelled of money for several months now.

Maciong got off hurriedly at Plaza Burgos. He pursued on the double a man carrying a *bayong*. He called the man by name. The man turned around. Each recognized the other.

"*Hoy,* Tasio, I have the ring with me. Is our buyer still interested?"

"*Abá*! eh . . . when did we last talk? A long time ago. That has completely escaped me. I thought you would not be able to get anything. What a pity, he has already bought one. Never mind, some other day perhaps."

Maciong could not draw out from his pocket the hand that gripped the ring firmly. He could recall echoing in his head "Never mind, some other day perhaps," which resembled the utterance "It seems I'll be forever frustrated." He stared at the riotous mill of people in Plaza Burgos. Everyone raced to board the trolley. Those whose knees were feeble and whose weak arms could not push or jostle, failed to get in. The women made allowances for others in such turmoil; they didn't mind the vise of muscular arms that squeezed their bodies; their backs, their chests, almost got flattened up. His throbbing breast shook up his polo shirt which was soaked with sweat.

To Maciong's sight the sun's rays still possessed color. But its brilliant color was slowly fading on account of the thick-woven darkness that mantled the summits of lofty buildings.

Maciong trodded on the polished face of asphalt road that had just been sprinkled with evening dew. The light vengefully flung by luxurious houses seemed like sharp arrows piercing the smooth face of streets that Maciong followed.

"*Baluuuut . . . baluuut . . . baluuuut . . . baluuuut!*"

"*Putooo . . . putooo . . . putoooo . . . puto . . . !*"

"Maciong, do eat now. Was your profit yesterday big?" Luisita asked. "You didn't even give me any *balato*. I want some money to buy a pair of shoes."

Maciong grinned. He knew that Luisita was kidding or scorning him.

"Maciong, stop that accursed buy-and-sell business. You're thin, you can't even earn enough to buy your own cigarettes. You're always walking . . . straight on . . . walking . . . straight on . . . toward a thousand nothings. Where's your 'lion's share'? You always eat my 'chicken feed.' You're always eating what I've earned from washing clothes. . . . You're like a fledgling waiting for worms from the mother bird's beak."

"Luisita, you can say anything because that's what you can see. Your mind cannot grasp the reason why Pedrong Makunat is now the manager of Lucky Spot Real Estate Agency. Kamelong Palos, there . . . he owns a big office for steel, and the price of steel is ten times more than his investment. They all began from nothing, like me. Ruperto, Mariano, they too have their own houses now. Didn't those devils start like me from nothing but paper and pencil? . . . and Calixto, Melanio, *abá*! you might be dazzled by the jewels they're wearing.

You can look down on them, but they have their own bankbooks for you to reckon with. They all started ahead of me, I've been slow in getting ahead of them. They don't know what my ingenuity really is."

"Spare me that, Maciong. Because of your *abilidad,* you'll starve. Go and eat now. The hot ginger tea will soon be cool. Your partners may be impatient waiting for you."

"I know what I'm doing. My fortune is held by my two palms. The world exists inside my brain."

"*Naku*! do stop now. You'll see. You're fit only to cultivate the soil. Go and dig in the middle of the rice fields, and your profit is assured. You'll not feed us by your 'swing-swing.' We cannot eat that damned list. Your children will grow up stupid and ignorant."

Maciong ate quietly. He swallowed a few mouthfuls and sipped coffee-corn once or twice. Soon Maciong counted himself again among the army of those who bought and sold what they did not own, and what they did not possess as yet.

"Are you sure of what you said? Is it far? 'Pick up,' is it?"

"Yes, 'pick up.' It's near. Let's go."

Those conversing grouped in islands. Each conducted their own haggling and bargaining. Some touched the ring. Some peeped and scrutinized the small chips of diamonds with a lens. Peep . . . look . . . haggle . . . peep . . . look . . . haggle. . . .

"Maciong, what's your 'line' now? Do you have a buyer for truck tires. I have twenty of them."

"Me? Whatever is profitable. Do you really have tires? How much? Is it far? Let's take a look," Maciong said.

"Not far, just on the wayside. The value of each is a thousand pesos."

"Just near by? Let's go. Let's have a look. But of course I'm already fed up with you. You often offer something that simply doesn't exist. I'm often caught in compromising situations whenever I negotiate with you. I should see it first before I offer it to anyone."

"The trouble with you is that you are so dull-witted," the other thrust back. "I offered you the flour, you neglected it. Nails, trucks, machines, and typewriters. You're too slow, eh . . . !"

They had not yet removed themselves far from those selling nothing when Maciong encountered a former acquaintance, Tasiong Abuloy, whom he loathed whenever he recalled his chagrin with the ring.

"Do you have something for me there?" Tasio opened the conversation.

"Do you have a buyer for tires?"

"I've been searching for one. Where . . . how many . . . how much . . . ?"

"Twenty . . . one thousand two hundred and one pesos each : they're very near."

"Sold. If I can stretch your quoted price, the rest is mine, ha? I have nothing to do with a price higher than that. . . . It's good to be clear in this matter," Tasio reminded him.

"Come on. It's all yours. *Hoy, tsiko,* what you told me is that it's only for a thousand," Maciong whispered. "You've nothing to do with what exceeds that amount. There . . . you're hearing it. Don't say anything about prices, just leave it to me. I'll answer for it."

Two nods of approval were the response of Maciong's partner. They entered a narrow alley and crept into the first floor of a house. Thick cobwebs hung criss-crossed from the ceiling. Rats scampered and scurried in panic. The odor of old furniture turned the stomach. The vendor turned over a few sheets of iron; to their skeptical eyes were disclosed twenty·truck tires wrapped in paper.

Tasio suddenly went out to call someone by telephone. Maciong recognized Tacio's "connections" when a truck came to haul all the tires. Maciong beheld clearly a fly caught in a cobweb thread, swathed and wrapped round by a shroud spun by a spider. While he gazed entranced by the gossamer fiber dangling from the moss-covered rotten beams of that lower floor which made the room ugly, Maciong could not cease reflecting on the cause why he found in that hole the fortune denied to him by the sunlight's colorful radiance.

Maciong's attention soared. He heard the ringing of the telephone. He listened to the voice inquiring whether Manager Maximo Kabangis was there, whether he wanted to buy tires, nails, oil, iron sheets, trucks, machines, houses, lots. Maciong felt his exhausted and aborted hopes slowly reclining on a soft bed. His eyes were focused on a morning newspaper, astonished at a triumph he had been eagerly hoping for, completely baffled when such a triumph came. Maciong heard the song from the radio, heard the sound distinctly: *"Tindig, aking Inang Bayan; Lahing pili sa Silangan"* ("Stand up, my motherland; Chosen race of the Orient").

Maciong thought of hurling the rolls of ten-peso bills onto Luisita's grimy lap. He would awe and stun Luisita. He would no longer purchase old clothes at the corner of Asuncion-Azcarraga for his four children; just a while ago he could not afford new clothes for them. He would confront Luisita with the fact that he had *abilidad.*

Maciong gasped while hastening back home that noon. He felt the sudden bloating of his pockets which, in his quick strides, kept bumping against his thighs. He threaded his way through the thick crowds of vendors selling what they did not have, but he was oblivious to all the haggling and appointments—the direct path to enormous profit and to bright prosperity. Maciong felt that the streets of Manila belonged to him—all of Manila.

"*Mama . . . mama . . .** genuine Camel, sir . . . genuine . . . gen . . . "

"*Hoy,* give me some," Maciong summoned the peddler. "How much?" he asked, digging into a pocket tightened by the rolls of ten-peso bills. The eyes of the boy selling Camels bulged when the rolls appeared. Maciong took three of the bills, gave them to the boy, took a pack of Camels, and left the boy in frozen amazement.

After a while the boy ran after him to give the change.

"Sir . . . your change . . ."

"Ah! never mind," Maciong replied, "it's yours. . . ." He raised his voice so that other pedestrians could hear what he said. He pulled up his shoulders, felt his pockets, lifted his face up to the sky while his cigarette smoke floated on amidst the din of haggling, the cacophony of buying and selling, the confused uproar and pandemonium of the streets.

The telephone kept on ringing. The hammering and pounding of steel from one end of Manila to the other went on and seemed to abide with the rhythm of life. The towering structures threatened to reach the zenith of the sky. The alcohol vapors from the streets seethed and surged up, inducing nausea. The *karitelas* were loaded. Streetcars were overspilling. Everyone rushed, flew, hustled breathlessly along the streets of Manila. All arms were moving, all minds, in fact the whole living body of Manila.

[* "Sir . . . sir . . .]

Alfredo S. Enriquez

(1912-60)

Born in Santa Maria, Bulacan, on January 12, 1912, during the era of
the golden age of Tagalog literature, Enriquez lived an unassuming,
quiet life, blessed with children and good fortune. Enriquez studied
at the Philippine Normal School; he received a bachelor's degree
in commerce from José Rizal College in 1937. Afterward he worked
at the College of Medicine, University of the Philippines, and then
for the firm of Litton and Company from 1954 up to his death on
May 27, 1960, at the age of forty-eight.

Enriquez served as secretary of the well-known literary group *Ilaw
ng Bayan* (Light of the Country) in 1938.

Among Enriquez's noted stories are "Hubad," "Tulay na Kahoy,"
"Sa Mga Yapak Mo, Panginoon," and "Bahay sa Dilim." His art is
characterized by a subtle, careful exploitation of the grotesque and
the absurd qualities of human experience. He has no equal in this
respect.

"The Head" ("Ang Ulo") may be found in Abadilla-Pineda's
collection of short stories *Maiikling Katha* (1957).

The Head

The Japanese with a grizzly face was kneeling with a stiffly erect body.
His head, exposed to the blazing heat of the sun, was bowed. His hands
were firmly bound with strong vines. Huge drops of sweat trickled
down his head, washing his face and neck, then disappearing underneath his thick woolen uniform.

He was a sergeant in the Imperial Army of Japan. On the early dawn
of that day he was one of four soldiers who got separated from their
large combat unit retreating from a cave, their last outpost, under
ceaseless savage attack from American forces and Filipino guerrillas.
And now he was the prisoner of a guerrilla group that they encountered

in the mountains. He was the only one who survived. Kneeling, he waited for death whose coming he was certain of.

Forming a circle around him were guerrillas thirsting for the blood of the enemy. On his figure were focused fierce, vindictive, spiteful glaring eyes.

With both hands Anong raised the big samurai sword they took from the prisoner. He awaited from his officer Lieutenant Clores the signal to behead the Japanese soldier.

"Let's not kill him at once. Let's batter him first with blows, let's torture him first!" one guerrilla spoke in an aggressive tone. In his voice could be felt the furious thirst for revenge.

"It would be good to pry out his eyes or scorch them with red-hot brands until he's blind!" urged another guerrilla.

"Chop the tongue off!" shouted another; his demand was affirmed by other voices: "Cut the tongue off! Cut the tongue off!" clamored the multitude.

"I'm going to chop his tongue off!" cried Anong. He grabbed the kneeling Japanese and forced him to stand. Anong's loathing for the Japanese stemmed from a cause: the Japanese had cut off the tongue of his brother (when he refused to betray the guerrillas by identifying them) until he died from loss of blood. The fire of vengeance seething in his heart drove him to join the guerrillas in the mountains.

"Put out your tongue," he ferociously commanded. Then he squeezed the prisoner's neck.

The hardened face of the Japanese did not manifest any change. He simply shook his head.

Anong's ears hummed at the prisoner's refusal to obey. The prisoner winced from the impact of Anong's violent slap.

"Hey, open his mouth!" Anong screamingly enjoined his comrades. Two men joined hands to force the struggling Japanese. Powerful fingers pressed on his jawbones and forced his mouth to open.

Anong snapped at the tongue of the Japanese and clipped it clean with the samurai.

A piercing shriek resounded throughout the mountainous region. The Japanese soldier had fainted. Blood spouted from his mouth.

"Let him regain consciousness and then pry out his eyes!" incited someone who was still unsatisfied.

"That's enough," ordered Lieutenant Clores. He had felt a scouring sensation in the pit of his stomach when Anong snipped the prisoner's tongue.

Anong hurled the piece of tongue far away and then wiped off his bloody hands on the grass.

A soldier splashed water on the captive's prostrate body. The Japanese soon became conscious. Gasping feeble groans and moans sounded from his blood-drenched mouth; they were not the groans of a human being.

Once more he was forced to genuflect on the grass soaked with the blood that gushed from his mouth. When Anong raised the samurai again, he mockingly asked the kneeling man: "Hey, do you have anything to say before you die?"

Anong's comrades burst into wild laughter. What a witty joke! Only Lieutenant Clores remained silent. With a nod the Lieutenant signaled Anong to execute his task: the sharp and heavy samurai swiftly dropped.

The head fell on the earth and rolled down the hill until it got caught by a big rock between two coconut trees.

The headless body fell with a thrust against the grass-carpeted soil. Abundant blood bubbled and flowed from the severed neck. The body convulsed once like a wriggling, quivering chicken; after a while it became still.

The lieutenant ordered the cadaver buried, together with the head, but the soldiers all protested.

"Let's bury the body, but let's bring the head home. The town-folk will rejoice on this occasion. In this way they will feel a little satisfaction from this fulfillment of vengeance against those who inflicted so much suffering on the people."

The leader approved the request of his men. He realized that he coul not control their thirst for revenge no matter how excessively cruel it showed itself.

The headless corpse was interred in a shallow hole. Anong directed the burial of the body. He was secretly pleased with it because he knew that the dogs would soon scratch the soil of the grave, then scuffle for the remains until all was reduced to scattered morsels of rotten flesh. The dogs will finish what we have left unfinished, he thought.

Anong himself picked up the head which was now covered with blood mixed with soil. Dark blood dripped from the part where the neck was split. Anong took his big handkerchief and slung it around the head.

The guerrillas began trekking back to the mountain trails, heading back toward their headquarters in town. Anong spearheaded the file, the head swinging and dangling from his right hand. Lieutenant Clores followed in the rear. His soldiers cheerfully and noisily celebrated. He understood why: they now had something to boast of before the town-folk: a large Japanese flag they found in the pocket of a soldier they killed, three Japanese rifles, three bayonets, a samurai sword, and, standing out among these sundry souvenirs, the head of the officer of the company, the company which they had completely annihilated.

Anong washed the head in a stream across which the guerrillas marched.

"What a shame if he greets his welcomers with a dirty face!" Anong contemptuously remarked.

His companions roared with glee.

When they arrived at the town they were welcomed by a huge crowd. Boys pursued them, everyone gathered pell-mell and hung about them when the crowd saw the head that Anong was carrying.

The guerrillas headed for their camp near the municipal center and plaza of the town. And in a place which was visible to everyone Anong propped the head of the Japanese on the flat surface of a large stone.

The news that the severed head of a Japanese was being exhibited in the plaza spread like fire throughout the town. Crowds came in an onrush of astonished wonder and curiosity to behold this unusual spectacle.

The head became the vessel of the people's pent-up hatred and vindictiveness. The wrath toward the enemy which everyone had concealed and restrained in himself for so many years was now suddenly released. The people cursed the head, spat on the face, threw well-aimed rocks on it. The children, urged by the elders, competed with one another in slinging pebbles on the face that showed not a trace of blood.

In his tent Lieutenant Clores fished from his pocket the leather wallet he got from the breast-pocket of the Japanese sergeant they killed. He opened the wallet and carefully examined its contents. He noticed an old photograph of the dead man accompanied by a youthful Japanese woman and two children, a boy about three years old and a girl about two. He could not read the Japanese script inscribed on it.

He then found a folded letter and read it. The following message was written in English: "Whoever finds this letter I pray that he send the wallet, together with the photograph and the letter to my wife. Thank you—Hitaro Tanaka, Sergeant, Imperial Army of Japan."

Another letter written in English fell from the wallet. The lieutenant read it: "My dearest wife: At the moment that you receive this (if it will be lucky enough to reach you) I am no longer here on this earth—perhaps my body lies already decayed in a spot nobody knows. Do not grieve my absence, if that is the case. My heart and deepest self protest against these circumstances, but what can I do? I am only a

mere soldier. Disobedience means sure death. That would be extremely shameful. This is better: to die with honor while on duty. Love our
children. Pray to God for my soul."

Lieutenant Clores carefully returned the letters to the leather case
and pocketed it. For a while he mused and meditated. . . .

When he emerged from his tent he saw a group of boys slinging
and throwing stones at the head. He forbade the children to continue;
immediately, the children obeyed. A skeleton-thin dog approached
the head, sniffed and then licked it. Lieutenant Clores shooed it away;
the dog scampered off.

The Lieutenant called one of his soldiers and ordered the head be
taken away from public exposure.

"Bury that deep, deep enough so that the dogs won't be able to dig
it up," he firmly directed the man, and then returned to his tent.

The soldier who was charged with the task promptly obeyed. He
wrapped the head in newspaper sheets and then brought it behind
their camp to bury it.

Only then did the people, who behaved as though they had been
witnessing a vaudeville or circus performance, leave the plaza.

Macario Pineda

(1912-50)

Born in Malolos, Bulacan, on April 10, 1912, Pineda resided in Bigaa until his death in Malolos on August 2, 1950. He studied at Bulacan High School (1931). Then he served as town treasurer of Calumpit, Bigaa, Pandi—all towns in the province of Bulacan—throughout the years 1934–46.

Pineda's stories have won universal acclaim: "Walang Maliw ang mga Bituin" was considered one of the best ten short stories in 1937. His "Suyuan sa Tubigan" was adjudged one of the best Tagalog short stories of 1943. His other well-known stories include "May Landas ang mga Bituin," "Harana," "Patayan sa Pulonggubat," and many others. His novels include *Ginto sa Makiling, Halina Sa Ating Bukas* (both published in the weekly *Aliwan*), *Dito sa Lupa Para ng sa Langit (Ilang-Ilang),* and *Isang Milyong Piso (Liwayway).*

Pineda's handling of the Tagalog language displays in its sensitive delicacy and nuance the native resources of a sensibility deeply rooted in the peasant life of the Filipino people, in the soil of his birthplace. His art is almost a transcript of the "fine web of sensibility" that constitutes the manners and psychic being of the Tagalog inhabitants of Bulacan.

"A Wedding in the Big House" ("Kasalan sa Malaking Bahay") is included in *Maiikling Katha* (1957) edited by Abadilla and P. B. P. Pineda.

A Wedding In The Big House

The sun was just beginning to shine when we farm folk arrived in front of the big house. We halted there and gazed for a while at that ancient edifice, home of the clan from which many of our own chiefs had descended.

Nana Tale scrutinized us one by one. "Are you all here now?" she inquired.

Tinong laughed. "Don't bother counting, *Nana* Tale. None among your maidens has escaped."

We young men all laughed, and even the girls could not restrain their spontaneous giggling.

Nana Tale knitted her brows, though her face was still all smiles. "This rascal Tinong—trying to make me angry this early."

"But that's what you were thinking of, *Nana* Tale," the bold Tinong defended himself. "Do you intend to take care of us men?"

Once more we burst into laughter.

I noticed Belen and Minang talking about something in connection with the big house. "Isn't that so?" Iting asked.

Doming and I approached the girls. "Who is that 'he' you're talking about?" I asked Belen.

"They say that this big house appears to be smiling today," she replied.

Doming laughed. "What do you mean 'smiling'? It's because it *is* clean, that's why. Don't you know that for two days we've been slaving hard to clean it?"

"It's true," intruded Taling who looked sharply at Doming. "It's true that the house is smiling. Observe! If you're not blind you'll see. . . ."

Beneath the rays of the morning sun it really seemed that the big house was in an odd, inexpressible way. The moss-covered tiles of the roof seemed to glow. The curtains fluttering in the soft breath of the wind also seemed to wave at us in tender welcome.

We didn't notice that *Doña* Isabela was just behind us. She, with some guests from Manila, had just come from the first mass in church.

"It's really smiling," she said with a smile. She watched her guests who were also on the verge of laughing at our childish talk. "Do you know if it's true that the dead can come back to visit us? I'm certain that my ancestors who have lived in that house for over a hundred years are now in it happily celebrating."

"That's the truth, *Doña* Isabel," one guest commented.

Martin touched me jerkily with a finger. "Those Manilans," he whispered, "however much I try to puzzle them out, I feel that they always talk without any heart. 'Did you hear them?'" He mimicked the guests. "'That's the truth, Doña Isabel.' 'You're right, Doña Isabel.' It's like a film in the cinema, a!"

I found myself laughing out loud.

We entered the big door when we heard *Doña* Isabel questioning *Nana* Tale. "Aren't the others coming, Tale? And the men? *Tandang* Tasyo, *Tandang* Pedro. . . ."

"A little later, after lunch, they'll be coming. The young men and women have come ahead in order to help in the preparations," *Nana* Tale said. "I had to come along because our young women ... " And she glanced at us men as though she suspected us of conspiring to grab the women and run off with them into faraway sinister hideouts.

"How about your father, Tonio?" *Doña* Isabel asked me.

I could not answer her at once. "Later, ma'am," I said, suddenly feeling a tightness of my throat.

Doña Isabel's eyes, for a second, became misty.

She smiled. "Perhaps you're all hungry by now. These young men have been suffering for three days now. . . ."

"Not really, ma'am. . . . That's nothing really," we all chorused.

Round the long table which, so they say, came from a sultan of Mindanao and accommodated fifty persons at the same time—a whole solid piece of *kamagong* wood without any joints, we came to dine together with the guests from Manila. Our young women from the farms could not join us because they all waited and served food.

When a guest raised an eyebrow at us peasants, *Doña* Isabel charmingly explained. "In the old days my father nearly struck me when once, in a party here, father forced our old tenants to dine with us. I was only a young girl then and because I had classmates from college as guests, I stamped my feet and objected. . . ."

For a second a spark of memory flashed in *Doña* Isabel's eyes. She laughed at herself. "I didn't know then those old folks who helped in the daily business of sustaining our means of livelihood."

The Manilans looked us over. Doming, with bowed head, frequently poked my thigh. Martin went on eating as though he heard nothing; his ears, however, had turned crimson. Tinong slackened his rapid chewing of the fried chicken. I felt my nose rubbing the bottom of the plate. I wanted very much to tell the Manilans: "Aha, now you know us, yes? You fancy that because we're only wearing slippers. . . ."

After eating we concentrated on our tasks. Before that all the work had been done. The girls had already arranged the plates, glasses, and all the other paraphernalia necessary for a big feast. About fifty chickens, fryers all, had their heads cut off and their feathers plucked clean from the skin. We men had slaughtered a cow and two pigs. We had filled up all the water jars, split an enormous pile of firewood, so that the cooks were all happy. Rightly so: *Nana* Tale resembled a foreman who rushed in—rushed out of the house, her mouth never ceasing from shouting instructions to anyone.

When lunch was over, Señorita Anita and Doctor Arturo arrived together with handsome young men and lovely young women from Manila.

Señorita Anita was so beautiful. It seemed as though her feet did not touch the floor at all when she walked. She kissed her mother, then they all moved to the spacious hall. *Nana* Tale's eyes filled with tears when she saw the couple-to-be-married leading each other with a warm intimate air. Doming eyed Taling from a distance while I looked at Belen. Minang continually fidgeted and bit her forefinger while she surveyed the scene.

Hurriedly we washed our faces and dressed up in *barong* Malabon. Doming and I went toward the girls scooping ice cream for the guests in the hall. "Let us men serve the ice cream," Doming proposed.

The girls all laughed. "Those hands will carry the trays? Do you think that you'll be carrying hoes inside?" Iting remarked.

"Come," I requested. "Actually we only want to be near Señorita Anita. In the feast last time I happened to be near her for a while when I served ice cream, *naku po,* how sweet!"

It so happened that the Señorita was coming when I spoke those last words. That was why the girls' eyes suddenly bulged in embarrassed surprise.

"Ah, you liked my perfume, Tonio?" I suddenly heard from behind me. "Don't worry, later I will give you a bottle of that perfume."

I swallowed many times before I attempted to reply in a hoarse, bass voice. "Thank you, Señorita."

Señorita Anita held me by the arm. "Tonio," she said, "isn't your father coming? Isn't he going to attend the party?"

"He'll be coming a little later," I answered, with my chest tightening. I forced myself to smile. "The truth, Señorita, is that even if you try to stop my father with knives still you won't keep him from attending your wedding. You know of course. . . ."

"Oh yes, I know that he could not attend our wedding, Arturo's and mine." The Señorita sighed before she smiled back at me. "Call me when he comes, okay?" she reminded me before she returned to the reception hall.

Taling and his companions approached me. "Give us some perfume, okay?" Taling said. "Me too, Tonio, ha?" Minang added. I glimpsed at Belen who stood stiff from a distance, seemingly deaf to all our exchanges.

I nodded to the girls' requests with a smile. After a while I stole away from them. I was apprehensive that they might by chance brush the spot on my arm which Señorita had held and the sensation of unequaled rapture I felt would then swiftly vanish.

I went in the direction of the large staircase. By that time numerous guests had arrived. The marble table was overflowing with gifts stacked on top of one another. The bouquets of flowers brought by the guests scattered an intense, pervasive fragrance throughout the house.

Doña Isabel and Doctor Arturo went out to the balcony. Your father's not yet here, Arturo," I heard *Doña* Isabel speak to the young man. "He's not yet here, mother. But he said that he and my sister would be coming this afternoon," the young man answered.

Doña Isabel caught sight of me. She came to me. "Your father's not yet here, Tonio," she addressed me.

"He's probably waiting in the church," I replied.

"*Abá,* I don't want that. It is my wish that he accompany us in taking down the children, Tonio; that's only fitting and proper. Better go and fetch him from the church."

I was not able to say anything as I hastily ran downstairs to carry out her suggestion.

In the church I found father who had just finished his prayers. "*Doña* Isabel asked me to fetch you, Father," I said. I was mindful of his anger since he might think I betrayed to *Doña* Isabel his intention of merely waiting in the church.

The old man quietly followed me. And we didn't speak a word until we had ascended the large staircase.

Doña Isabel was waiting for us; and when we were upstairs, the *Doña* put her arm around father's shoulder. "Why is it, Terong, that you have decided to wait in the church," she spoke with a slight undertone of resentment.

My father remained dumb. "Hummmm . . ." was his only reaction, blinking his eyes often. I then sensed that *Doña* Isabel was trying to suppress the tears in her eyes.

Everyone was ready to go to church. Four o'clock in the afternoon was already being tolled by the church bells when a large car stopped in front of the big door. Some young women emerged from the car bearing flowers and boxes of gifts. Doctor Arturo swiftly descended the stairs when he saw the last person getting down the car. The bridegroom's pace slackened, then halted.

Señorita Anita stepped out of the house and flew down the big stairs. She was almost holding Doctor Arturo up when they greeted the new arrivals. The numerous guests from Manila stuck their heads out; their whisperings resounded like shrill shouts.

The woman who got out of the car last was also the last to meet Señorita Anita. They embraced. And then the woman shook Doctor Arturo's hand.

"I wanted to hold a grudge against you, Anita," said the guest. "But I was thinking that perhaps my invitation got lost, didn't it?"

Those gathered around them laughed despite the feverish heat of the atmosphere.

"Let's go upstairs," Señorita Anita proposed. Then I observed that Doctor Arturo's face was sickly pale.

Señorita Anita clasped to her breast the cluster of flowers offered by the newly arrived guests. She seemed to inhale their fragrance. For once the woman who got off the car last tried to breathe in the sweet scent of the flowers. Her tears that dropped on the petals could not be concealed from me who stood near them. Doctor Arturo wiped his sweat, choosing to linger at the balcony.

Doña Isabel approached him. "How good she is, Arturo," softly confided *Doña* Isabel. "For Anita and Celia were actually close friends before they got separated from each other because of you."

The young man about to be married rubbed the sweat from his face once more. "I never expected her coming, mother," was his murmured answer.

Other guests—the father and the elder brother of Doctor Arturo—finally arrived on a jeep that had just parked in front of the big door.

Father and I went out to welcome Mang Alfonso. The old friends embraced each other. Father's tears brimmed, while Mang Alfonso's face brightened.

"Later, when we kneel in church, kneel down with us, Terong," whispered Mang Alfonso to father. "Imagine that forty years have returned, and our dreams now flourish more than ever."

"Earlier, in church," my father softly replied, "I prayed and forgave the late *Kapitan* Monang for his act of having me imprisoned in order to satisfy his hunger for revenge."

"Me too," mumbled Mang Alfonso. "I already forgave him." Now I realize that my departure from our town ages ago was predestined by the Creator especially for this day, Terong."

Mang Alfonso handed a bunch of flowers to the elder sister of Doctor Arturo. That cluster seemed so valuable a thing in the hands of Mang Alfonso.

Mang Alfonso and my father went up the stairs, myself softly treading behind. *Doña* Isabel, apparently leaning on the shoulder of Doctor Arturo, waited at the balcony.

Doña Isabel's cheeks were flushed. I sensed that the old woman would collapse without Doctor Arturo's support.

The guests from Manila apprehended nothing of all this. But for children of peasants and farmers, distant relatives of *Doña* Isabel, who were present on that memorable occasion, what was happening bore the profoundest significance.

Mang Alfonso smiled as he gave a bunch of flowers to *Doña* Isabel, but his eyes were blurred by tears. His voice, though gloomy, had an air of triumph.

"For you, Isabel," he spoke gently. "Today is 1906. My seventh and youngest child has rendered us back forty years of our lives. What has happened has happened, and can never be altered. But in dreams, Isabel, at the moment of the wedding of our children. . . ."

The tears in *Doña* Isabel's eyes smarted. "Yes, Ponso," she replied in a subdued voice.

Father rubbed his eyes with his fist.

In front of the altar at the wedding, bride and groom genuflected with stiffly erect postures. Stiffly erect also were the attitudes of the godfather and godmother—*Doña* Isabel and Mang Alfonso. Toward the rear of the pews my father bowed down in a rigid position.

"Anita, do you accept. . . ."

Nana Tale, who sat beside father and me, sobbed quietly. "Yes, I accept . . . I accept," sobbed-whispered Father's sister. "There's no *Kapitan* Monang who will destroy the love between two souls . . . there's nobody who will have my brother imprisoned for being the letter carrier of his friend. . . ."

How gladdening were the peals of the church bells. Perhaps, amidst the laughter of everyone, the big house of those who have been town chiefs all through the years was really smiling.

Epifanio G. Matute

(1908-)

Born in Tondo, Manila on April 7, 1908, Matute started writing in 1927 for *Taliba, Liwayway,* and other Tagalog periodicals. Then he joined the DMHM newspapers before the outbreak of World War II, serving as staff member in *Mabuhay* under the general editor Carlos P. Romulo. Then he was editor of *Sampaguita* (1933–35), *Mabuhay Magasin* (1935–41), *Mabuhay Extra;* and *Liwayway* (1941–44), where he served as fiction editor.

Matute has written numerous articles both in English and Tagalog for *Taliba, Liwayway, Philippines Free Press, Graphic, Bagong Buhay, Malaya,* and many other newspapers. After liberation, he edited *Malaya* (1946) and *Pagsilang* (1947). From 1948 to the present he has worked as chief of the script department of Dramatic Philippines. He wrote the popular satirical radio series *Kuwentong Kutsero,* later staged and filmed. He has also written several television plays.

With his wife Geneveva Edroza-Matute, he authored two textbooks which had been approved by the Bureau of Public Schools: *Pilipino sa Ika-3 Baitang* (For Tagalogs), and *Pilipino sa Ika-3 Baitang* (for non-Tagalogs).

"Impong Sela", first published in *Sampaguita Magazine* (1932), is included in *Mga Kuwentong Ginto* (1936) edited by Abadilla and Clodualdo del Mundo.

Impong Sela

Impong Sela was patiently tending her sixteen-year-old grandson, who lay sick. Beneath the white sheet he was stretched out like a corpse. He never stirred except perhaps for the occasional movement of his dry lips, which were like tallow in their whiteness. After a few moments, *Impong* Sela passed her palm lightly over the sick boy's brow. Her touch seemed to have startled the boy, but he went on sleeping just the same.

"*Maria Santissima!*" *Impong* Sela fearfully mumbled to herself, as she removed her hand from her grandson's forehead. "His fever has returned."

The old woman felt a surge of sadness in her breast. His fever had left him two days ago, thanks to the saint who was her namesake; but now. . . .

Blessed Mother of Mercy!

This worried her. She knew that a relapse would be fatal. What if her grandson, her dearest Pepè. . . . Merciful Heaven!

Why, wasn't she the person who brought up her grandson? *Impong* Sela poured upon her first grandson, her only son's son, all the love and attention of a grandmother. His parents almost did not know how the boy grew up. *Laki sa nuno,* he was called. And true to his name, Pepe grew up, spoiled by his grandmother's lavish care and attention. He was the cause of the frequent quarrels between Conrado and *Impong* Sela. There were times when mother and son exchanged bitter words, but the old woman had always won out. She could never permit the father to lay a finger on *her* Pepe.

And then, now. . . .

Impong Sela started to think deeply. Pepe must be saved from death by all means. In her confusion she thought of the saints; novenas and devotional prayers entered her mind. . . .

Ah . . . !

"Dearest Jesus of Nazarene," she whispered softly, as she raised her eyes heavenward. "I beseech You! Please don't let my grandson die. And together we will go to Quiapo Church for nine Fridays! Please don't take him away from me!"

She remembered that the same vow had saved her own son, Pepe's father, when he was only seven years old. Maybe it would also save her grandson!

By and by, the sick boy stirred. Slowly, he opened his eyes as if he were still dreaming and gazed around him. It was not long before he saw the grandmother beside him. He slipped his right hand out of the sheet that covered him and took the old woman's hand.

"*Lola,*" he called out weakly.

"Yes, what is it, *hijo*?" said *Impong* Sela, as she turned to her grandson and leaned down in order to catch what Pepe was saying.

"I'm hungry."

"I'll get you some milk."

"I don't want milk! I'm tired of it."

The old woman hesitated. Milk, meat broth, orange juice, tea, and nothing more. These only could be given him, the doctor had said so.

"Do you want some broth, son?"

"No!"

"Orange juice?" It was only this morning that he roughly pushed away the glass of juice she had offered him, causing it to spill on the floor. And Pepe never liked tea, not even when he was well.

"*Lola,* I'm hungry!" Pepe's voice was tinged with impatience.

"Just a minute, *hijo,*" The old woman stood up and left the room.

After a while, *Impong* Sela returned with a plate of rice soaked in meat broth, and a spoon in her hand.

"Here, son, but don't eat plenty, *hane*?"

When Pepe saw the food he struggled to sit up, but he fell back on the pillow. The old woman quickly supported her much-weakened grandson.

"Don't strain yourself, *hijo,*" she said, while she arranged the pillow against the wall. "You rest your back here."

With his grandmother's help, Pepe was finally able to recline on the pillows. Then *Impong* Sela started to spoonfeed him. One spoonful. Two spoonfuls. Three. Four. Like a starved being, Pepe almost grabbed at every dole from his grandmother.

"Mother! What are you. . . ." Conrado ran into the room and tried to take away the plate of rice from *Impong* Sela, but he was too late. The plate was almost empty.

"Mother! Don't you have enough sense?" Conrado said in his anger. "Don't you know that the doctor ordered that. . . ."

'Ow, let me alone!" the old woman quickly interrupted him. "I know what I'm doing. How will the child get well if you let him starve? He won't die because of the little rice that he ate. If he is going to die, at least let him die with his eyes closed and not wide open. Totoooooy! Neneeeee!"

Pepe's small brother and sister ran into the room.

"Don't run! Your brother is sick. Here, eat this," and the old woman offered Pepe's leftovers to the children. "It's a shame to throw away God's grace."

"Don't!" Conrado shouted. "Mother, don't you realize that Pepe has typhoid fever?"

"Eh, so what! The children will catch it, isn't it?" she said in a challenging tone. "The trouble with you is that you believe in everything that the Americans have brought here. The children might catch Pepe's sickness because of the microbes in the food. . . . *Tse*! Why is it that during our time we did not boil our drinking water, there were no artesian wells, the water we used came from an ordinary well, which contained pond scum at times. Look at me. How old do you think I am now? If the microbes which you are talking about exist, why am I still alive? You sprouts of this modern era, who are so *delicado* about everything, how many of you ever reach our age? What you are saying is all rubbish. If God wills you to die, you have no other choice but to die—even if you consult a thousand doctors. Have faith in Him, not in a lot of rubbish." She turned to her grandchildren. "You eat this, and don't stand there like a couple of wooden posts."

Totoy and Nene hesitated and looked at their father, who, after the long "sermon" of their *lola,* could not do anything but remain silent.

"Why, are you afraid?" *Impong* Sela asked her grandchildren as she threw a withering glance at her son. And then she took hold of a slipper from her foot, "Let's see who is the master in this house! You eat this, or else. . . ."

Trembling, the children obeyed, while their father looked out the window.

The next morning Pepe was delirious. The high fever made the poor boy toss about restlessly. He felt as if he were being roasted, he kept moving in his bed and his moans were pitiful to hear. His mother's eyes mirrored a mute suffering which only a mother could feel in those moments, as she witnessed the heartrending condition of her son. *Impong* Sela was also there, but she was quiet. Very quiet.

"I am positive that he had eaten something bad for him. Perhaps you did not follow my orders," the doctor said, after their efforts to cover up *Impong* Sela's doings. "He is in critical condition."

The doctor was not mistaken. Within a few hours Pepe began to toss about wildly in his bed; he kept shouting things which made the onlookers bite their lips. Sinang's teeth gritted together. Meanwhile, *Impong* Sela kept murmuring long prayers.

"Sinang," the man called softly to his wife. "Don't cry. I think we better take the boy to the hospital."

"Hospital?" *Impong* Sela burst out in the middle of her novena. "So that he will die there? Never! Don't you ever bring my Pepe to the hospital. If you are tired of caring for him then let us alone. I can take care of him myself. A good father you are. When you were small I always cared for you whenever you got sick; I never let you out of my sight. If now you cannot do likewise for your son—I will do it!"

"But mother!" Conrado's voice was pleading. "What can we do here? We lack the necessary equipment, whereas in the hospital. . . ."

"Whereas in the hospital. . . ." When *Impong* Sela started mimicking anybody she was ready to fight. "In the charity ward, especially, they will attend to you only when they feel like it. What is a sick boy to them, when he is not even their relative? If he dies, what is it to them? Look at what happened to *Kumareng* Paula. She stayed in the hospital for only one day and yet. . . . *Ave Maria Purissima!* Don't you dare touch my grandson! I won't let you!"

The blood suddenly rushed to Conrado's face. He wanted to shout, he wanted to rebel, he wanted sky and earth to meet!

But from his trembling lips nothing came except a stifled "My God!" In the midst of her tears, Sinang approached her husband and gave him a let-Mother-be-glance. With a deep sigh Conrado dropped into a nearby chair. All talk ceased.

Very early the next morning, they were all surprised to discover *Impong* Sela crying to herself in a corner. She had not even shed a tear when Pepe's condition was worsening, but now that he had already quieted down, thanks to the serum that the doctor had given him, she. . . .

"Why, mother?" Conrado wondered.

"I was just thinking," she sobbed. "Juan's young daughter died last week."

"Oh, what of it?" Her son was more surprised than ever. He could not see the connection between the death of Juan's daughter and his mother's tears.

"Rosita and Pepe are almost of the same age," explained *Impong* Sela, "and if a girl dies in one place, a boy will also die in the same place."

"Nonsense! You are so superstitious. What is the use of . . . " and Conrado almost burst out laughing at his mother.

"That's true! Don't laugh at the old superstition. I have seen many cases; it has never failed."

"Perhaps all you have observed were coincidences. Don't clutter your mind with such nonsense."

"Another thing more," continued the old woman without paying any attention to him. "Last night the hens started cackling. That also happened on the eve of your late father's death. My poor Pe . . . ppeeee!" And *Impong* Sela cried afresh.

And. . . .

Surprisingly enough or not at all, the tears of *Impong* Sela continued to fall until the green grass on the grave of her dearly loved grandson was almost a hand's breadth high.

Cornelio S. Reyes

(1911-   )

Born in Tondo, Manila, on March 31, 1911, Reyes studied in the
public elementary schools (1919–26) and the Manila North High
School (1927–30). After studying engineering for a year at the University
of Santo Tomás (1931), he enrolled at the University of the Philippines, receiving his Ph.B. in April, 1939. In December, 1941, he
studied at the National University and then at the Far Eastern University where he finished his M.A. courses in April, 1950.

Reyes has a wide journalistic background, having worked with the
Monday Mail (1939–41), *Taliba* (1942–43), *Malaya Magazine* (1945–
46), *The Manila Post* (1946–48), and the *Saturday Post Magazine*
as associate editor (1946–48). Reyes taught English at the Lipa City
Colleges in 1948–50; and since 1950 he has been associated with the
Boy Scouts of the Philippines as editorial assistant and then as public
relations officer (1961–65). As scholar of the Boy Scouts and the Asia
Foundation, Reyes observed scouting activities in America, England,
Europe, Asia, and in every important city in the world.

Reyes has written over forty stories in English and over twenty
stories and poems in Tagalog. His story "Blood and Brain" ("Dugo
at Utak"), which first appeared in *Liwayway* (1942), draws its material
from his experience of traveling around the country as a laborer.
After his father died in 1933, and through the depression years of 1933–
37, Reyes worked with the telegraph section of the Bureau of Posts,
laying down cables in the Visayas and Mindanao seas, in order to
support his studies and his family. In "Blood and Brain," he reconciles
the differences between art and life.

Blood and Brain

A sudden burst of light between life and death. A sudden burst of
light from the wild swinging of the arm-sized cable, and its crashing

on Korbo's skull. A sudden burst of light from his brain's heaven-reaching cry of protest, his brain in the same instant bursting forth and scattering around the spool of the iron cable.

The brain is the receptacle of my dreams, the complete book of my life. In it are written my joys which I relive over and over again, in my dreams. In it are always locked, never to be reopened, the pages of my sorrows.

The brain, the eyes that witnessed your beauty, the ears that heard you profess your love, the nose that smelled your fragance, the lips that felt the passion of your lips. The brain was the arm that enfolded you to my breast and knitted our bodies together so that we might be in oneness with the earth and the sky, with the stars and the universe.

In a sudden burst of light the blood pools and the sticky bits of soft, grayish brainmatter are rendered useless. Trash to be swept away and thrown into the trash can.

In the sudden burst of light through which Korbo saw the wild swing of the cable which was bringing him death, and felt it, a lightning-like protest of his whole being traveled the length of his mind. A sudden burst of light and singled out in his brain were the joys, the sorrows, Karelia, his adopted son, Dando, only to end a fiery and blinding flash.

"Don't! Wait, Mr. Cable. It isn't fair! There's no justice in it!"

It would not be long now and the sun would be at its highest. The heat was scorching.

Nothing could be seen except the far reaches of the sea on both sides of which were—like thin shadows of some invisible islands—the blue sky, the silvery clouds.

The cable ship *Apo* was calmly hauling up the cut cables from the sea bottom in order to patch them up and again lay them down in the sea; so that the cities of Manila, Cebu, Iloilo, and Zamboanga—the communication among the islands resumed—could be joined again.

The windlass on the deck was steadily heaving up the cables and depositing these into the dark belly of the ship's hold.

They were twenty men in the dark depths of the cable locker. They were twenty and each one, after the other, when his turn came, approached like one fulfilling a vow; the arm-sized iron cable streamed in endlessly. Its ferocity, its hardness and heaviness, its protesting swerves and swings which announced an ominous power to crush and destroy everything it hit—they subdued with their arms until the cable was tamely laid out and arranged in the locker upon which they stood.

Their approach singly to the incoming cable and their endless circling, with heads bowed, round the locker of darkness seemed like an offering of themselves to a mysterious God.

They were twenty, and the angry flesh of their arms, body, and thighs was painful and almost swollen to ripeness in its ceaseless protest against weariness. Their lungs seemed to be rent to pieces in their unending demand for air, the air which seemed to be always insufficient.

In the meanwhile, their hands, which tightly grasped the cable, were swollen with blood and with numerous wounds, repeatedly cut by the barnacles that clung to the cable insulators. Those cuts cried in pain and were itchy from the various poisons that had come from the bottom of the sea.

After making his round, Korbo eagerly looked at the tiny patch of sky which he could see from the hole in the deck wherein came the endless procession of cable. His painter's soul thirsted for that patch of blue, the only thing of beauty in the dark, tomblike cable platform.

For two weeks the cable ship *Apo* had not reached any land, and for two weeks Korbo and his companions had lived under the deck.

Two weeks in the darkness accompanied by the mute protest of the body and soul against slavery to the cable. Two weeks as long as two hundred years.

I'm afraid that my hands might not know how to paint again.

I'm afraid that I have already forgotten the color of the plants and flowers, the color of the sea, the color of the earth. I'm afraid that I have already forgotten the feel of the sun's rays upon my body, the feel of the breeze on my face and hair.

My heart leaps up in anxiety that I might not know anymore your loveliness, the feel of your palm against my palm, the feel of your lips against my lips.

Because if all this beauty were gone from me, my hands will no more wield the brush and my soul will cease to be. Life will have become a veritable grave.

At last the cable ship *Apo* docked.

Korbo's thirsty soul, which had been satisfied with the patch of blue seen from the hole of the deck, drank the breadth and expanse of the sky.

At a shop he smilingly gazed for some time at a chain from which hung a tiny and mysterious god whom he could not recognize.

"How much?" he asked the shopkeeper.

The man told him the price.

"If only I have enough money!" Korbo said.

"That was made from pure gold. It is not expensive at all."

Korbo laughed outright.

"Karelia will like that," he said. When he saw the puzzled look in the man's eyes, he added, "My wife is fond of collecting small images of different gods. Isn't it nice to see that tiny god's wide and mysterious eyes that seem to embrace in one glance all the universe?"

It was the shopkeeper's turn to smile. This customer is funny. What does he mean? The only value of the chain lies in the gold. The medallion is an ugly sight.

"Because of this unusual hobby of your wife's, I'll let you have this object for half its price."

Korbo mentally counted the contents of his pocket.

"Please wrap it up before I change my mind."

"It was nothing," he said to himself. Karelia would be pleased with what he was bringing her.

After everything had been prepared, and after joining together the ends of the repaired cable at the seashore, the cable ship *Apo* calmly proceeded to lay down the cables toward another island. After the cable-laying, the ship would return to Manila. The sailing was slow and careful because it was important that it be attuned to the machine on the deck which pulled at the cable coming from the ship's hold and laid it down into the sea.

All the danger signals were readied. Three short blasts meant the cessation of all activities, the stopping of all machines.

They were twenty men in the cable locker. Each one carefully supported the cable, which was now being veered out from the platform they stood on.

Forty eyes were glued on every upward surge of the iron cable.

But somebody had made a mistake, somebody had made a wrong start in the winding of the cable, somebody had been careless!

The cable swung wildly and two arms were all but wrenched from their sockets.

Forty eyes registered forty kinds of horror.

Three short blasts. Again! And again! And again!

Danger! Danger! Stop all machines!

The cable swung and smashed to pieces a skull, letting out bits of brain matter which littered the cable platform.

All activities ceased. Everything became stifled into silence. The whole length of the cable had suddenly lost all strength; now it hung down limply, all its danger gone.

Korbo saw the cable slip from its mooring. When it swung its entire length, in a flash he saw it coming toward him.

And within that sudden burst of light, from the instant it slipped until the time he felt its pressure on his body, his life with Karelia unfolded in his mind.

His soul rent the heavens with the violence of its protest.

Don't! Wait, Mr. Cable! See if there's justice in it!

The whole flaming sky seemed to break into pieces with the setting of the sun.

The world had stopped moving: The big chunks of clouds. Vegetation. The quiet sea which repeated in the reflection of its limitless expanse the revolt of the skies.

Korbo found Karelia waiting at their meeting place. She was seated on a big rock, watching the wavelets creeping along the sand.

When he looked at her face he saw sadness in it and a few traces of tears.

He sat beside Karelia and gazed at the smoldering sun which was going down behind the dark mountain beyond the limitless water.

"Then you know," he said. "I did not get the job at the factory you had told me about. So many people are without work. We were very many who applied, yet only one man was needed."

"I did not know," Karelia said. "But I know that you haven't any interest in that kind of work. I know that your heart is in your painting. I feared that you would only eat your heart out if you were accepted at that factory."

"Ah, you are angry with me, Karelia, although it is not my fault that I am a painter. Is it a sin to feel and see beauty and love it with all my being, to paint it in order that others may feel and see it? If other people scoff at such an occupation, because I cannot earn enough to buy rice, it only means that they do not recognize truth. If rice is presumed to be the most precious commodity, that is not the product of reality, but the result of the prevalence of poverty brought about by what we call progress. Beauty is one of the values that have apparently lost their meanings to us. Love is another."

He laughed. "Ah, I am lecturing to you again. You're to blame. You touched on my favorite subject again."

Gradually the red sun disappeared.

"Korbo," Karelia said. "I'm afraid that my brothers and sisters are not receiving enough nourishment. Pepe is sick again. I give them very little help. Father is out of a job again."

A small portion was all that was left of the sun.

"Korbo," Karelia said, "We have been engaged for two years. You know Dando. He proposed to me."

The sun had totally disappeared and the darkness gradually settled everywhere.

"Do you love Dando?" Korbo asked.

From the remaining light he saw the onrush of blood in the veins of Karelia's cheeks.

"Dando has enough means to help my brothers and sisters," Karelia said. "Dando can afford to get married."

Korbo felt the slap that was the answer to his stinging questions.

"It's already dark," Korbo said. "I'll take you home. They might be waiting for you."

A sudden burst of light between life and death. Then the leaves of memory rapidly, and in parts, unfolded in his mind.

When Karelia had gone life to him seemed to have lost all its significance and meaning. His feelings were seemingly paralyzed. Gone was the beauty of the world.

The flowers were no longer devoted prayers. The shimmer of the stars was no longer repeated avowals of love.

The canvas on his last frame had become old without even tasting a drop of color from the brush.

Fast was the current of the clear waters that glinted in the stones at the bottom of the shallow river.

A woman was washing clothes beside it. Korbo recognized Karelia.

Karelia occasionally glanced at the sleeping baby in a crib under a bamboo clump on the river bank.

Korbo approached the crib and watched the sleeping baby for a long while. When he turned to look at Karelia again, he saw that she had stopped washing the clothes and was now gazing at him as if she still could not believe that he was there.

Smiling, he walked toward Karelia. He sat on a rock, took off his hat and mopped the perspiration on his brow with a handkerchief.

"Your *barrio* is so far from the town," Korbo said. "I got tired looking for it."

He looked down at his shoes which were already white with dust. One heel had worn itself out. He planted it firmly on the ground so that Karelia would not notice it.

"How did you find this place?" Karelia asked. Korbo saw that he had not successfully hidden the worn-down condition of his shoes from Karelia.

"Your brother showed me the way," he said.

He liked Karelia's eyes. A mysterious depth lurked in them.

"When I heard that you had married Dando, I went to see you," Korbo said. "Your brother told me that your father hit you and then drove you from the house."

"I wrote you a few days after our quarrel," Karelia said. "I went to your place. You have moved and did not leave your new address."

"I got a job as a laborer in the ship which repairs the cables in the Visayas and Mindanao. In the weariness of my body I could forget my memories."

"I wrote in my letters that during those moments, when we were together, I seemed to catch a glimpse of the meaning of life," Karelia said as if she wanted to laugh at the memory. "I wrote that in those moments I was filled with the feeling that life had a meaning only because you were there."

Karelia continued to scrub the dirty clothes. Her cheeks now had a heightened color. Her shoulders, left uncovered by the neckline of her dress, were burnt by the sun.

Korbo could not find a phase in his life wherein Karelia was not included. In his mind he believed that it had happened even before the creation of the universe.

It seemed to him that life on earth was just beginning when a maiden came near him while he was painting and she wonderingly watched the strokes of his brush.

He was then on a wild spot. And the woman was, he guessed, one of the group of picnickers.

After a long attempt at an understanding of his canvas, the woman turned to him smiling.

"Are you painting the bamboo clumps over there?"

"Ah, you guessed it at last," he laughingly said.

The girl laughed also.

"Forgive me," she said. "But your bamboo clumps are hardly recognizable; what attracts most in your canvas is the mysterious color, which, try as I could to see, does not appear in the bamboo clumps over there."

His spirits soared higher.

"Ah, if you could only be in my place and see and then paint the silvery flash and depth of your eyes, the roses in your cheeks and the redness of your lips; then you would also believe that colors speak their own language which the heart understands."

The woman laughed.

"What I understand only is your very unusual and odd way of saying that a woman is beautiful."

Their laughter rang together.

The baby cried in its crib under the bamboo clumps at the river bank.

Karelia left the clothes she was washing and approached the baby. She got it out of its crib and rocked it in her arms. But it would not stop crying.

Korbo followed and asked Karelia for the baby.

"Let me," he said, smiling as he eagerly held out his arms.

Karelia gave the baby to him; it stopped crying when Korbo's big arms enfolded it. It went back to sleep again.

"Our ship will leave again next week," he said softly, so as not to disturb the sleeping baby from whose face he never took his eyes. "I am renting a house in Manila. If you'd pack now, we'll reach it before it gets dark. Tomorrow we can get married."

Just a sudden burst of light between life and death. Within that instant can the whole life of a human being be lived again?

Is it possible to pick out and put together the crushed brain particles that tell of the sorrows and those that tell of the joys, so that in the reconstructed picture the meaning of life can be read?

Among the brain particles was included a gold chain with an image of a tiny and mysterious god. Its eyes were big and wide, and they seemed to embrace at a glance all that could be seen in the universe.

Ponciano B. Peralta-Pineda

(1922-   )

Born in San Antonio, Nueva Ecija, on December 2, 1927, Pineda studied at the Nueva Ecija High School (1948), and then at the University of Santo Tomás where he earned his A.A. in 1949. He received his A.B. (1963) and LL.B. (1952) from the Manuel Quezon University. He passed the government bar examination in 1953.

Pineda served as editor of various journals: *The Varsitarian, The Quezonian,* and the *MLQ Law Quarterly.* He has also edited an anthology of Tagalog short stories and two college textbooks on Pilipino. Pineda taught journalism and creative writing in Tagalog at the Lyceum of the Philippines, after which he moved to the faculty of the Manuel L. Quezon University. He is at present director of the Institute of National Language.

Among Pineda's distinguished stories are: "Malalim ang Gabi" (1954), "Ginto, Kamanyang at Mina" (*Malaya,* 1945), "Sa Iyong Pagsilang" (*Sinag-Tala,* 1945), "Pag-ibig ng Isang Matanda," "Uhaw," "Huling Angkan," and many others. His essay on labor-capital relations, "Kapayapaang Industriyal," won first prize and the Magsaysay Trophy in 1957.

Pineda organized the *Kadipan,* a literary guild of college students, of which he was president for three consecutive years. He helped form the Association of College Professors of Pilipino. Pneda was the recipient of a Colombo Plan scholarship (1965–66); he received an M.A. in linguistics from the University of British Columbia, Vancouver, Canada.

"The Fisherman" ("Ang Mangingisda") won first prize in the Palanca Literary Award for the short story in 1960.

The Fisherman

Even when the dynamite had exploded in his hand still Don Cesar's launches, which remained immobile despite the impact of the waves, danced in his mind. The noise of his motor, to his intent hearing, seemed like music floating from the radio in the well-lighted pier of Fides.

Those things comprised his power and hope: the boats of Don Cesar and the port of Fides. They brought into being his deepest desires which never for a moment vanished from his mind. And the desires inspired by the pier and the boats were profoundly colored by events that surrounded his life. Like what happened recently.

Just a while ago, when he loaded his motor with gasoline at Fides's landing, what he wanted above all to escape from recurred: applying for another loan from Fides.

"If it's possible, could you add this to my earlier debts, ha, Fides?"

Fides simply gazed at him. She didn't move at all but simply wrote something on her list of debts.

He understood the truth signified by those two narrowing eyes: doubt about the fulfillment of his promise. He caught the tail of that meaningful glance, which was slightly tinged with reproach.

When he went out yesterday, just as in the past two days, he was not able to catch enough to provide for his mother's needs and to repay his debt. Early that morning he had already apologized to Fides's mother for his delinquency in payment.

"Eh, but what can we do if you failed to catch enough?" Fides's mother retorted with exasperated warning.

"I was unlucky," he muttered. "Fortune might be generous to me tonight, though."

He blurted that sentence by way of rationalizing: in order to beg for another loan; in order that, by all means, he might wash off his shame and embarrassment with expressions of gratitude and gentle pleas.

But he could not conceive of repaying his debt to Fides. His mother early that morning reminded him to "pay your debts at the pier, son." He fully realized that they had nothing at all, nothing at all.

He knew how Fides and her mother pursued him with heavy stares when he bade goodbye. He didn't hear at all what Fides's mother was accustomed to uttering when fishermen who inveterately asked for loans could not pay back even a single centavo: "*Abá,* eh, what about us, when it's always like this? Every one of us is compromised. . . ."

But now his hope loomed large before him. He put absolute faith in himself and the sea.

"Tomorrow I feel sure I can pay them back."

It was already evening when he disembarked from Tangos.

He was bound to the sea. But not for once did it occur to his mind to escape—to free himself. He had simply chosen to live with the sea, for the sea—to hold dominion over the sea, like the owner of those fishing boats at the side of the big landing.

Ever since he gave attention to the first launch of Don Cesar he felt a strange throb in his breast: he wanted to acquire a launch—someday. With a launch he would not be needing a small canoe; he would not be using a tiny motor; the slightest anxiety would not touch him anymore, though the west wind rage or the storm in the sea heave in mighty fury. He would no longer sail toward the deeps for only a few hours. He could then be able to reach the distance that Don Cesar's launch covered. Besides, he could go out on Sundays. And upon returning he would unload hundreds of baskets teeming with fish. No longer would his mother despair at his inability to pay Fides for gasoline and oil. He would lift his face up with confidence. He would look directly at Fides's narrowing eyes. He would have so many liters of gasoline loaded into the tank of his boat. When his boat sped by Don Cesar's, he would be able to exchange warm pleasantries with the Don's fishermen. "How many days will you be out, ha?" he would inquire. They would respond; he would answer, "As for me, I'll be out for thirty days."

His ambition resembled a sturdy plant with leaves densely flourishing, with the loveliness of its growth intensifying in the passage of days. During the night, when he was stretched flat on the floor, the whirr of the motors and machines whining as they sped toward mid-sea tickled him. The hum of the launches was a reservoir of power that poured strength into his body.

"Someday, Mother," he confessed one night," I shall buy a launch."

His mother warned him not to indulge in such a dream.

"Let us be content with a small boat which 'delivers' our daily bread from day to day."

"We're going to haul in a lot of money, mother. We shall never be found wanting. You'll find yourself placed in a more comfortable situation."

Seated by the window facing the sea, they could view the brightening pier of Fides and the launches of Don Cesar tied to their moorings. The echo of boisterous laughter from people killing time at the pier floated up to their dark house.

His eyes glowed. His heart teemed with impetuous hope.

"I'm really going to buy a launch, mother."

His mother, however, urged him to make the small boat suffice for his needs.

"The happiness of man, my son. . . ."

He could no longer understand the tail of his mother's sentence. His spirit was already far away. Far out in mid-sea, in the bosom of the waves. . . .

A long chain of years passed in his life as a fisherman before he was able to save enough money to buy a motor. That day was a historical event, a significant occurrence in his life. He considered it already a token of triumph without equal, an honor both to his mother and himself.

"I will no longer be so fatigued by paddling the boat when I go out to fish. This is the beginning now, mother. . . ."

The mother understood the joy which overflowed in her son's heart.

"Do not forget Divine Providence, my son," his mother said. Divine Providence was always the constant distracting consolation. Divine Providence amidst poverty, illness, an instant gaiety. At moments he seemed to have lost faith. Especially when he was in bad luck. As, for instance, these last three days.

He had also bought a new boat to which he transferred his motor. Perhaps Don Cesar also experienced a similar joy and pride when he acquired his first fishing vessel—he told himself.

His ambition turned into a frenzied grasping when he observed two boats in the pier.

He often asked himself why there were already two boats in the opposite shore; while he himself, until now, didn't own even one. This realization seized his whole being whenever he would think of it. And the more he could not explain his state when he would encompass with his gaze the northern part of the river; there one found the pier, factories, gigantic boats, precious merchandise, launches, ships; but toward the south—around their hovel—were nipa makeshift constructions protruding across the river bank, small wretched canoes, laborers, fishermen who took in only a measly percentage of their daily catch.

His self-questionings were answered by an illustrious dream as dazzling as the fishing vessels of Don Cesar and the luminous port of Fides!

Soon Don Cesar had three launches. Fides's area for anchorage grew larger and larger. And he—his craving for a boat intensified; his wonder at the pier knew no bounds.

Once he heard his fellow fishermen mention the amount of money that Don Cesar's fishing boats hauled in.

"One venture of Don Cesar's new boat, and the money invested is almost all recovered," one man reported.

"And the profit for one fishing journey of Don Cesar's boat we shall earn in a year, that is, if we're lucky," another fisherman said.

"Ow, we shall not earn that much . . ." another ventured.

Such conversation inflamed his one desire.

He told his mother all the news he had picked up from such gatherings.

"So you see, mother," he boasted, "just consider that! You will no longer suffer . . . "

His mother could not utter a word.

". . . You'll no longer work. . . ."

His mother merely tried to hold back the tears brimming in her eyes, her eyes which the darkness gently veiled.

Irked impatience did not desert him for these past three days.

"What bad luck," he mumbled, "the worst luck ever!"

Perhaps, he thought, if he used a launch in fishing he would not return so empty-handed. If he had a launch he would course farther out; he would struggle against the weather; he could travel to the deeper fishing grounds; he would then possess all the fish in the sea. He would not return home without a catch. Even though the winds rage in fuming wrath. Despite a storm. He would return with plenty of fish . . . a heavy load. His mother would rejoice. They would no longer endure the ravage of painful want.

A while ago, when he left their house in order to load gasoline at the pier, he had already decided to pawn or sell his motor so that he could pay all his debts. But he was not able to carry out that decision. He loved his motor so much, he wouldn't sell it to anyone. His motor was in fact synonymous with the launch that was the goal of all his yearnings.

Today he would not go home without abundant fish: this was his strong resolve. Without fail he would bring home plenty of fish. He expressed this determination to Fides's mother.

"Tomorrow I'm certain that I'll be able to repay you."

He did not want to carry out his plan. He knew what consequence it could bring about. He knew that it was strictly forbidden by law.

But in those past days he was forced to join those who used such a method. For only a number of times. And nobody in their group was harmed. They were not caught, they returned home with plenty of fish. How large was their earning then!

Now: the coast guard patrol would not drift into the area he was headed for, he mused. No doubt there won't be any hindrance; none will catch me; nobody will inform against me; nobody will prohibit it. Besides this will only be for now.

He expended great caution in wrapping the two fat dynamite

packages underneath his canvas-covered seat. He would not use them—if . . . he was lucky. . . .

He was now in mid-sea. The wind seemed to toss up and seethe as the night deepened. Darkness shrouded everything. The fishermen's lamps twinkled in the immense expanse of water. Still he had no catch. He was already fatigued by the repeated casting of his net. Nonetheless he was feeling strange. A queer sense of expectation arose in his breast. He caught sight of a school of fish. It was certain that he would be compensated by this school. He flung back his net. How beautiful was the spread of its leaded edge. He was happy. He detected the school. His experience would not mislead him. He would bring home an enormous load of fish. He would take pride in his big catch. His heart leaped. He tugged the net. Heavy! He shook it again. He exerted all his strength. How heavy! Again he tugged. Tugged. And the net was suddenly loosened by a powerful hand that seemed to be pulling it at the other end and competing with him. The net was ripped! Torn!

Now he resolved to go home. He wanted to reach Tangos. He wanted to rest now. His consciousness arrived first at Tangos. It had gone back home to Tangos. It seemed as though a curtain was lifted in his mind. He could perceive Don Cesar's launches all in glorious array at the touch of the illumination from the merry pier of Fides. For a second his vision focused on the water. He smiled. He sighted another school of fish. His deepest self was provoked. He groped for the bundled-up dynamite sticks. He tore apart the wrappings. How beautiful those two objects were to his sight! Now he would be able to go home with plenty of fish. Now he could pay Fides. The explosion would only take a second. He would mend the ripped-up net. He would fill up his boat before the patrol arrived at this part of the coast. He stopped his motor for a second. He could hear the noise of the motors in other fishing vessels. But he could not hear the sound of the patrol boat. He switched on his motor. He was no longer vexed. Ecstasy gripped him. The hum of his motor sounded like caressing music. His launch moved on. Then he stopped the engine. The short fuses of the dynamite sticks were white. He twined the two fuses carefully and kneaded up the bundle. His mother would rejoice when she woke up in the morning. "I was lucky, mother," he would shout. "Ay, thank God!" his mother would respond. He would not confess that he used dynamite. She would only be aggrieved. "I was lucky, mother . . . I was lucky. . . ." He struck a match. The sparks of the size of sand grains leaped and scattered. The matchstick would not light up. He squeezed the match in his armpit. It got warm. He struck it again. The wind snuffed the flame. He concealed the match behind the deck of the boat; fire bit the matchstick. He brought it nearer the dynamites, touched it firmly to the end of the short fuse which he tightly, steadily, grasped with his right hand; it sizzled, for a twinkling of an eye, for a swift instant, rapidly, rapidly sizzled—like lightning that tore the sky, and the simultaneous flash that wounded the dark night appeared together with a deafening boom that cracked the wholeness of that immeasurable expanse of sea.

Pedro S. Dandan

(1917-   )

Born in Tondo, Manila, on June 30, 1917, the second of seven children of parents who came from Baliwag, Bulacan, Dandan started writing early while studying in high school in 1934. His first published poems appeared in the weekly magazine *Mabuhay* (1938), and his short stories appeared in other periodicals before World War II broke out in December, 1941. Inspired by his association with pioneers of Tagalog fiction writing like Dr. Buenaventura Medina and Jesus A. Arceo, Dandan was encouraged to write; he later won the praises of Tagalog critics for his artistry, for the skill and subtlety of his handling of the short story form.

Among his well-known pieces that have merited critical acclaim are: "At Nupling ang Isang Lunting Halaman," which won first prize in the first *Linggo ng Wika* (1947); "Pamahiin" (*Mabuhay,* 1938); "May Buhay sa Looban," chosen by Agoncillo as one of the best stories within the period 1886–1948; "Kawalang Malay" and "Kabaong," two of the best stories of 1939. His stories and plays have consistently won prizes in the annual Carlos Palanca Memorial Award for Literature. His novels include: *Ito ang Pag-ibig* (*Malaya,* 1946), *Bungang Ipinagbabawal* (*Balaklak,* 1965), and two unpublished novels, "Adiong Sikat ng Tundo: Bagong Dimas" and "Ibong Pipit sa Tuktok ng Taon."

At present Dandan earns his living as traffic supervisor for the Philippine National Railways.

"A Dog and Her Five Puppies" ("Inahing Aso at Limang Tuta") derives from Dandan's experience during the war years.

The Dog And Her Five Puppies

The dog followed the woman in front of the bush and brushed its side on her skirt. The woman bent and stroked the canine's head.

The dog wagged its tail, and its soft bark floated through the quiet of the evening.

The woman lifted the pot of gruel from the stove and laid it on the bamboo holder. She poured the gruel into four bowls. She got a portion of her share and added the rest into the biggest bowl for her youngest, Doming.

The dog tailed behind her, while she placed the bowls one by one on the low table. Now and then she would glance at the dog and would shake her head.

Lauro, Into, and Doming sat before the table. They had not yet touched the spoon laid beside the bowl. Before meals they would wait for their mother to clasp her emaciated fingers and murmur a short prayer.

Before the woman could conclude her prayer, Doming had grabbed his spoon. His mother hurled a reproaching glance at him, and Doming dropped his face as though he were a bud plucked from the stem. The woman grieved within herself.

From the four bowls of gruel white steam rose. Into burned his lips when he suddenly mouthed a spoonful, so that one eye moistened. He opened his mouth so that thin porridge would not touch his lips and spill all over. He looked about fearing some one might have noticed him, and he saw Lauro smiling.

The dog was behind Lauro, looking at them. It would rise, then it seemed that it would burst its hide. Its looks were meaningful. Its barks sounded plaintive.

In her mind the dog was a strong link with the husband who was away. . . . Missing for five months, he suddenly came calling out one midnight. When the woman opened the door she saw the man with a huge dog, the handle of his gun slipping out of the back pocket, and carrying a buri bag containing rice, bananas, and sweet *camotes.*

The woman laid down the oil lamp and took the bag from her husband. Behind her were the three children who has just risen, blinking. Doming did not readily recognize his father: the beard was almost as long and thick as the hair that hung out of the fiber hat; and weed flowers had clung to his clothes. Seconds had passed before the children kissed their father's hand.

After kissing the forehead of the youngest, the man brought in the dog. The children's eyes lit with joy, and Into even shouted: "Wow! Now we have a beautiful dog!"

Quickly the woman covered the mouth of her son, whispering: "Not so loud; somebody might know your father has come."

"Why, is it bad?" Doming quietly asked. "Yes, it is bad," Lauro answered as if he knew what endangered his father.

Before the break of dawn, the man bade farewell. He asked his wife to take care of the dog, which was a gift to him by a close guerrilla friend who was killed by the Japanese in one of their skirmishes. He promised his family that he would come back ... would certainly come back.

Since then a year had passed. The dog had become attached to the family, had become a living reminder of the far-away loved one. It had also become the symbol of time's exigencies—the slow tightening of the clutch of hunger.

Meanwhile, the woman had come to recognize with firmness the picture of life that passed before her eyes: the struggle of the dog against its own kind and sometimes against man to be able to fill its empty stomach with anything from the garbage cans, pit or backyards of markets, the patient ambushing of rats or mice in the middle of the night under the huts, and afterward the final act of cuddling its five young ones and offering life's juice within its breast.

These things made the woman even stronger before the inevitable adversities. She did not mind her backache nor her nocturnal coughs. Early at dawn she would rise. With Lauro, her eldest, she would go to the town market to buy vegetables which they would resell, while Into and Doming would peddle peanuts or cuts of roasted coconut meat in crowded corners.

They lived this way every day until the price of rice rose to the skies. They had to be content with coconut in the morning, gruel at noon and at night. The dog would rarely get what the family ate. In its own way the dog would eke out a living, but sometimes the woman would leave something for it out of her own share.

That evening she did not finish her gruel. She placed what she left over in the coconut shell for the dog. She poured a little water, and the moment she left the dog rushed to it. She could hear the noise made by the dog's throat while it gulped the food.

After cleaning the dishes, Into prepared the box he used for peddling peanuts. Doming approached the five puppies in a corner of the hut and happily ogled at the little eyes that had not yet opened. Lauro leaned against one face of the chest to read the book he used in school before the outbreak of the war.

The dog lay on the floor after devouring all the contents of the shell. Then it rose and went to the puppies Doming was playing with. The puppies whimpered as they sought the breast of the drooping dog.

Doming yawned. He moved on his hinds and placed his head on his mother's lap while she continued making a sleeveless shirt out of jute. She could see the five puppies sucking life's juice from the breast of the dog. . . .

That was the last night of the bitch in their company. When the next day dawned she had disappeared. They could not find her. She could have been caught by the men of the city pound who often made the rounds pushing a cart they wanted filled with dogs that roamed the streets.

Even if it was very difficult to earn money, the woman tried to save enough to retrieve the dog. That of course meant decreasing what should normally be spent for their own food. But then, almost anything could be bought. A dog would cost from two to three hundred pesos. And the woman lost hope that she would even recover the "reminder" left her by her husband.

The orphaned five puppies became a problem to the family. Although they subsisted on coconut even at noon and took gruel only at night, she would still put aside a little for the puppies. She would place the thin porridge in a wide piece of cloth, wind this and squeeze it into the mouths of the puppies.

On the sixth day after the dog disappeared, three of the puppies died, one after the other. It was then that she heard Doming suggest that they better cook the other two left.

She feigned not hearing her youngest child. But when she glanced around, she saw in her children the pale image of death, and she felt the sudden shattering of her reason. Nonetheless she did not give up the memory of the man in the mountains.

What was left of the coconut meat being peddled by Into and Doming that afternoon, the woman laid on the table. As usual, she offered a short prayer of thanksgiving to God, and then each of them took his share from the plate. She could not look at her children while eating.

Doming was the first to finish eating. He went to the chest where the puppies lay, and feeling that the two were stiff, he shouted: "Mother, these two are dead! You should have cooked them!"

The three children helped her bury the five puppies under the stairs. The children dug with their own hands until they were able to cover the five puppies with earth, thus making a little grave.

Doming was the last to go up the house. He cast a last glance at the grave of the five puppies before he finally closed the door. . . .

The woman laid the mat early. In deep slumber they would forget the bitterness inside their stomachs. She lay beside her youngest, and after a few moments of thinking about the uncertainty of their existence, her tired mind finally rested.

In the middle of the night she woke up feeling for her child. She missed the warmth of the little boy beside her, and when she realized he was gone anxiety gripped her heart.

She saw their door ajar. At once she rose and in one step reached the door. The moon was bright. She saw etched on the ground the shadow of Doming who was squatting under the stairs, scratching the earth.

That moment her heart could feel the delicate feeling that gnawed her youngest son. She placed a hand on one of his shoulders. Very lightly. The boy was surprised and immediately hid behind him what he held. She demanded it insistently. Doming embraced her and crying, said: "I'm hungry, mother . . . I'm hungry. . . ."

The woman only bit her lips. She carried her son and brought him up into the hut. She sat on the chest and sang the child to sleep. Within her she tried to believe that another morning would come, and her singing for Doming grew lovelier.

ANDRES CRISTOBAL CRUZ

(1929-   )

Born in Dagupan City, Pangasinan, on November 30, 1929, Cruz grew up in Tondo, a slum district of Manila. He studied at Torres High School and the University of the Philippines where he received his A.B. in 1953. He edited the literary section of the *Philippine Collegian,* and the *Literary Apprentice* published by the University of the Philippines' Writers Club. Then he worked for the Liwayway Publications, Inc., and helped set up the first Tagalog Writers Applied Workshop in Bataan. Afterward, he served as confidential secretary of Manila Mayor Antonio Villegas. At present he directs the Phoenix Publishing House in Manila.

For his works—*Estero Poems* (1958); *Tondo by Two* (1959), a collection of short stories; critical reviews, and so on—he won the Outstanding Young Man Award in 1962 sponsored by the *Manila Times* and the Philippine Junior Chamber of Commerce. For his collection of stories in English, Cruz received the Republic Cultural Heritage Award in 1964.

Cruz, in a letter to the editor, expressed his wish to change the original title of the story "The Ancient Well" ("Ang Matandang Balon") to "The Inherited Well" ("Kinagisnang Balon") since the well has been inherited by generations who have lived in Tibag. "Tibag," the locale, means "eroded." Cruz believes that "erosion in society" is due to inherited conditions. The story, Cruz states, is "affirmationist," an example of "nationalist realism." Narsing, the protagonist, sees the hope of salvation in "the backyard which he must cultivate," for "in our own backyard is our salvation, although the place is no longer our own. He must persevere and be resigned, as Sisyphus is resigned." Cruz adds that the baptism scene at the end of the story would indicate Narsing's acceptance by his own generation.

Cruz, who prides himself as a "controversial" personality for his anti-United States sentiments and for belonging to the group of writers who espouse a literature of engagement, considers his story written in Pilipino, not Tagalog.

He would like to dedicate the story to Gerald and Berenice Harris of New York, whom he met in Bataan on July 4, 1959; this dedication is, as Cruz says, a part of the story.

"The Ancient Well" ("Ang Matandang Balon"), which won the first prize in the 1959 Palanca Literary Award, first appeared in *The Literary Apprentice* (1958).

The Ancient Well

It is said that in the district of Tibag there is no diaper that is not washed in the water drawn from its deep, large and ancient well.

It is said that nobody has ever cooked food and cleaned the dishes who did not use the water of that well in Tibag.

It is said that no one in Tibag took a bath without pouring on himself the clean cool water that is the gift of that old cistern.

And further it can be said that there is none buried in Tibag who did not drink, or was blessed with, the water taken from the well of that community.

If one ponders about it, one can conclude that the life and death of the people in Tibag rests on that old well.

Undoubtedly the well is important, but the people do not pay much attention to this fact. For to them the well is part of their lives and their world; part of the legends they have inherited, of the beliefs and superstitions that would illumine the visions of their children, and that would illumine also the minds of the generations to come.

Nobody knows exactly the time when that well was dug.

"Since the time of the Spaniards," said the elders.

"Before you became men, that well was already there," ventured others.

And as proof the curious would examine the bits of stone and brickwork around it. These bits were said to be of the same quality, of the same hardness as those in the walls of Intramuros or those in the Catholic churches of antiquity.

Others would contend that the well was dug, or in more accurate terms, was ordered to be dug by the authorities during the early rule of the Americans. The evidence lies in the fact that one can find in many towns in the Philippines, particularly in Luzon, wells similar to that in Tibag. And the reason why these wells can be found in the outskirts of the old towns is that the authorities thought it would momentarily check and suppress cholera which had so often become an epidemic which killed thousands throughout the islands.

Though these conjectures are confusing, the curious observer contents himself with them. Just believe in them, they said, and "the story's finished."

That is the same retort which the irascible elders would shout if you contradict their scary fantasies. They say that on dark nights, when the moon is "dead," an enigma appears near the well.

Hide—they say—and then peek from the *kakawate* trees. If you're lucky, you'll witness a most beautiful woman appear near the well. She is trying to glimpse—they say—at the face of a lover who drowned, or was drowned by others, during the Spanish times. Once—they say—all sorts of animals emerged from the well groaning and shrieking.

And what other mysteries! Once a crowd of boys conceived the idea of spending the night concealed behind the clump of trees nearby. And what did they discover? He who frightens others, was himself frightened. And when masks were torn off and secrets revealed publicly, a man who was groping in the ground looking for something bolted and fled, pursued by the spying boys. The witty conversation and gossip reigned for a long time when the two "phantoms," none other than the only widower and the only aging spinster in Tibag, were married.

That is only one of the happy incidents surrounding the well of Tibag. Near the well the young women and the wives and mothers bathe, and wash their dirty clothes. When the maidens are there, the young men are also present continually soaking and washing their feet. There one finds the "stealing" of coy glances, looks; metaphoric eloquence paid for by a douse of water; or of threats and warnings that became a matter of course and were not actually carried out. The banter and noise of kids bathing in crowds, of water-cans striking the edge of the well, the restrained giggles of the women, the wild frolic of the girls. . . .

It can be said that in Tibag, the daily routine of life is inherited and found already "there" like the old well, a manner of life received by the children and bequeathed in turn to the offspring of those who are now still young.

One of those who can affirm this truth is old Owenyo the water carrier. He is the only water carrier of Tibag. Those who fetch water with tin cans and pole use the water for domestic purposes. The women who carry pots and tin drums also fetch water for home consumption.

It is old Owenyo's occupation to draw water from the well and deliver it to the houses. He performs this service for several big households in Tibag while filling the drums of his old customers. These customers are those who, during the fiesta, provide the largest

assortment of food and entertain the largest number of guests, those
who acted as "hermanos" or those who were chosen to manage the
feast as member of the committee. These people were also the
customers of old Owenyo's ancestors.

Old Owenyo is about fifty years old. With ash-gray hair cropped
short, of medium height, he always wears a tight polo shirt with long
sleeves. Muscular and well developed was his body in his early years.

"Why not, when his bones have been so well exercised in drawing
up water even in his youth," said a few.

"When he was only a young man," added others, "he was already
a water carrier."

"How about Ba Meroy—isn't he one too?"

"Ah, that's true!"

Old Owenyo's father, named Ba Meroy, died during the Japanese
occupation.

"But even before the war," others asserted, "old Owenyo was
already pumping water."

"He inherited that profession."

"Eh, how about *Nana* Pisyang the midwife? Wasn't it near the
well that they. . . ."

"Ah, yes. That is where old Owenyo courted *Nana* Pisyang.
Inquire from others about this fact."

"Was *Nana* Pisyang already a washerwoman?"

"Yes, she was. The water old Owenyo drew from the well was what
Nana Pisyang used. That's why their story is really interesting, eh."

"How about Da Felisa the midwife?"

Yes, she was also then already a washer of clothes. She taught her
child to be a midwife—and she's *Nana* Pisyang."

"Consider how the course of life runs. . . ."

"Is there such a thing in America?"

"Ah, but that's America!"

"And this is the Philippines. Surely here one's trade is inherited."

"Everything here is inherited."

"Ba Meroy was a water carrier, therefore, his son old Meroy is
also a water carrier."

"And *Nana* Pisyang, Da Felisa's daughter, is also a washer of
clothes."

"But *Nana* Pisyang also massages—she's also a midwife."

"Oh, but what's that? It's not every day that someone delivers a
child. Moreover, just give *Nana* Pisyang some small change for a cup
of coffee, and everything's okay."

"They already have someone to whom they can bequeath the pride of their occupation."

"Isn't her daughter Enyang already *Nana* Pisyang's helper in washing and delivering the clean clothes? They already have a child studying in the sixth grade."

"And their Narsing?"

"Ah, Narsing? What a pity. He has finished high school, but he's unable to continue."

"Oh, that's enough. Whether you've finished or not, everything's the same."

"Narsing has a good head. He always carries a book around!"

"They say he borrows from the library in town, and also reads there."

"Once I saw him clasping a book in his arm. I asked him what that was."

"And what was it?"

"*Florante and Laura*," he said.

"Look at that. A boy gone to waste. He even has some brains."

"I've heard he doesn't want to be a water carrier."

"Possibly he's ashamed of it. Think how he has nearly reached college—and then everything ends up in his working as a water carrier. How about others who, though they only know "carabao English," are now big bosses and VIPs."

"Why be surprised? Don't always feel astonished at the situation here in the Philippines. That's because they have strong connections."

"And so Narsing falls back to his lot as water carrier!"

Narsing rebelled. He refused to shoulder the bamboo pole. It's true that he still fetches water; but that's only for use at home. Moreover he would rather pick up the two tin cans of water by hand than use a pole.

The old women who wash near the well declare that if Narsing would use the pole he would be mistaken for Old Owenyo in his adolescence. That was also the opinion of cockfighting *aficionados* who were training their roosters, of the gossipers at the *sari-sari* store in front of the old chapel.

Whenever Narsing hears these exchanges, the more he flames up in revolt. And this is usually accompanied by extreme resentment.

"Why did I study and go to high school," he said, raging at himself, "when after all I shall end up a mere water carrier?"

His mother was hanging out clothes to dry in the sun when, one morning, he bade farewell. The four tautly drawn wires were sagging on account of the big heavy clothes. Narsing did not see how the laundry lines soon had no clothes on them, how the lawn at the edge of the bamboo enclosure had no clothes laid out to dry. On the other side of the fence up to the path leading to the rice field, the *camotes* crawled with shoots all pruned, its leaves almost bare because of daily harvest. There's a small lattice on which the upo plant clings and entwines itself.

Nana Pisyang, his mother, gave Narsing some money to tide him over in his journey. This sum had been saved from the payment of washing and ironing, from the sale of a few fruits, and it was really being reserved for the coming school needs of the children.

Narsing boarded with an aunt in Tondo, at Velásquez Street. In the daytime he would go around looking for work. Whatever the job, so long as it was not that of water carrier. He felt pain from hunger and fatigue, but he endured it. He tried all sorts of companies and factories. In all of these establishments there hung at the doors and gates the sign NO VACANCY.

He was of course not the only one who was disappointed. He would often mingle with others, job-seekers all, who were even graduates in education and commerce. These companions even had letters from this senator or that congressman. Narsing wanted to laugh and cry at the same time. People, it seemed, took no notice of the signatures of politicians. Perhaps even if it were King Pilate who inscribed his signature, nobody would give Narsing a job in any of the offices he visited.

One day Narsing passed by a large vegetable garden owned by a Chinese. Let's try this finally, he told himself; he entered the one-hectare yard of vegetables enclosed by a barbed-wire fence. He spoke to the Chinese whom he encountered balancing with a pole two water containers made of wood. Picker of worms, shoveler, or digger, Narsing suggested to the Chinese.

"No can do," answered the Chinese, "that my only work. All that my own planting, watering."

"Oh, then, there's really nothing for me to do here?" said Narsing; he felt his voice stiffening. He seemed angered.

"You like now so only daytime, ha," said the Chinese, smiling awkwardly, "I want only help from you."

"Oh, so then, what?"

"You fetch water, get from well, sprinkle little. You like?"

The Chinese then handed Narsing the water sprinkler and water container he was carrying with a pole.

In the afternoon of the next day Narsing bade goodbye to his aunt who resided at Velásquez Street. He boarded a bus headed for his home town in the province in Tibag. It was a common occurrence in Tibag for someone to fail in obtaining a job in Manila, especially in a new occupation and one not inherited. On the way he pondered how he could evade the profession he was going to inherit, which earned only enough for daily subsistence, a situation that demanded the endurance of suffering from beginning to end; without relief, full of hardships, and always contingent if not on the good hearts of a few on the exploitation by the many.

It would have been better, Narsing told himself, if I did not go to school anymore. It seemed as though his mind and imagination awakened him to be a witness to a thousand mysteries of nature and the thousand challenges of life over which he could not conceive of triumphing.

It was almost dusk when he arrived in Tibag. The kids rushed to him, asking if he had brought them presents. Nothing, he had nothing with him.

Enyang, the child next to him, was then quietly setting supper on the old low table. While they were eating, Narsing could sense that his father and mother were both waiting for other matters that he would relate in connection with his search for a job in Manila. What else could he tell them that they did not yet know concerning the difficulties of job-seeking?

His mother constantly offered him food, solicitously trying to feed him well. It seemed as though he had actually starved in Manila. He glanced now and then at his father seated at the head of the table. His deepest self kindled with emotion as he witnessed how the young strove to grab the food from one another's hand. His father and mother brought less and less food to their mouths: they gulped more water than cooked rice. Their viand consisted of tomatoes and salty shrimp-sauce with camote shoots, a saucer of pickled mustard, and a couple of fried milkfish. Now and then his mother scolded the kids who fought like cats and dogs as they reached for food. In all Tibag perhaps they were the only family who never left rice pellets on the table. In earlier days the situation was different. But now, when they cook broth with fish or, once a month, with meat, a whole pail of water had to be poured in to have more to eat. While the swallows of the younger children grew bigger and faster, the father's and mother's chewing slackened bit by bit. Even he seemed to be following their ways.

At that scene he raged in revolt. Then he recalled his feelings when he observed how brothers and sisters secretly tried on the good clothes that their mother took in to wash and iron everyday. That scene evoked his protest at the multiplying wrinkles on his father's forehead after he was through with the day's job of fetching water; he would burst in revolt when he saw his father shouldering two large cans of water, his father who resembled Christ in his stoop, subject to afflictions that seem to have no consummation at hand.

That very same night he and his father exchanged searing words. Narsing sat on the first step at the top of their low ladder, his gaze fixed at the far end of their yard. He was planning to cultivate their vegetable garden in the meantime when he sensed his father standing behind.

"If that's the case," advised his father in the mildest tone, "and you desire to work, try fetching water."

His father had still something to add when Narsing, no longer able to restrain himself, answered with a violent pitch.

"What's the matter with you, Sir. You're already a water carrier, you still want me also to be a water carrier!"

His father retreated, shocked. His mother rushed in frantically, asking what happened and why.

His father began cursing him. "Why?" he declared, possessed by heaving emotions, his voice shaking.

"What's wrong with being a water carrier? That's how I have sustained your lives!"

Narsing was preparing to leave when his father lunged, grabbed and slapped him with a jolting impact. Narsing felt his face ripped apart. He lifted one hand to ward off another blow; he saw his father's eyes ablaze.

His mother screamed, wept; she embraced him tightly, warning him not to raise a fist against his father and commit an outrage. The children began to weep convulsively, sobbing like small cuddly animals.

His father stepped aside, his body leaning on one side of the nipa wall. His utterance still sounded clear as before.

"What a waste—you have even gone to school. Hey, if you want to do something, go on. I'm not stopping you. The day will come when you'll experience . . . you'll also learn . . ."

Throughout Tibag all sorts of news spread quickly. When Narsing went to fetch water from the well, no one greeted him nor took notice of him at all unlike before. His father likewise ignored him. It seemed that people were too shy and timid to ask, but they were not subtle in bartering gossips and mistaken conjectures.

A week after the quarrel between father and son, Old Owenyo had an accident at the well. He slipped—and what good luck for him that it happened outside the well. If not, he would have died then and there. The old man's chest struck the tin cans, maiming him. One of his elbows got twisted in the fall. Many believed that the old man got dizzy, others that he grew oblivious for a while of what he was doing.

Old Owenyo suffered an attack of fever afterward. The best skilled midwife from the town across the river was then summoned to treat him. The customers of Old Owenyo requested others to perform his job for them. When will the old man fetch water again, they repeatedly inquired. Narsing's mother did not have any idea what to do. Their enormous debt to Da Utay's store was slowly accumulating because of the old water carrier's sickness.

One afternoon, when Narsing was drawing water for home use, somebody had the courage to ask whether his father had already recovered. Why doesn't he himself go to fetch water. What a pity, they say, if the money his father used to earn would only go to someone else.

Those statements were uttered without the slightest innuendo of mockery or insult. In Narsing's judgment what he heard were proofs of the common belief that he would certainly inherit his father's occupation.

When the next day came, what Narsing expected to happen did not happen. He was not ridiculed nor laughed at. The blisters on his shoulders burst, the skin was torn off; all through the night his bones ached after the ascent and descent along steep stairs, after the drawing up and transporting of water from place to place. Indeed he was already performing the job of a water carrier.

Supine on the wooden floor, Narsing restlessly rocked to and fro on his side. He could perceive the distant stars. He listened to the hum of tiny animals and the creak of bamboo trees pushed and pulled by the wind. From afar a dog barked as though it caught sight of a ghost or apparition. He could not sleep. He thought of many things. He remembered the time when he was in high school. Before he dozed off, he saw in fancy his own self exactly like his father who, Christlike, shouldered the pole with two heavy cans suspended from it. He also thought of cultivating their yard and planting all sorts of plants, although now they were renting that land which they formerly owned.

It was still grayish dawn when Narsing left the house to draw water once more. His shoulders smarted with piercing pain. He gasped as though he could not straighten his knees anymore.

In the afternoon of that day, Narsing waited for his turn at the old well of Tibag. Around the well young men and women continuously joked; others laughed, saying that their new water carrier had just been christened.

"Christen Narsing! Christen Narsing!" shouted those huddled around the well, and someone even dared to splash water.

Buenaventura S. Medina, Jr.

(1927-   )

Born in Tondo, Manila, on December 1, 1927, Medina received his A.B. and LL.B. from Far Eastern University. He has been professor of English and Tagalog literature in the same university for several years now. Among the honors Medina has won are the following: prizes in the Palanca Short Story contests seven times, with three first prizes; first prize in the National Contest in the short story sponsored by the Institute of National Language, and third prize for an essay, "Saan Patutungo ang Langay-langayan?," in a competition sponsored by the literary organization Panitikan.

Medina has served as member of the board of judges for the Republic Cultural Heritage Award for 1962 and 1963; he is a member of the Philippine Center, International PEN. At present he works as editor of the *Philippines Free Press in Pilipino.* Medina is married and has three sons.

"The Cat at My Window" ("Pusa Sa Aking Durungawan") is included in the *Palanca Prize-Winning Short Stories: 1950–55* (1957).

In a letter to the editor, Medina writes: "Thoughts about my craft? We bred in English think more in English and then write. When I feel a story will turn out better in English, I use English. When I think it will also be good in Tagalog, I rewrite (*not* translate!) the same story in Tagalog. Of course, I feel more at home in Tagalog. At least, I may principally be called a Tagalog writer. Although people would call me bilingual. (But who isn't among us bred in English?)."

The Cat at My Window

That incident is part of a historical process that will occur again and again. I know. I know, and now I feel that it will happen once more.

I was the cause of it all. I and those who are like me.

I allowed the light coming from the electric lamp hung to the post outside to lick the darkness that reigned for some time in my room. A moment ago the window was shut tight. I did not want any recollection (of Ida, Ida, Ida) to escape this room where my anguished mind revolved. But my mind revolted: Ida, our tryst the night before, in a room where for some moments light greedily withheld from it its grace—memories that refused to wander away, intensifying the throb of my breast and the beat of my heart, urged me to flee the darkness. Quickly I flung myself forward; at once I parted the two lids of my window. Instantly the radiance washed into my room.

I returned to my bed: my bedsheets and mosquito net were still folded, and the pillows were still stacked up. I did not disturb them; it was enough to attend to the confusion in my mind so as to forget the order of all these objects.

But then I could not stare for long on the blurred brightness of my room. (Also I could not stand the illumination that flowed into our room, Ida's and mine, in the past night after several minutes had elapsed in our imprisonment in the gloom.) I thought of escaping from the encroaching weak light so that even for a moment I could shake off Ida's image; I lay down on the bed, burying my head in the pillows that were still neatly piled up in order. Then I heard the sound of something which clung to the beams and alighted on the sill. I bolted upright: on the window sat a cat.

Sensing perhaps my foreknowledge of her sudden approach to my window, the cat abruptly leaped and lunged toward the nook underneath the sideboard in the corner. I stood up. I did not want anything to heighten the turmoil that raged within me. The cat's meow was shrill as I moved toward the sideboard. I did not wish to come closer; I only wanted to reach for the door in order to push it open and give the cat an opening through which she could escape.

I shooed the cat away. She meowed again. In her quick departure from my room she created a soft scraping on the floor.

I was going to push the door of my room when suddenly my aunt called:

What's that?

My aunt was sleeping in the living room. I knew that the cat went into her room. She would never find an exit through which she could flee: all the windows and doors there were closed. My aunt would surely see her.

It's the cat, aunt.

I heard the click of the lightswitch. The living room brightened. I shoved my door closed. I did not want the light to stream into my

room. It's certain I would hear my aunt's curses. She's usually maddened by cats. By that cat, above all. That's the mother cat. She's
the mother of the three kittens which my aunt was extremely afraid of.

Throw her out. Waylay her. Keep her away from me. Those were
my aunt's words this morning. She could not clean the living room
because there, in one corner, sat the mother cat and her three kittens.
I do not want to see them, for heaven's sake.

To gratify her I obeyed my aunt's wishes. I felt that my conduct
was an acknowledgment of my spiritual debt to her—a recognition
of a debt to an old woman who had been my mother during these days.

But the mother cat was agile and shrewd. Probably apprehending
the dawning catastrophe, she rapidly took her kittens away from
the living room. But she left footprints, nauseating traces on the
wooden floor which led to the kitchen.

My Aunt cursed vehemently. What a nuisance! Keep her out! Throw
them! What a shameless cat. . . . devil!

I found the kittens on top of a pile of firewood beneath the platform for stoves and cooking utensils. Swiftly I picked up the kittens
when the mother cat was absent. The cries of the kittens were feeble,
they felt like rolls of cotton in my hands. I placed them all in a paper
bag.

The mother cat searched continually for her offspring. I was sure of
this. She looked in every place where she had placed her brood. I was
thankful for those moments of annoyance and distraction, for a while
I forgot the disturbance in my mind. But on catching sight because
of the open window through which poured the light of the electric
bulb at the post, the anguish returned. Darkness returned too. Radiance returned. . . . And the window: I left it shut for some time before
I flung the lids open. . . .

No no maybe not now it's not yet time please consider what my condition will be is your love like that your love ha ha ha but but but—

Ida's voice was sweet to my ears but I could not understand what
she was saying: my desires deafened me, darkness deafened me, the
truth that was then fulfilled deafened me.

Ida wept. I left her for a while. I approached the window and pushed
the lids apart: brightness from the electric bulb at the post outside
streamed in. When I faced Ida, she had stopped crying. She was com-
forted by the dim light that penetrated the room. During those moments anxiety slid into my heart. Anxiety clutched fiercely at my
heart. It accompanied me when we left that room.

I did not note Ida's appearance when we left that room. We stepped down hastily along the narrow stairway as though we wanted to escape something we terribly feared. Only there inside the taxi we took, in a hidden glance, with the help of the light from the electric post, I observed Ida: I witnessed calm shrouding her face—a serenity which forbode turbulence, that dread which would later envelop me.

Passing along the seashore I opened the window of the car beside me. Freely, spontaneously, the wind rushed in. The wind sucked the tension of the moment: Ida stirred, squeezed herself toward the farther corner of the taxi.

Are you feeling cold? Why don't you edge closer to me?

Ida crept closer to my side. I felt the warmth of her body. I clasped her palms. I do not know if the chill of her hands were caused by the wind playing wildly with the ferocious night.

You're not saying anything. Are you angry?

Ida remained quiet. What she answered me was a slow quivering, a trembling in her seat because of the sudden gusts of wind. When suddenly she let go and leaned on me, I caught her warm sigh escaping.

I took Ida back home. Nobody was overcurious in their family. They knew me very well. The gentleman is easily recognized, my son, her father told me, may you not violate good manners. Yes, sir.

I waited only for Ida to enter their house before I bid the chauffeur to speed up, speed up fast, the velocity of the car.

The sudden closing of the door in the living room echoed with a bang, followed by the sharp shrill curses of my aunt. The curses smashed into bits the congealing silence of my room. I seemed to have been pulled upright.

What's the matter, aunt? I opened the door of my room. Is the cat there?

Shameless! Shameless!

Go to sleep now, aunt. Go to sleep.

Shameless! Shameless! Without fear in God! the devil! the she-devil!

Aunt, that's only a cat. . . . Go to sleep now.

No, son, not the cat. I'm mad about what happened this night. There at the street corner, near the dumpyard. What a pitiful baby! After being murdered the baby was thrown away. . . .

I leaned without a thought on the door which slowly closed, and before my eyes loomed the radiance of the electric bulb at the post, the dazzling brightness flooding my room.

I still hear my aunt: Possibly she's an unwed mother, it's certain she's ashamed that other people might learn that she is with child. Pregnant with child but without a husband! That's what I've been saying, that's what I've been saying . . . the young today . . . they have no fear in God!

No please now now no no but my situation nonetheless nonetheless Aunt!

My utterance grew louder. Go to sleep now.

My aunt immediately quieted down. Immediately there rose in my heart a dreadful anxiety.

I advanced toward the window. I swiftly pulled the panels together tightly. I resolved to force myself to forget the luminous flood and the continuous flow of the light into my room. I shall force myself to forget whatever memories the darkness of the room nourished and preserved. I shall forget everything. (Ida, Ida, Ida: everything I shall forget. But how . . .?)

Once more I reclined on the bed. I closed my eyes, but the confusion, anxiety, Ida, could not be torn away from consciousness. Ida, anxiety, confusion, all were shuttling back and forth in my mind. And the incident this night only increased the turmoil that was oppressing me.

Aunt!

Why? My aunt was surprised.

What happened at the streetcorner?

Utter shamelessness! A baby killed and thrown on the garbage heap. Pitiful! Pitiful!

What a pity! Really!

Ha? The devil! the devil!

Pitiful, yes, but who? My aunt did not speak anymore. She was probably fast asleep now. I know that it would be difficult for her to forget that incident. She's like me, perhaps. Perhaps.

I heard the scraping on the beam. The cat's cries were piercing. That cat whom my aunt strongly loathed and feared was there again. She alighted on the windowsill. She scratched the panel of the window lids. I was conscious of all that. But I did not budge at all. I was scared to move. (The fear that gripped my heart crawled along my body, it sucked my strength.) I fear seeing that cat. But the cat's cries halted. Tirelessly she dragged her claws on the wooden panel. I could almost feel the nails on my flesh—heavily thrusting, cutting into my flesh.

I bolted upright, anguished by the insistent sounds. I was exhausted from carrying the burden of the massive darkness in my room. I was fatigued by the recollection of Ida, Ida, Ida.

What's that?

That was my aunt. But I was already exhausted. I did not want to answer anymore. I had lost my voice. My throat had grown hoarse from responding to all the questions torturing my mind. How how now now

And the cat's desire to enter my room heightened. She continued scraping the window lid with its sharp claws. She continued making appealing noises. But I was being hurt.

What's that?

I heard the thud of my aunt's feet, she was approaching my door. What's that?

The cat. The cat on my windowsill. She's looking for her kittens. She's searching. Her children. Aunt, aunt, aunt, she'll never find her kittens again. I killed them all.

And I heard the footsteps moving farther away.

Genoveva Edroza-Matute

(1915–)

Born in Sta. Cruz, Manila, on January 3, 1915, Mrs. Matute received her B.S.E. (1946), her M.A. (1949) and her Ph.D. (1964) from the University of Santo Tomás. She has been writing stories in English and Tagalog since 1936. Her collection of stories and essays in Tagalog, *Ako'y Isang Tinig* (1952), is one of the important books of fiction in the language. It was given a token of recognition by the Institute of National Language in 1957.

Mrs. Matute's stories and essays have been published by various journals and magazines like *Taliba, Bagong Buhay, Malaya, Mabuhay, Liwayway,* and many others. She has written radio scripts many of which have been filmed. She has won the Palanca Memorial Awards four times, with three first prizes and one third prize. Among her distinguished stories are "Pagbabalik" (1952), "Paglalayag sa Puso ng Isang Bata" (1955), and "Parusa" (1961).

Mrs. Matute has written twenty-five books in Tagalog. Three are used as textbooks, and many are approved supplementary readers in the schools.

She is at present chairman of the Department of Pilipino, Philippine Normal College, Manila. She also acts as adviser of the Pilipino section of *The Torch;* editor of *Sibol,* a literary journal; and contributing editor to several publications like *Philippine Journal of Education, In the Grade School, Salaysay, Bansa, School Time,* and *Progressive Teachers.*

"Twilight Embrace" is included in *Philippine Literature* (1964) by Buenaventura Medina, Jr., and Teofilo del Castillo.

Twilight Embrace

She first learned about it from Lydia.

'La, said Lydia, who sat on her lap and laid her palms on her nape, are you really leaving us, 'La?

Leaving? But where shall I go? she asked with light laughter. I can't even move—with this cursed rheumatism. How can I leave?

That's nice! Nice! Lydia could not have sounded happier. Releasing her hold on her grandmother's nape, she clapped her hands. That's what I said, you won't ever go to Odet's!

The light laughter that made her show the toothless gums slowly vanished as she squinted peering into her grandchild's face.

This sprite, what mouthfuls of nonsense! Where did you learn them? Why should I go to Odet's—I don't even know where they live? I've been to them only twice . . . and God knows when!

But Lydia was no longer listening to her. She had quickly jumped out of her grandmother's lap as she heard the first warning squeak of the door that revealed the child's pretty mother.

Lydia, pretty Carmen called. The voice that grandmother heard was not harsh, not angry. Cool. Cool. Pretty Carmen was brought up in the convent. She never heard her voice ever become harsh, angry. It was cool. Cool. Lydia quickly left the kitchen. Her mother followed. From the wheelchair, the grandmother followed mother and child with her eyes.

Pretty Carmen was soaping hard Lydia's arms and hands.

It was from her eldest that she learned about it again. Mother, Ramon gently said, Rey would like you to stay with them—his daughter Odet would like to have her grandmother with them. If you'd just think of it, you have not really known your grandchildren by your youngest. Soft laughter without sparkle accompanied Ramon's words. And I said that Carmen and I would not allow him to take you away from us, but. . . .

And I don't want to be there. It was you who said that I didn't even know my grandchildren—nor my daughter-in-law—by Rey. . . .

. . . But, Ramon continued . . . Rey might get hurt. So I said, Carmen and I would allow that . . . you spend your vacation with them.

Ramon's eyes grew restless. They did not want to meet the furrowed face that looked up at him, the eyes and their fading light that focused on him.

Spend my vacation . . . at the home . . . of my youngest? Through her mind crossed lazily the words just spoken by her eldest. Her bony fingers gently caressed her hair now turned silver. Did her eldest say she was going to spend her vacation? With Rey? Where does my youngest stay? What is the name of the girl he married? Odet must be my granddaughter by my youngest child. I cannot even recall her face. Ah, but Lydia's different. I know Lydia. The youngest by my eldest. Her mother is pretty. She washes clean the little hands of Lydia. But why? Will my children really visit me? Their father has long been dead. . . .

Mother, are you listening? The voice of Ramon rang through the million thoughts that lumbered through her brain. Why would such thoughts now frequent her mind? When she was still young. . . . If I should leave ahead of you, do not take it to heart so much: you have two sons anyway. . . .

Heavy were the hands that touched her shoulder. Carmen and I have discussed this, Mother. We have agreed to consider Rey's wishes.

Now she was beginning to understand things better. You said I would spend my vacation at Rey's? The fading light of her eyes sought the face that was looking at her a while ago, but now she was alone. She turned the wheels of her chair toward the door. She clutched at the knob. The door would not move. It remained locked.

Beyond the locked door she overheard Ramon's voice. Loud. But the words were vague, shut off by the thick door. She could hardly hear Carmen's voice. Gentle. Not angry. Cool. The voice's coolness penetrated the closed door.

She fell drowsy listening to these voices. Why would she get sleepy often now even during the day? As often as the hovering thoughts in her mind that was getting slow in understanding the words said by Ramon. By Lydia. By the other children. By the maids. Pretty Carmen had not talked with her for so long now.

With the drowsiness that fell over her came hovering a million thoughts. Thoughts or memories? Memories or imaginings?

We have two sons anyway. The voice would rise above the years. It would come back to her in its gentleness. In its deep lovingness. We have put them through college. They can start growing roots by themselves. And we can travel together—even just until Mindanao, just until the Ilocos. I would wish to see our home town before we die.

Oh, but we will do that—you know I just love to travel. But they still need us. No, it is wrong to give them all they need—and spend on them the little that is left of our savings. They might turn selfish. . . . That voice in its gentleness, in its deep lovingness, was beclouded with doubt. But this doubt was readily banished by the blinding light of her faith: My sons, grown selfish? Oh, but you do not really know them—as I know them!

First there was Ramon. A big portion of their savings went to the establishment of a nice law office for him. Handsomeness that attracted handsome clients, cases of delicate matter about delicate people, which brought him success, and the convent-bred and pretty Carmen. Then next came Rey. The rest of their savings introduced Rey to the society where he found an heiress from the south.

The morning after the wedding, that voice returned to the silence where it had sprung. A mishap clutched and stilled forever that voice in the fragile twilight of her life.

Do not cry, mother. That was Ramon. You will stay with us. Carmen is kind, and soon you will have grandchildren. . . .

Grandchildren? Soft footsteps that were uncertain as to what direction . . . running steps . . . shrill voices. . . .

The ball . . . I . . . t! A moment's silence that broke into spills of voices.

What could it be? The grandmother stirred in her wheelchair, emerging from a momentary drowsiness. Had she fallen asleep? Had she dreamt . . .?

Tinay, the maid, was coming to her. She was holding a teaspoon of medicine and a glass of water.

Lola, you take medicine—for your skin. Here, quickly drink water— your medicine is very bitter. Tinay glanced at the scales on the old woman's arms. O God, suppose I get old, will my skin be scaly like yours? Tinay laughed. But before she left she told her something.

Lola, Mrs. and Mrs. Valli are coming.

Who?

That Mrs., the comadre of Nyora Carmen—the one who says when she sees you that she almost sees her mother who had died long ago. She says that Lydia is fortunate because she has a grandmother— her child does not have any. . . .

Oh, is she the one?

Tinay left, taking away with her the teaspoon and the glass that was now empty. She closed the door behind her. Beyond the room resounded no longer the timber of Ramon's loud voice. Nor the cool voice of Carmen.

It was drizzling that afternoon when Rey's car drove through the front gate. It was Tinay, the maid, who told her about the arrival.

But *lola,* Tinay said laughing. What guests are you talking about? That was Mang Rey! Your own son, don't you know? Tinay laughed again.

Something suddenly sang inside grandmother. Something danced about. Something shone bright. She peered with the fading light of her eyes at the tall and husky figure that went straight into the living room. Like a ray of sun that shone by her was the face of the father who would worry so much about her—in case she would be left behind.

As swift as her memory was the way she turned the wheels of her chair toward where her youngest went. The memory of that voice so gentle and loving: But you—you love the younger of the two better. And her voice when she answered: Oh, but I am not like you who play favorites. Don't I know you favor the elder?

Her voice now would span the space between life and death, and now she was addressing the father of her sons: You see, you don't have to worry, even if you left me behind. Our youngest will take me away. To their home in the south. See? You don't have to worry. . . .

She intended to move her chair into the room where her youngest had gone. Her bony fingers would love very much to touch that face akin to her dear departed, her eyes with their fading light would love very much to see the figure that she once cradled in her young arms.

At the door she was halted by the raucous voices of her eldest and her youngest. The turning of her wheelchair stopped as her own world ceased revolving.

All through the years we took care of her. Now that it is your turn, you have many excuses. . . .

Now that you don't get anything from her, is that it? And didn't I tell you that we would be traveling around the world? How could we?

Pretty Carmen's voice came next. A cool voice which she could not understand. A cool voice that sank through the marrow of her bones.

As cool as the droplets of rain that pelted her as she moved her chair into the terrace. As cool as the twilight that embraced her body of bones.

It was Tinay, the maid, who saw her in the terrace.

O God, this old woman . . . why get soaked in the rain? Come inside. What are you whispering? Mrs. Valli . . . Mrs. Valli . . . Mrs. Valli . . . O God, *lola* must be acting like a child again. Come inside. . . .

There was a whole world of gentleness, of candor, in the voice of the maid.

Teodoro A. Agoncillo

(1912-   )

Born in Taal, Batangas, on November 19, 1912, Agoncillo studied at the public schools and then at the University of the Philippines where he received his Ph. B. (1934) and M.A. (1935) in history and political science. He began writing in Tagalog at fourteen years and English at sixteen. He has written poems, short stories, biography, history, and literary criticism in Tagalog.

Agoncillo served as technical adviser to the Institute of National Language (1937–41); he became linguistic assistant and then chief of the Research Division of the Institute in 1948. In 1945–46 he edited the distinguished periodical *Malaya*. He was appointed by President Magsaysay as assistant to the director, and then head, of the Philippine Information Agency in 1945–56. In 1956 he was appointed professor and chairman of the Department of History, University of the Philippines.

Agoncillo is today the leading historian in the Philippines. He wrote a history of the country in Tagalog which won a Commonwealth Prize in 1940. His books include: *The Revolt of the Masses* (1956), *Malolos: The Crisis of the Republic* (1960), *Philippine History* (1961), and others. His latest work is *The Fateful Years: Japan's Adventure in the Philippines 1941–45,* which appeared May, 1965.

Agoncillo is also the leading critic of Tagalog literature by virtue of past performance.

"The Dawn Is Still Dark" ("Madilim pa ang Umaga") was chosen as one of the twenty-five best stories of 1943 and is included in the collection *Ang 25 Pinakamabuting Maikling Kathang Pilipino ng 1943* (1944).

The Dawn Is Still Dark

He was no longer the elegant but cowardly man. The caress of the misty cold morning, which brought the western breeze that swept against the thick clusters of yellowish *palay* stooping from their heavy load, had faded from his sight. It was no longer gentleness of heart that appeared in the windows of his eyes. Not anymore. He was now sprightly bold, he was no longer shy as he used to be. Now his eyes flashed with collected decisiveness in them; there was a light that scorched everything his eyes gazed upon. But his gaze was not that over which young women have grown mad or lustily crazy. The light in his eyes now imaged happenings and profound changes.

No one noticed the alteration in Ruben's character.

His friends and intimate companions believed that he was still his same old self—the playboy. But Ruben, who lay in bed with no beloved companion with him but the darkness of his room, was himself astonished at his new personality. He could not conceive how he was able to make such a change in his life. For a while he doubted himself deeply.

He heard the grunt, gradually becoming loud cries, of a child from the next room. He heard the dry cough of a woman from a distance. He did not pity himself. He understood that it was his duty to change, even though this decision would tremendously affect his character. He was determined to shed his "flashiness."

He was slightly surprised when he heard the two successive peals of a neighbor's clock. But he was not yet sleepy. He wanted to fall asleep at once so that he would not be late going to the office tomorrow. But however much he shut his eyes with desperate effort still he could not doze off. It seemed early still, though there was not a flicker of light in his room and the second hour of the night had already rung. He could perceive, in his fancy, the darkness of his bedroom slowly approaching him. He was on the verge of screaming in order to drive away the confused things that crowded his consciousness. But he could do nothing. He could hear from the approaching gloom the voices that he did not want to hear because they were not real, but he could still hear them. He had not the strength of will to confess the truth. He knew that he would only be laughed at. They would attach to him words like "greedy." Or "he didn't want to tell the truth because he didn't want people to borrow from him," and other accusations of a similar nature. Until now the shadow of poverty still danced around him.

The next morning he prepared to go to the office. But now, unlike the days before, his body felt weak and sluggish. He himself grew aware of a slothfulness weighing on him. It was a laziness born out of his anxiety and restless anguish during the night. Nonetheless, he was not much concerned with his condition; one thought dominated his mind. He must go to work; he will compel his body to become healthy enough, energetic enough. He would strive to perform some service in whatever way.

In all his life it was only that day that he felt a stinging pain in his heart. Not a sting that injected a kind of grief squeezed from a deep sigh, because he still did not understand the larger significance of a joy-suffused shedding of tears. He had not yet suffered any disappointment. How many women had he addressed with vows of sweet dedication—words, yes, but not words that expressed the mood of the heart mirrored in his eyes, his eyes that now had lost all sheen, all glimmer of light that once penetrated the thin breasts of those women he courted with fiery, passioned, honey-filled language. Only one vision hounded him; one concern troubled his mind; one duty afflicted the shoulders on which it was placed. In the early days, his shoulders scarcely stooped to the ground; now he was bent drooping to the ground. He was no longer the Ruben known to all when he was still a carefree playboy.

When Ruben arrived in the office, his face displayed the bleakest dejection. Everyone noticed his halting, slow movement. The men and women in the office would simply look at one another nonplussed everytime he fumbled in his work. Ruben was always pondering something. He was comparing the past with the present. He remembered his long-deceased father. Before his eyes passed the long procession of events: he will never forget that day which had grown so important to his life, that day, that afternoon which bestowed on him a task, an outlook, a duty, that day, which became the frontier of his past—his past that had stored no souvenirs—and his present. For on that day his father was buried.

He did not notice the repeated crackling laughter of his companions in the office. And when he stirred from his reveries, he seemed to be struck dumb, dazed, at whatever object or topic his companions discussed with noisy display.

"Oy," Nena called, almost hollering. "Why don't you laugh with us? It's bad for anyone to be always thinking."

Ruben acknowledged with a dry smile. He didn't budge from his seat; he held a book, his finger marking the page he had just read in between his periods of meditation. He envied the innocence of his companions, but he was aggrieved at their merrymaking. He secretly raged at the thought that he was a prisoner of his own selfless sacrifices in order that afterward many men might lead happy lives.

He considered the book in his hand, turned over the pages, and then looked again at the title. The ugly image of society traced its features in his mind: one day, while walking along Rizal Avenue, he witnessed both extremes of society—the two classes he was not aware of before when he was just trying to compose the body of his past. On one side lived the laughing comfortable rich, eating, conversing about their social positions, profits, business, and so forth, while on the other side, near them, were the impoverished poor—dirty, foul smelling, muck-smeared, wrinkled palms laid out, trembling perhaps because of hunger—the rich: laughing, sniggering, gorging food and wine, expensive wine. But not one threw a glance at the beggars, at the pitiful groaning men and women, the downtrodden poor whispering for some refuse or debris to be flung upon them by merciful chance. In Quiapo, in Sta. Cruz Bridge, in Plaza Goiti, Plaza Burgos, in the corner of Azcarraga and Rizal avenues, in Plaza Sta. Cruz, here, there, everywhere Ruben perceived the difference between heaven and earth. He wanted to scream. He wanted to bring heaven down for the sake of "the scum of the earth," but he was only a humble employee.

Ruben spent the whole afternoon in such reflections. He did not pay attention to the scornful innuendos of his office mates. To Lydia's teasing remark—"Won't you confide to us the problem of your heart, for we believe that you are thinking with your heart, not with your head. . . ."—Ruben had contrived no answer but a dubious smile, a response halfway between a smile and a laugh. The clerk who handed out their salaries arrived. Ruben didn't notice him, although his arrival was the only event the others had long been expecting. His friends suspected that perhaps he was harboring some feeling that he would not want to disclose to the critical eyes of the public.

"Do you have a headache?" asked Nene.

"No," Ruben softly replied.

"Is your heart sick?" Lydia insinuated.

Everytime this matter was mentioned Ruben would simply shake his head.

"I will never marry," was Ruben's comment.

His companions reacted with shattering raucous laughter.

Ruben felt a pungent cut in his breast. Their laughter had driven him to recall the convulsed guffaws of the aristocrats. This class of men was howling with glee, not realizing that beside them were souls waiting for a dawn without a cloud stain; those miserable creatures had souls that groped in the dawn that was still dark. Spasms shook his breast. He heard clearly the pounding throbs in his chest. There flashed in his memory the evening that had just passed: a child crying, groans from the other room, parched coughs, and the night stretched out beyond endurance. Before his eyes loomed jet-black darkness— approaching closer, closer, closer, until he felt himself strangled, embalmed by blackness, and then shaken so hard that he woke up to find the darkness gone, the terrifying darkness which crept toward him, encroached and choked him, wrapped itself around to suffocate him.

Even though the fourth peal of the clock had not yet sounded, Ruben quickly sprang up and dashed downstairs. He walked swiftly, not daring to look back. He squeezed himself amid the jostling crowd near the bus station, the mass of people that drifted toward Sta. Cruz. Ruben didn't notice the bustle of other employees with him. One object engraved itself in his mind: one duty reposed on his shoulders. In the complex memories that struggled appealing for attention, one particular word filtered through the innuendos and criticism of his intimate friends: greedy. "We're not going to ask you for a loan. . . ."

His heart bled, wounded by these accusations. His head ached whenever this fact would come to his mind. Fresh in his mind lingered his response to such innuendos: a dry dubious smile, dubious because halfway between a smile and a laugh.

He didn't know that everyone in the bus had already gotten off, and if he did not hear the loud "It's already Sta. Cruz!" he would not have stirred from his paralyzing reflections.

Directly in front of the bus station were two stores both of which were almost concealed by the bustling throng; Ruben entered one store. He acted like a blind man, ignoring the painted women huddled near the doorway. He did not care whether acquaintances waiting for their bus near the store had seen him. He whispered to a waiter in the restaurant, glanced here and there before he finally sat down in an out-of-the-way corner. A piece of bread, a cup of coffee without milk. Ruben paused for a moment. He seemed to hear the criticism of his friends; and if they would catch him in that store where the cheapest food for the lower class was being sold, perhaps they would laugh wickedly and heap monstrous accusations on him.

Before he emerged from the store he bought some groceries: a bag of *chicos,* a box of crackers, and bread. . . . He went out of the store, the mellow light of hope playing on his countenance.

Outside, toward Rizal Avenue, he encountered a dirty man whose fixed gaze locked with his: when the man halted, Ruben halted too.

"Mister," blurted the fellow.

Ruben kept quiet, waiting for him to speak again. He observed the man from head to foot, finding him not as filthy as a first impression would suggest. The man's shoes were extremely worn out, no longer brushed or polished since they were bought or begged from somebody. The coat seemed newly washed though visibly faded from years of usage; it disclosed reddening spots; its sleeves were completely frayed at the edges.

"Mister," repeated the man, "I'll forsake all sense of shame before you. I want you to know that I have five children, my wife is sick, and we have no money with which to buy medicine. I have had no work for a long time now. But . . ."

Ruben felt the paper bag he clasped with his arm; he wanted to give everything to the poor fellow, but he remembered that there were others waiting for them.

"Consider it an act of mercy," the man pleaded, "or would you like it better if I were to steal. . . ."

Ruben felt unable to stand it, so he grabbed some coins and handed them to the man whose face now mirrored Ruben's own confused thoughts. Quickly Ruben fled from him and headed to the trolley station. While waiting there he cast his gaze around him. Like before, over there prevailed mocking laughter. Here a man read a newspaper. There, people howled, totally oblivious of their surroundings. In one restaurant people whispered, talked, smoked expensive cigars, luxuriously drank coffee of the best quality, or costly chocolate. Empty plates lay before them. And by the door of the restaurant, about a few steps away from the moneyed class who laughed, smoked costly cigars, and drank the most expensive wines—there, there watched in vigil "the scum of the earth" with open palms, waiting for refuse, leavings of food, whatever can be pushed down the cold hollow stomach. His hair standing, all bristling, Ruben sprinted to the train that had just arrived.

Ruben didn't notice that he was already home. For the first time in his life, in that place where he rented a room—the district of nipa houses—did he give sympathetic attention to the condition of the place through which he passed: a muddy path along both sides of which stood lean-tos, crumbling makeshifts of squatters . . . those shacks adjoined one another in so close a manner that there was actually no breathing space among them: the murmurings and hushed voices in one shack were heard in the others. The ground floor of these houses was filthy muck-filled mire on which, miraculously, families lived and thrived. But those impoverished inhabitants resembled their own houses: their hearts and feelings throbbed warmly, embracing one another, intimately sharing the agonies experienced by others, their sufferings penetrating to the heart's core. One man's groans were heard and taken up by the groans of others. Only now, yes, only now did Ruben realize well all those truths—the despair and distress of destitution that reigned tyrannically over their place.

Ruben advanced to his house almost darting through the labyrinth of shacks and mud. Outside the door he began shouting.

"Isang, Sisa, Gloria, Juanita, Carling, Fe, Totoy! . . ."

The others came out running without waiting to be called.

"Totoy, take this to your mother," Ruben said, while he handed to the boy the *chicos* and crackers.

Brigido C. Batungbakal

(1910–)

Born in Pulilan, Bulacan, on May 5, 1910, Batungbakal spent most of his life in Sampaloc, Manila. He studied at the National University in 1932. He received an A.A. degree from Arellano University in 1947 and finished the course requirements in Foreign Service at the Far Eastern University in 1949.

Batungbakal worked as editor of *Mabuhay Extra* (1939), and then helped edit *Ang Bayan,* with Lope K. Santos, in 1945; afterward, he worked for *Balita* and then for *Liwayway* from 1948 to 1961. He was literary editor of *Daigdig* in 1947. Apart from writing radio plays, he has earned his living as staff member of the newspaper *Mabuhay* since 1962.

In 1937 Batungbakal won a prize from *Taliba* for his story "Busilak ang Sampagita." He won the only prize given by the Commonwealth Literature Awards (1940) for his collection of short stories entitled *Pula Ang Kulay Ng Dugo.* Two of his stories, "Kadakilaan: Sa Tugatog ng Bundok" and "Ikaw, Siya, at Ako," were chosen by a national committee as two of the twenty-five best short stories of 1943. His other noted stories are "Nagbihis ang Nayon," "Tatlong Katyaw, Isang Dumalaga at si Myrna," "Siya sa Ibabaw ng Daigdig," and others. His novels include *Uhaw, Mapagpalang Lupa* (both serialized in *Liwayway*), and *Tulay na Bato.*

"Light: From the Smoke of Gunshots" ("Liwanag: Sa Usok ng Punlo") is included in *Mga Piling Katha* (1948), edited by Abadilla.

Light: From the Smoke of Gunshots

Moments had elapsed since Kadyo flung away the pistol, but still he could not abandon the place. He felt a force compelling him to return and retrieve the gun. In a wild glance which Kadyo cast on that spot, he saw the pistol roll, making exactly the same movement as at the time when he first got it, when they fought an MP (Military Police) detachment that they ambushed. The pistol was thrown a few strides away from the corpse of the soldier of the patrol they gunned down as it passed their hideout.

Between the instant his gaze nailed itself on the pistol that slid along the earth and the instant he detached his gaze from it, a history formed just as swiftly in his mind. It was surprising how the first occasion, when he caught sight of the MP patrol from his sentry's nest, returned to his mind. But Kadyo could not recall how his attention was attracted by the noisy soldiers. The only thing that he found engraved in his consciousness was what he had heard from one soldier. He was arguing with his officer, and until now Kadyo could hear his arguments.

"The government is to blame for the fact that the citizens are like this. Why is it that before the war there were no Huks, though there were people who were considered Communists? There's a reason for all these—now, the government has forgotten its duties. The officials have forgotten that the poor are also human beings who need to live comfortably."

A scornful laughter was the only response Kadyo heard from the leader of the patrol. Then the leader spoke: "Ah, even you have been infected, my friend. If you were not only a soldier of the MP, I would readily call you a Huk."

"Who will not side with them? We also are Huks," Kadyo heard from the soldier. "All those forgotten men should be aware of those principles for which the Huks are struggling; we soldiers are ignored, lacking decent wages but always fighting against death despite our miserable condition. If I am going to die, what will happen to those whom I am leaving?"

The officer's laughter was shrill, hysterical. Then he declared that the guardians of peace must be ready to sacrifice themselves. Heroes should not become wealthy; they should bear all sufferings in order to be fit for heroism. And the officer's brittle laugh had not yet completely ebbed away when Kadyo joined to its echo the staccato beat of his gun.

The burst of his Thompson spread out rapidly throughout the length of the provincial road. Like the cackle of gamecocks and roosters answered by roosting hens disturbed in the silence of the night. Their shots were returned by a few sporadic bursts of bullets from the revolvers of MP soldiers.

After a while they walked toward the bodies of MPs scattered around and then began searching their uniforms. The first body Kadyo approached was that of the youngest MP. In one pocket he found a picture together with a few paper bills which, after being counted, amounted only to seven pesos.

A bitter smile traced itself on Kadyo's lips. Kadyo mused that the sum was the only reason for the soldier's death, the tribute of his life in the service of the government. In Kadyo's judgment, their fighting had more sense because they were waging it for the belief that one should embrace a just cause for the sake of deprived citizens. Whether their revolt was just or not, Kadyo could not definitely state outright. After they had ransacked and gathered the property of the MP soldiers, they retreated, trudging on the spacious rice fields until they reached their camp at the foot of a mountain.

That night Kadyo did not sleep soundly. A thousand thoughts seized his consciousness, and the more he tried to forget them the more they rooted themselves deeply in the recesses of his mind. The voice of the MP soldier he slew flooded his ears; his last utterance that all those who belong to the lower social class may be regarded as Huks, blared and clangored in his mind. But these last words were abruptly cut when he freed the lethal bullets from his Thompson submachine gun.

The sharp laughter of the MP chief seemed to despise him, as though it asked what profit they obtained from killing them, until the soldier's words would again echo in his mind.

The sun had not yet appeared in the East when he arose, stretched himself slightly, and then headed to the loftiest hilltop of their encampment. The town was also awake; it resembled a seated old man smoking a cigarette. Kadyo searched his pockets for a cigarette, but when he drew out his hand a picture confronted him.

A portrait of an old woman. At the back of that picture was written the name and address of the old woman. Kadyo could not stand the blurred vision of the portrait; he felt those eyes reproaching him. Kadyo then remembered his old mother who vehemently objected to his joining the ranks of armed Huks. But his decision nonetheless prevailed. He didn't even pay heed to the pleadings of his mother who then had only a few days to live. Looking at the picture of the old woman, Kadyo imagined that the soldier and the mother also experienced the same conflict. Perhaps the mother vigorously objected to her son's enlistment in the army; but in the belief that he could serve the country in such an act of participation, the mother resigned herself to her son's wish.

Kadyo threw a wild glance on the town which seemed burning on account of the smoke that diffused itself throughout. Then he sat on a rock and from there surveyed the shape of the town below. Kadyo felt a surge of anxiety, so he quickly returned to the camp.

On his return he met his companions who had just awakened. They were talking about the encounter with the MPs. Everyone showed what bits of property he had salvaged from the ambushed soldiers.

Their raucous laughter sounded like the roar of thunder in his ears. Unable to endure the happy conversation of his companions, he left them so as not to hear anything more about the incident. In his solitude he seemed to hear the soldier's voice, declaring that all those in the lower classes of society should join the Huks; abruptly his Thompson exploded.

After a while he approached their leader and announced his resolve to go down to the city in order to spy on the enemy's movements. Since Kadyo was the one assigned to do espionage work in the city, his desire was granted. He prepared himself, put on presentable clothes, and then walked down in a dash to the town.

Kadyo did not become impatient as he walked on until he reached the center of town. Everyone he met respectfully greeted him. Not because he was a Huk but because he still counted among those citizens whom the people elected as a councilor for their town, and when the war ended, he was included among those chosen to be the mayor of the town.

One of his friends said hello: "It seems that the councilor is going to the city," to which he assented with a nod before he got on the truck headed for Manila.

In the truck he listened to the chatter of passengers concerning the ambush of the MP group. The corpses had just been discovered on the lower slope of the provincial road. Kadyo's flesh felt stings and pricks. The more he forced himself to forget the incident, the more the scene dominated his consciousness. But he didn't feel so desperate, for soon the truck arrived in Manila.

Instead of darting to the dense districts of the city, Kadyo proceeded to an unfrequented street. Soon he found himself standing in front of a small house in an impoverished corner of Tondo. There he faced an old woman on whose cheeks were the traces of tears, though her voice betrayed a calm spirit.

"And what do they want?" the old woman asked Kadyo.

"Is this where Pedro de Jesús lives, ma'am?" replied Kadyo with another question.

"Yes, sir, do they want something from him?"

"Kadyo is my name, ma'am. I am a friend of his," Kadyo said as he bowed his head.

The old woman invited him to come up before she confessed that she was the mother of the friend he had been looking for. When Kadyo was seated, the woman began to narrate what had happened to Pedro de Jesús.

"Your friend was killed while serving with a squad of MPs stationed in a town where the Huks were rampant. I can blame nobody but him; he himself told me that to serve the army is a duty to the country. Furthermore he affirmed that one must serve the country so that peace among creeds might be restored," she said, and then related how she received the news about her son's death.

Kadyo looked fitfully around the tiny room. There he saw a picture of Pedro de Jesús wearing a helmet, a Thompson slung on his shoulder. Before the picture a candle burned as though praying for the soul of the deceased.

"Though the Huks have killed my son," the old woman asserted, "you must believe that they cannot destroy his spirit because the willingness to dedicate yourself to your country is an inheritance sown in the heart of every Filipino."

Kadyo conveyed news reports to the old woman which were all denials of the truth he knew about her son. So that after a time he drew out of his pocket the money left by Pedro de Jesús, saying that she should please make allowances and let the poor remembrance that he could afford be a fitting and sufficient token of his condolence.

Kadyo did not stay long. He told the old woman that he would be late for the office. Perhaps he would return some day to learn all about what really happened concerning the death of his friend.

And from then on he experienced a bewildering anguish. Whenever they would engage the MPs, he had felt a desire to counsel his comrades to temper their savage wrath. The Military Police, he would say to himself, were also like them in that they were all fighting for the restoration of peace to the citizens whom the MPs wanted to safeguard. Why could they not unite to restore the peace that had been wrested away from everyone. . . . But he fancied witnessing this prayer answered by the guffaws of his comrades, until later on Kadyo decided finally to turn his back to them.

That morning Kadyo did not turn to look back when he threw his pistol away so as not to be able to grasp it and make it a weapon of death. But even before he had swung around he heard a few shots; then the sirens of a weapons carrier blew. The burst of gunfire was repeated, every bullet relentlessly piercing the body almost two steps away from the pistol that lay flat on the soil, while the first rays of the sun kissed the abundant overflowing blood.

Edgardo M. Reyes

(1936–   )

Born in San Ildefonso, Bulacan, on September 20, 1936, Reyes relates how he finished elementary and high school with an abundant share of "75" percent marks as habitual grades for his courses. Later, he studied journalism at the Far Eastern University; afterward, he entered Manuel L. Quezon University where he edited the college paper, *The Quezonian.*

Although Reyes, in his shy manner, confesses that formal schooling had greatly disillusioned him, he has excelled in writing to a degree unmatched by others who have earned degrees in college. Reyes has won the Palanca Literary Award three times for his stories, among them "Di Maabot ng Kawalang-malay" (1960), "Emmanuel," and others. Such prizes he values not for their honor but for the blessing of cash which he believes so necessary to live and do better work in the future.

Reyes asserts the objectivity and sincerity of art: "The writer should write without pity; those who have compassionate hearts should join the Social Welfare organization. . . . One should write without bowing to any religion or morality because these two forces impede the natural, spontaneous flow of the feelings. It is all right to cry, but let us not weep over our own bitterness; let us lament, in our writings, the tragedy of the world. Extremely hateful are those writers who create characters that reflect their own egos; the selfish writer shamelessly shouts his own resentments—let the world then take care of his problems."

"Decline and Fall of a Town" ("Lugmok na ang Nayon") is included in the anthology *Mga Agos sa Disyerto* (1964).

Decline and Fall of a Town

The skin smarted from the heat of the sun and the wind felt like the breath of a fevered invalid.

"Is it still far?" I gaspingly asked Vic. We were both trailing the cracked earth blanketed by wet rotten hay. "It seems that we've been walking for almost two hours now. Perhaps without our knowing it we're already in Siberia."

Though unable to catch his breath, Vic was still able to smile. "We are almost near to having covered half the distance," he said.

"Really?"

"Yes, really."

Astonished, I scratched my head.

The petrified landscape around us intensified my fatigue and nausea. To my knowledge the place where we were then was entirely left out from the daily revolution of the world—it was like a heart gone dead, mute; like a brook gone dry.

From the east the green wavy mountains seemed like a crawling monster. To the west and before us stretched the rocky plain of rice fields dotted with solitary trees and clusters of bamboo. Once in a while I could catch a glimpse of a bird thrusting out into the skies beyond.

"Let's rest for a while," I said.

We slumped down, helplessly prostrate, and smoked cigarettes in the shade of a gaunt tree that grew near the side of twin termite hills.

I took off my polo shirt and shook it with impatient roughness. My sweat-soaked skipper stuck fast to my skin. On the peak of the last bamboo grove that we passed by I could perceive the spire of the church belfry in San Manuel. "Tomorrow I will go back home," Vic told me yesterday. "Since it would be Sunday, why don't you come along with me so that you can see what our town is like."

I said why not, but it was absolutely not in my mind to undergo an act of penitence out of season. The reason for this is that I thought we were headed for the municipal center of San Manuel—more than a hundred kilometers from Manila—because Vic had lived there before they became our neighbors in Sta. Mesa for some years now. So that's it, what we were going to visit was the farthest *barrio* that lurked in the outermost fringe of San Manuel.

"It'll be ten o'clock now," Vic said, gazing at his wristwatch. "Let's go now so that we can reach Sapang-Putol by lunchtime."

We trudged on. My black shoes were now "immaculate" with dust. Sweat gushed down my face and legs. My throat was terribly parched. Owing to my severe thirst, perhaps I will not change for a beautiful woman a glass of water with sparkling ice cubes floating in it.

If one cares to judge our situation, the fatigue we experienced would exceed in value the purpose of our journey. According to Vic we were going to ask for some chickens from his relatives in Sapang-Putol on the occasion of the wedding, this coming Saturday, of his *Kuya* Selmo ; and it is necessary to give a feast. But how much would we really get?

"Isn't what we're going to do quite embarrassing?" I asked. "We have to barge in here simply to beg. . . ."

"But we're not even going to utter a single word," Vic replied. "Simply telling them the news about my *Kuya* Selmo's wedding would be enough for them to know what to do."

"They sense it pretty quick, don't they?"

"Not really. The fact is they've been used to it because townspeople and city folk like us often approach them. Just drop a word that you're going to celebrate a baptism, marriage, vigil, or whatever occasion demands a festivity or party, and they already know what you need."

Our conversation distracted our minds from the wearisome walk.

Bit by bit there formed in my sight a gloomy and impoverished landscape. Houses remote from one another, dwindling in size, some inclined woefully, all made up of cogon grass and bamboo, seemed threatening to fall and grovel supine at any moment now. In the freely coursing wind mingled the barking of dogs, the clacking of chickens and ducks, moans of *carabaos,* creaking of lofty bamboo, flapping of leaves of mango trees, *santol, duhat, kamatsile,* and others. On the rugged path two shoddy and dirty boys were trying to play with cashew seeds. On the ladder of a hut sat on each step three women who, it seemed, were picking lice from each other's hair. This probably is the most miserable town I've ever seen. This is Sapang-Putol.

"We're going first to Tata Pilo," Vic said. "He's mother's first cousin."

The *madre-de-cacao* that hedged the circular yard we entered spread its abundant blossoms. From the long trellis at one end hung elongated *upo* fruits. There was also a towering conical heap of hay. The two *carabaos* that reclined in the corral stared at us. The front window of the house was flung open, but I could not perceive any single person inside. Near the trunk of the bamboo stairs two chickens anxiously scratched the barren ground. In the gutter nearby three pigs foraged for food with snouts buried in loam. Underneath the house a wooden mortar cart, tools, harrow, and plow were all neatly arranged beside each other.

Vic didn't even call anyone. He went straight up the ladder leading to the *batalan.* I followed him.

"Caught—all of you!" Vic shouted in a terrifying tone as soon as we came to the threshold upstairs.

Inside the people who were eating took fright and, a little dazed, gazed blankly at us. They were all sitting on the bamboo floor (others had a knee raised up), spread round the *dulang*. The old man with sunburned skin, the veins in his arms bulging, would not be less than fifty years old. The old thin woman with hair bunched behind would be about forty-five years of age. There were also a young man, a young woman, two adolescents the eldest of whom would be difficult to guess, and three children whose heights were in a declining sequence. The littlest one, a girl about five years old, looked at us with mouth agape; the cooked rice she was clutching trickled from her hand; round her mouth stuck rice pellets. The table overflowed with rice, but their viand consisted of nothing more but boiled eggplants and shrimp sauce. Nonetheless all of them were richly sweating, as though relishing their delicious meal.

"*Abá, Inte!*" blurted the old man.

I smiled. So Vicente was called *Inte* here; so it seemed that only in Manila did he become *Vic*.

All of them stood up, vigorously and expectantly approached us in welcoming gestures. Vic kissed the hands of the elderly couple. It seemed that in their happiness and fervent greetings they had completely forgotten me. I gulped when my eyes focused on a sweating earthen jar full of water.

"Has your mother been ill these days?"

"Not at all, sir."

"And how's your father?"

"Still working in the railroad, sir."

Finally, Vic introduced me and I at last came to meet all of them. The old man was *Tata* Pilo, the old woman *Nana* Buro. The young man was named Oding, the young woman Ising. The others were not at all important.

"Well, let's go inside now. We'll finish eating so that we can prepare something for you," said *Tata* Pilo. "You must surely be hungry, aren't you."

"And extremely thirsty, sir," I confessed with a smile.

Ising fetched us some water in cups made from cut beer bottles; I drained down three glassfuls. I didn't at all like the taste of the water, but that seemed to be the sweetest drink I had ever had.

We entered the narrow interior of the house. Since there was only one chair inside Vic took it upon himself to sit on a bulging sack standing up in a corner; I believe the sack contained *palay*. The floor was made of bamboo strips with slits between them. On the *sawali* sidings were pasted in a slovenly, haphazard manner the pictures of movie stars, prints torn from supplements of magazines. In one tiny room I caught sight of clothes hung up sloppily and a disorderly pile of pillows and mats.

"So we'll be going home tomorrow," Vic laughingly muttered.

"Ha?" I retorted. "We have office work tomorrow."

"Oh, then what?" Vic nonchalantly responded, "since our work's in the afternoon. We still have many places to visit here. When you come to visit a place such as this, even your most distant relatives would resent it if you failed to see them. Folks say that there are things you glance at and things you gaze at."

I didn't say a word anymore. After a while, from down beneath the floor of the house, I heard the choked cough of chickens suddenly grabbed. I felt my stomach turn.

It was past one o'clock when we started eating lunch. The lard of the fried chicken on the porcelain plate shone brightly. There was no spoon available—but then, when the food was that tempting, it was better to use your hands.

"Eh, before I forget, how's your *Kuya* Selmo?" *Tata* Pilo inquired as he sat on the window sill observing us. "Has he not thought of taking a wife?"

"That's why we trod to this place," returned Vic. "*Kuya* Selmo's wedding will take place on Saturday, sir. Mother told me that if you can go to Manila. . . ."

Tata Pilo excused himself with his work at his melon fields. The conversation ranged in all kinds of subjects. Vic's schooling was touched upon.

"If there's no foolishness intruding," I ventured, "perhaps after two years more you'll have a lawyer for a nephew."

"We're both in the same boat," Vic said with his nose pointing at me.

"You're all blessed with good fortune now that you're pursuing your careers," *Tato* Pilo spoke with a voice weighted with joy and bitterness. "Among these children of mine none ever even reached high school. It's because the town's so far and the kids just won't bear the ordeal of walking. And the governor's promise to put a high school here, until now, is unfulfilled."

After eating we rested for a while before looking for relatives in Sapang-Putol. Oding accompanied us. Every house we entered welcomed us with spontaneous hospitality, as though our visit were a great honor and joy to them. I didn't even hear any word from Vic asking for something; instead he extended to everyone an invitation to attend his brother's wedding. And we never left any house without being persuaded to eat something—boiled *sago,* boiled *camotes.* All of them loudly exhorted us to eat supper and spend the night with them.

In the afternoon Oding urged us to go with him to a store nearby. It seemed that the girl who was selling goods there—her name was Eda—was the prettiest girl in Sapang-Putol.

Eda's oval face was truly very lovely. Her pitch-black eyes were keenly vibrant. She wore her hair long; her lips were naturally red. But only her face was beautiful. Her legs, her feet, her arms, the fingers of her hands, even her chest, seemed to have been damaged by the arduous toil in the fields. It occurred to me that the physical surrounding is important to the nature and character of any human being. If Eda, for instance, were the daughter of wealthy parents and reared in Manila, perhaps her beauty would not have been so marred. Eda's beauty— how pitifully wasted.

I observed too that Eda's goods were few: several packs of the cheapest cigarettes, some bottles of soft drinks, three jars of cookies, a jar of candy. Perhaps if I would buy wholesale all that Eda was selling, my ten pesos would even yield some change.

While we wandered about, aside from perceiving the gracious regard of the inhabitants there, I felt and witnessed the poverty that reduced the town into abject servility. How can a town so far removed from bustling civilization ever progress? What future awaits those children who, in times when they should all be in school, are on the backs of *carabaos*?

During the night, although I was rendered immobile by paralyzing fatigue, I could not sleep. All sorts of thoughts flitted in my mind. All of us were lying down on the mat spread on the floor. Vic and I lay beside each other. *Tata* Pilo's house was filled to capacity: like a can of sardines without gravy, they say. In the inner room all the women were gathered; in the outer part all the men.

There's no privacy at all, I reflected. Ising was already a young woman; what if by chance I become naughty at night? All the houses into which we've been invited had no bedrooms: but how about the newly married? Or just the ordinary married couple?

Next morning Vic and I woke up early, but, even then, we were still the last persons to get up from the mat. In the *batalan* I hesitated to wash my face because I could not find any soap. So I simply doused my face with cold water.

We had not yet sat down for breakfast when one by one the "guests" whom Vic invited arrived at *Tata* Pilo's house. They brought with them assorted and sundry things. This is Vic's account of everything we received: a half-filled sack of "Milagrosa" rice, a pig of roasting size, two goats, a cageful of chickens, eight ducks, two turkeys, and two nipa bags full of different vegetables.

"How can we carry all those?" I asked. I did not imagine we would receive so much.

"We'll use *Tata* Pilo's cart," Vic said.

A few moments more, after expressing our gratitude to all—I could not look at them straight in the eyes—we bade goodbye. We got up the cart which was already yoked to a *carabao;* Oding grasped tightly the reins of the beast.

The happiness I could discern in the faces of everyone was a sincere delight. As the cart was edging away slowly, the people were still confiding to us their good wishes, reminders, counsels.

"Just say 'hello' to them."

"Tell your mother to visit us sometime."

"Convey to the bride and groom our congratulations."

"Tell them to please forgive these few things that we are able to give."

The whine of the cartwheels penetrated my gums with a piercing pain. How far we've gone now. To my view Sapang-Putol was now only a dark wilderness. I surveyed the contents of the cart. All these things constituted a great wealth to the poor folk of the town, I fancied. And on Saturday, the multitude from the city would come to satiate themselves by devouring them.

Liwayway Arceo-Bautista

(1924–   )

Born in Manila on January 1, 1924, Liwayway Arceo-Bautista belongs to a distinguished family of writers. Her brother is Jesus A. Arceo, the leading fiction writer in the 1920s and 1930s.

Arceo-Bautista first became well known with her story "Uhaw ang Tigang na Lupa" published in *Liwayway,* 1943, and chosen by a national committee of Tagalog writers as the second best story of the year. Among her noted pieces are "Alaala," "Ikakasal ang Ninang Ko," "Lalaki man ay Umiiyak Din," "Nadya," "Maganda ang Ninang Ko," and "Sining Din ang Buhay"—the last two are included in Abadilla's anthology *Mga Piling Katha* (1948). In 1962 she won a Palanca award for her story "Banyaga." Her novels include: *Mahal Ko, Sa Bawa't Buhay,* and *Nasaan ang Ligaya.*

"Thirsty Is the Arid Land" ("Uhaw ang Tigang na Lupa") is included in Castillo-Medina's *Philippine Literature* (1964).

Thirsty Is The Arid Land

1

Many nights I slept beside her. Like a child I gathered warmth from her breast and listened to the pulse of her heart. But I continued wondering about her deep sighs, her pained stare at everything, her suppressed sobs. . . .

2

I had not gone to the library for many days now: I had not seen for many days now the image so dear to me: round face, wide forehead, hair parted on the left, slanted eyes, nose not so high, lips that cradled a smile of profound joy. . . . His were my forehead and my eyes. My lean face, my nose like a parrot's beak, and thin lips, were mother's.

205

3

Mother spoke rarely: she was a woman of few words. She never gave me orders to follow. She rarely scolded me and if she did her words were brief: Stay aside . . . And she should not see me anymore. I should not see anymore the anger that would flash in her eyes. I should not see anymore the biting of her lips. I should not see anymore the trembling of her hands. These would also mean the strong *don't* when she would not want me to do anything.

Mother's smile was rain in summer: my child's heart was arid land. . . .

4

Not once did I hear my father argue with her, although I could never believe that a couple would never quarrel. It must be because each had a broad sense of understanding: respect for each other was not forgotten.

5

Evenings I would seek the joy imparted by a father who would tell tales of giants and gnomes and of beautiful nymphs and princes. By a mother observing and smiling, by a group of beautiful and happy listening children.

But instead I would see father when he wrote, when he typed, when he read. I would see how he would knit his brows; how he would puff smoke from his cigar; how he would look at me as though seeking for something; how he would close his eyes; how he would go on writing. . . .

Mother was a pretty picture when she would be darning clothes: when she would fix the buttons of father's shirts. When she embroidered my chemise and handkerchiefs—in the movements of her fingers—I would read an exciting story. But the excitement would vanish.

My aloneness wearied me, and I longed for a companion at home: a child in his mischievous age or a lovely baby, with a smile of innocence, with sweet breath, with little feet and hands so tempting to pinch, with cheeks and lips unstained with sin and nice to kiss, or a sister only a year or two younger in whom I could confide. . . .

6

Whether mother and father ever quarreled, the fact is they never let me know. I missed the affectionate exchange of deep stares, of smiles, of teases.

Enough was a cold *I'm going* when father would leave. Enough was *the collector had come for the electricity* or *for the water* or *for the*

phone to last the evening meal. Enough was the furtive look to show
that he had heard.

I could count with the fingers of my two hands the times when we
went out together: father, mother, and I. Often I was taken along by
mother: I never saw the two of them alone.

7

Even if sometimes father would come home when it was almost
daybreak, I never saw any change in mother. She would go to bed
when it was time to retire, but I never was certain whether she was able
to sleep or not.

*Perhaps this is truly what is felt by the spouse of a man who is
possessed by a public.*

But there was no bitterness in her voice.

8

A few years had gone since our washerwoman returned a small
book: she said she found it in a pocket of father's coat. I gave it to
mother: it was father's diary.

The next morning tears had scarred mother's eyes. Since then she
had even become more quiet. To me she looked even more sad.

What was in the diary?

9

Father was inebriated. Father would usually come home drunk, but
his intoxication was different tonight. Mother washed his face with
warm tea, but this did not assuage his delirium.

Mother was silent as usual: in her eyes was protest unexpressed.

*Because I wanted to write . . . because I would die of this grief . . .
because . . . because . . . because. . . .*

10

Now father complained of his chest and head: he said he could not
breathe well.

Perhaps you have a cold, mother said. You are feverish.

I wound a cold compress around father's head. He did not object to
what I did: his eyes followed all my movements.

His arms, from elbow to palms, and his legs, from knee to foot, I
bathed many times in tepid water which I thought he could bear—water
in which were boiled leaves of *alagaw*. I covered him with thick
blankets after he had drunk the hot *calamansi* juice I gave him.

Father smiled: *my young woman is now a doctor.*

I laughed demurely in answer to his smile: father had never teased me before.

I wished I was mother then: I would then consider my joy even more precious. . . .

11

My expectations were wrong: father was ill for days. Mother never left his side: dark lines had encircled her eyes. The doctor said he would do his best. But he would not tell me what ailed father.

12

Father asked his desk to be fixed. I cleaned his typewriter. I pasted the clippings of his recently published stories. I put together the sheets of paper inside the drawers. The lowest left-hand drawer of his desk gave me a great puzzle: a box of pink felt and a stack of letters. Minute and rounded letters in blue ink spelled father's name and his office address on the envelopes.

13

The photograph in the box of felt was not that of the lean face, with an aquiline nose, with fragile lips. At the back of it were rounded letters in blue ink: *Because I cannot forget. . . .* The picture was unsigned, but at once I began to hate her and learned to nurture a resentment against father.

14

Why did we meet only now? I could have been more at peace within had you not come into my life, although I could not perhaps bear but exchange complacency with love. How true it is that one's station in life often becomes the barrier to his happiness.

15

We are past the age of rashness: we can no longer be deceived by our feelings. But drawn between us is the gaping truth that arrests happiness; what we cannot realize, let us now only relive in the mind. Let us now only retain in the memory the sweetness of a dream; and wish that we never awaken to reality.

16

I saw her in my dream last night; she was reproaching me. But I did not intend to ruin a home. I could not covet her happiness; I

*could not let her weep because of me. I also love her whom you feel
part of your life; I cannot allow anyone I love to weep.*

17

*This love is a play in which I enact the principal role; because I began
it, I should bring it to an end. Think of me as a dream fading upon
waking. Allow me to banish this grief that strangles me. . . .*

18

But why is it so hard to forget?

19

I felt mother's hand on my right shoulder: it was only then I realized
somebody had come into the library. She saw the picture inside the box
of pink felt. She was able to read the letters that were scattered on father's
desk.

Mother came and left without saying a word. But on her way out her
hand once more felt my shoulder and I could still feel the caress of her
fingers—their warmth, the weight of their touch. . . .

20

The silence that sprang between mother and me had not vanished yet.
I was now evading her eyes: I could not stand the sadness I saw in them.

21

Father asked for his pen and notebook. But after I had convinced him
that rising would not be good for him, he said: *Now it would be my
daughter who would write about me. . . .* And he said that skillful hands
would inscribe his life in black marble. But I could not express the
protest that almost smothered me.

The cold earth is my glory!

I would never claim that my hands had etched those few words.

22

*Do not be deceived by the ardor of emotion; the first pulse of the
heart is not always. . . . I was almost your age when your mother and
I were wed. . . . How very young were eighteen years. . . . Never give
yourself the sadness that will torment you all your life. . . .*

Once more I felt the tight bond that joined father's feelings with mine.

23

I feared father's frequent loss of consciousness.

Mother went on without speaking any word to me: went on with only morsels for meals, went on with sleeplessness; went on with private grief. . . .

24

Mother touched father's forehead with her right hand and frustrated a trapped feeling from escaping by the clash of incisors and lips.

She sat on the edge of father's bed and held his right hand in her palms.

I'm well now, my love . . . I'm well now . . . when you come again tell me where we can go together . . . I'll tear down these walls that imprison me . . . in whatever way . . . in whatever. . . .

The warm beads that bordered mother's eyes broke and pelted father's arms. Father strove to open his heavy lids and, in meeting mother's eyes, a smile filled with hope graced his dying lips. Again the windows of his soul were drawn together, and he did not see the eyes welling with tears: reflections of the hurt unspoken.

Father's right hand was still in mother's palms: *Tell me, my love, that I may claim now my joy. . . .*

Mother bit hard her lips, and when she spoke I could not believe the voice was hers: *You may, my love!*

The warmth of mother's lips came with peace that descended on father's lips and even if in her eyes was the gleam of having failed to wield life, no tears flowed: she was certain now of the contentment of the departed soul. . . .

Appendix I

Time and the Human Spirit in Philippine Literature

BY EPIFANIO DE LOS SANTOS CRISTOBAL

Before the conquest the Filipinos had a literature written in characters of their own. Its manifestations in verse consisted in maxims (*sabi*), proverbs (*sawikain*), boat songs (*soliranin, talindaw*), nuptial songs *(diona, uyayi, awit,* and others of the kind, the only difference being in the music), and a kind of farce representing and criticizing local customs (*duplo, karagatan,* in which riddles or *bugtongs* play a considerable role, and epic-dithyrambical tales called *dalits*); war songs, love song *(kundiman),* and so on. A considerable number of these can still be gathered from the Tagalog grammars and vocabularies of the seventeenth and eighteenth centuries, and even of the nineteenth century.

In prose there are still codes of a religious and criminological character, in which a marked Malayo-Mohammedan influence is noticeable.

The conquest being effected by Castilians of the sixteenth century, the golden century of their literature, impregnated with the Renaissance, was transplanted to the Philippine Islands. Owing to special circumstances, the Castilian influence was reflected first in the dialects of the country before it appeared in the Spanish language, which became fashionable at the outset of the conquest.

The fact that the dialects, principally the Tagalog, already had a literary character before the conquest, rendered possible the xylographic publication of the *Doctrina cristiana tagalo-espanola,* attributed to Plasencia, in 1593, in which Chirino, a Greek and Latin scholar, places the Tagalog *Ave Maria* above the Greek, Latin, and Spanish. The most noteworthy in this piece of literature is that it is devoid of all Spanish influence in its vocabulary and grammar, which denotes anonymous collaboration on the part of the islander.

Beginning with the *Memorial* of Blancas de San José, 1606, the name of a Filipino author appears: this is Don Fernando Bagongbanta, who versified in octosyllabic romance in Spanish and Tagalog. In 1610, Tomas Pinpín published his *Librong . . . ,* and besides attaining the title of prince of the Filipino typographers and engravers, he made himself a reputation as philologist and humanist and typified the emerging class of Filipino manufacturers. He was an author in two languages. His prose as well as his verse mark an epoch.

Bagongbanta made use of the romance of eight syllables. Pinpín, in one composition, combined *romancillos* of five, six, and seven syllables. The meter of these two writers is the one which became at length the accepted fashion in all native literature.

In the comedies and compositions of a heroic character, double verses of six and seven were used, and in some epigrams of a popular character, double verses of five. These latter may have either nine or ten syllables. They have nine if the ninth syllable, with which the verse ends, is accented, because the final syllable, accented in Tagalog only in exceptional cases, counts for two. If the tenth syllable is accented the verse has ten syllables for Filipinos and eleven for Spaniards. The two great divisions of Filipino poetry are clearly marked in the Filipino bibliography. The *awit,* or chivalric-heroic poems, are written in Filipino dodecasyllabic verse or in Spanish double verses of six, and the *corridos,* legendary and religious poems, in Filipino octosyllabic verse. I say Filipino, because in these dodecasyllabic verses there is no synalepha between the vowel with which the sixth syllable terminates and the vowel beginning the seventh. The caesura in the sixth must invariably be in the sixth, and the first hemistiches can not be of five or seven syllables, as in Spanish, and it is a real pause rather than a caesura. This sixth syllable completes the sense of the verse, and the word to which it belongs has only in exceptional cases any grammatical connection with the one next following. The rhyme and especially the rhythm are entirely different from those of the twelve-syllable Spanish verse; the rhythm is unisonous with the *kumintang,* a purely Tagalog musical air which is generally used as accompaniment to these dodecasyllabic verses and has a sexasyllabic movement, similar to the monorhythmic *romancerillo* of six syllables. Although the Filipino dodecasyllabic verse may look monotonous to the eye, yet, if read in Tagalog, the variety of the rhythm and of the final articulated sounds gives it grace and at times ineffable sweetness, reminding one of the exceedingly soft adagios of Beethoven and certain epic pieces of Wagner.

In the course of time, the five-, six-, and seven-syllable verses took possession of conundrums, proverbs, and popular tales, such as the "Tale of the Turtle and the Monkey." Those of nine, ten, and fourteen syllables began to disappear in the seventeenth century. Exceptions are to be found in the nineteenth century in only one author, I believe, who uses different meters and combinations: in the *Libro nang Martir sa Golgota,* by Juan Evangelista (1886). So much for the Filipinos. The Spaniards and the members of the religious orders used almost exclusively the octosyllabic verse, and, as an exception, the dodecasyllabic. Among the Filipinos the proportion of the octosyllabic verses to the dodecasyllabic is scarcely eight to the hundred.

Though we have no *Bibliographia Poetica* like Ritson's, which catalogues some six hundred English poets of the fifteenth and sixteenth centuries, 99 percent of whom are mere shadows of names and some simply initials, it can be affirmed that the Philippine Islands have had a considerable number of poets. The Spanish chroniclers are agreed that the Filipinos are born poets as well as musicians and that poetry is very pleasing to them. And in order not to repeat what I have already written with regard to the vernacular literature, especially the Tagalog, both in prose and in verse, I shall merely reproduce here a general opinion on the character and tendency of their poetry, which is also applicable to the prose and to the Spanish literature as well, with slight differences as regards the character and the time of their apogee.

The inexhaustible playfulness, the graciousness, the parabolic acuteness, the grace and primeval freshness that distinguish the always picturesque style of the ancient poets had a certain influence on the style of the erudite and sovereign masters at the beginning and middle of the nineteenth century who, broadening the scope of the characteristic models they found, added variety of shades and tone to their poetical language, assimilating those conquests of Occidental civilization which are its greatest pride and glory. A broader field of life and the conflict of ideas enhanced the dramatic interest of their works, which were already possessed of powerful organic unity, and moral elevation, religious tolerance, and noble patriotic indignation found for the first time expression in them.

Beginning with 1872, and especially from 1882 to 1896, the poets, due to the imperative force of the circumstances, derived their inspiration from sources unknown to their predecessors. Priests and disciples of the new gospel rather than poets, they seized the scourge of ridicule and sarcasm and with it plied the tyrants' backs. Their rugged stanzas, which awakened the national conscience, still echo faithfully the din of the battle and the vigorous onslaught of the combatants. In them we find neither freshness of spring nor ingenuous playfulness, but the strife and fanaticism of the struggle for liberty.

The historical period from 1896 to 1899 is the one in which lyrical enthusiasm reached its highest degree of effervescence. The poets had then, besides the national heroes Burgos, Gomez, and Zamora, the national hero by antonomasia, the Great Filipino (Rizal), the Great Plebeian (Andres Bonifacio), and glorious national dates: Noveleta, the 13th of August, 1898, the Declaration of Independence, and the inauguration of the Filipino Republic, and they were able to sing to and write for a public made up of heroes, capable of refreshing the laurels won by their ancestors.

Beginning with 1900, however, the bellic fires died down and the salvos of the batteries and strong places thundered only to commemorate some patriotic date or episode or to salute the triumph or advent of the arts of peace. Metrical innovations and a desire to enrich the vernacular tongues predominated, but the poets, instead of studying the old models or placing themselves in direct contact with the people, reflected what is agitating modern society and invented, or thought they invented, words, turns of speech, and phrases wherewith to express it. They aspired to being hierophants of the people, and in their hands the generous and noble patriotic indignation was transformed into the less noble and generous expression of factional and political strife.

Then the Tagalog theater went forth in quest of new worlds to conquer. Its plays now were based on contemporaneous history, and this not being of an established order, they reflect the changes. They showed also a tendency toward symbolism and, to a certain degree, toward the restoration of everything purely national.

As to the literature in Spanish, I have already mentioned that Bagongbanta, in 1606, and Pinpín, in 1610, wrote in two languages, Tagalog and Spanish, the latter of these authors with a command of the Castilian tongue of which there are but few examples.

Chirino (1604) says that in Spanish the Filipinos "write as well as we, and even better, because they are so skilful that they learn everything with great ease." Blancas de San José (1606) was astonished to see that at his time there was scarcely a woman who was not able to read books in Spanish, which he considered "hard to believe for anybody who had not seen it," and this not only among the inhabitants of the plains, but also among the hill dwellers, the Negritos. In 1611, a Negrito seven years of age lauded San Ignacio de Loyola "in Latin and Spanish as gracefully as any eloquent orator."

The sciences then taught were institutes, theology, philosophy, canons, grammar, civil law, and laws of the Indies, and the predominant careers the priesthood and law. Through Dr. Francisco Lopez Adan (1737) we know that at the universities of Santo Tomás and of the Jesuits, the Filipinos, who but yesterday were mere students, acted very soon as "teachers and professors" with a competency making them worthy "not only of the professorial chairs of these Islands, but even of the first of Europe."

Thus it was not strange that Filipinos occupied the highest positions in society. There were many Filipino bishops; one acted as governor general and president of the Real Audiencia. Father Pedro Bello was elected provincial of the Jesuits. The Filipino jurists did not remain behind the priests.

As the dominant castes (which did not appear until the middle of the nineteenth century) were then unknown and the government of the pueblos was in the hands of good sons of the soil, the influence of the country could not have been more edifying and democratic than it was in those days. The ideas and everything that agitates, worries, and cheers university life were reproduced in the pueblos and found an echo in the hut of the husbandman. On Sundays and holidays, and particularly on the patron saint's day, all the inhabitants of a region would make a pilgrimage to hear and hang on the lips of the noted sacred orator who had been brought from Manila, or wherever else he was, at the expense of much trouble and gold The subjects on which he spoke were not confined to those suggested by the life of the saint of the day: often, leaving the theological, philosophical, or juridical field, he would enter fully upon a discussion of the current topics of the moment, using language replete with pearls of erudition. The town was then quickly converted into a live academy. All the features of the sermon or philippic, whichever it was, were discussed dramatically, with commentaries by the unisity students of the pueblo home on a vacation, or by the university graduates of the adjacent pueblos and provinces. From the town proper the lyrical discussion migrated to the outlying *barrios,* and thence, by a bound, it would translate itself to the rustic hut and from it to the shelter of the herder tending the cattle.

And, of course, during the three centuries that the Latin-Spanish culture had for diffusing itself, however slowly the process took place, that culture was bound to become thoroughly diffused and to germinate and bear rich fruit for the sons of the Archipelago of Legaspi. This culture was not due to books, to the press, to clubs, to schools, to lectures, but a special atmosphere, like the special atmosphere and sky of Holland, which shaped a Rembrandt, a Potter, in short, what is known as the Flemish School. It stimulated the natural genius, the natural sagacity of the Filipino, helping him along on the rough path of theological, philosophical, and juridical studies, and created and fortified the unity of ideas and sentiments of the Filipino people, infusing it with the critical spirit that distinguishes it and which, though perhaps confined within narrow bounds before the revolution, was nevertheless sufficiently formidable to confound the adversary with his own arguments. It did not produce writers in abundance during the time when political conditions prevented it, but it brought forth subtle improvisators, ingenious conversationalists, and that exquisiteness in social intercourse which brightens and cheers life and is so highly spoken of by the foreigner who has had an opportunity to become more closely acquainted with it.

By a happy combination of circumstances and qualities, innate as well as acquired, the Filipino has become like the Italian and southern Frenchman, whom Taine describes as "si sobres, si prompts d'esprit, qui, naturellement, savent parler, causer, mimer leur pensée, avoir du goût, atteindre à l'élégance, et sans effort, comme le Provençaux du XII siècle et les Florentins du XIV, se trouvent cultivés, civilisés, achevés du premier coup."

Now, just throw a people with these qualities into the arms of a movement like the French Revolution, so that, touched by the dew, sun and soil will enter upon feverish activity and productivity, without any impediment whatever, surrounded by a vivifying, favorable atmosphere in which the materials and the current of ideas serve as stimulant and divine nourishment to the creative power, and you will find them capable of conquering new worlds.

Indeed, the beautiful gems of Cecilio Apostol, Fernando Ma. Guerrereo, José Palma, Clemente J. Zulueta, Honorio Valenzuela, and others, belong to that historical period of 1895–1900, unequaled in the annals of the Philippine Islands in freshness, passion, and spontaneousness, all essential qualities in every art, but principally in poetry.

Long before the atmosphere had begun to be favorable to individual inspiration, these poets had had a certain technical skill in their art, a certain mastery of the proper use of stops and shorts and of that rare manner of joining together words, phrases, and poetical periods, sometimes in a natural and at others in an artificial way. They were masters of a more or less rich poetical dialect—in other words, they were poets of measure and number.

Thus Zuleta's *Afectos a la Virgen,* a tropical flower that was awarded a silver lily by the Academia Bibliografico-Mariana of Lerida, Spain, dates of 1895; *El Kundiman,* by J. Palma, a savory fruit of the native orchard fertilized with the soil of the garden of Rueda, of 1895; Guerrero's inspired "Mi Patria," which first saw light in *La Independencia* in 1898, was written in 1897. Many compositions, for instance

Apostol's, written prior to 1898, would lose nothing by a comparison with other poems of his of a later date, except with that dedicated to *Los martires anonimos de la Patria* and *La Siesta* (1898) which, though they remind one of *El nido de condores,* by the Argentine poet Andrade, and of Nuñez de Arce's *Idilio,* are not only the best in Apostol's repertoire and would grace any anthology, but are superior to the poems of the poets cited by us, because of the lyrical impetuousness and the coloring of the tropical landscape which these lack. They held, besides, periodical *tertulias* (evening parties), modest academies where everything was read, discussed, and commented upon disinterestedly, and in which Jaime C. de Veyra, Zulueta, and Macario Adriatico began to show their critical gifts.

The revolutionary time was for the Filipinos what the Elizabethan era was for the English. The difference, aside from the natural and circumstancial differences, which need no explanation, is that a large part of what was sown, grown, and harvested during the revolution remained in the fields of labor, as there was a lack of time for gathering all the grain. This grain, however, is not of the kind that will rot in the field, but it may become lost, and for this reason it has since 1900 been hurriedly gathered and polished in order to enhance its value. Seed of another kind, brought to us from America, has also been cast into the furrow and has taken root. It is hoped that the buds which are already beginning to show will soon ripen into fruit.

Much has been done; much headway has been made. However, Spaniards, Filipinos, and Americans must bear in mind that the work was and will be everybody's. Nobody is entitled to claim the exclusive privilege. All must cooperate in the work already begun and labor without cessation, with the eyes turned toward that celestial city of which Goethe speaks, because what has been done is very little compared with what still remains to be accomplished:

> Das wenige verschwindet leicht dem Blicke
> Der Vorwärts sieht, wie viel noch übrig
> bleibt.

And with the good wishes of your devoted servant and colleague in letters, "ingatan po cayo nang Dios at ni Guinoong Santa Maria." ("May God and the Virgin Mary protect you"), as the pious Modesto de Castro would have said.

[This essay, a translation from the Spanish original, first appeared as "Short History of Tagalog literature" in M.M. Norton, ed., *Builders of a Nation,* Manila, 1914.]

Appendix II

Balagtás: A Voice in the Wilderness

BY TEODORO AGONCILLO

No Filipino writer within memory has been so profusely praised and so roundly abused as Francisco Baltazár. Some Tagalog writers, more enthusiastic than discriminating, compare the Filipino bard to Chaucer, Tennyson, Goethe, and even Shakespeare. On the other extreme are those who, not having read Baltazár's *Florante at Laura,* console themselves by spending their leisure denouncing the work as a "glorified *corrido*," a literary trash as impossible as it is bizarre. Perhaps one can learn from the errors of these two extremes and strike a note that will respond to the music that Baltazár himself had composed for his time and place. Baltazár exploited his raw material to express, through the written symbols, his reaction to a regime shot through with injustice, hypocrisy, and intolerance.

Francisco Baltazár, popularly known as Balagtás, lived in an age in which freedom, at least for the Filipinos, was a fiction not even to be read or dreamed about, nor yet to be hoped for, but to be shunned as a leprous idea. It was an age of innocence beneath which lurked the ugly monster of ignorance. The writers of the period, hampered and restricted within a narrow tradition with a predominantly religious background, satisfied their urge for creative expression by putting out works that only served to deepen and broaden what the learned Dr. Trinidad H. Pardo de Tavera contemptuously called "the heritage of ignorance." The whole period of Filipino literature under Spain may be characterized as the period of medieval romances and religious plays.

The pre-Spanish plays—or what passed for plays—the *karagatan* and the *tibaw,* were transformed by the early Spaniards into the *duplo,* which, during the American occupation, was infused with a new element to become the *balagtasan,* a word coined after the name of the poet, Balagtás. The religious zeal of the early Spanish missionaries which culminated in the destruction of practically all written Filipino records of pagan provenance bore fruit in the introduction into the

Philippines of the *cenaculo,* a sort of religious play depicting the passion and death of the Lord Jesus, and, more important, in the translation into the Philippine languages of the Christian prayers and the metrical romances of medieval Europe. The discarded literary types of Europe continued to trickle into the Philippines, and so the *comedia de capa y espada* (cloak-and-dagger play) took firm root on Philippine soil. This *comedia,* now transplanted, was engrafted into an ancient Filipino play and produced a hybrid form, the *moro-moro.* The latter, originally an Oriental play or dance characterized by a superabundant display of jerky bodily movements, took on a new form and content under the Spaniards and thus became, with the infusion of the religious sentiment, tone, and color, a melodrama of combat between the Christians and the Moors—with the latter invariably at the receiving end.

Meanwhile, the metrical romances were also introduced into the Philippines, and their development, under the new climate, was directed like the drama, by the religious. Adapted to Filipino airs, the Philippine metrical romances branched off into two categories: the one named after an ancient Filipino song, the *awit,* and the other named after an old Spanish ballad, the *corrido.* Generally, the former was heroic, in dodecasyllables, the latter legendary-religious, in octosyllables. Yet, even in the heroic verse the religious tone and atmosphere predominated, for the clerics, exercising the function of censors even before the actual establishment of the Board of Censors in 1856, brooked no departure from the established order. Consequently, the Filipino creative writers sheepishly "toed the line" and wrote according to the accepted mores of the period. Hence the thousands of literary-religious works which tended, in one direction, to instill the fear of God in the Filipinos, and in another, to constrict their thoughts into a narrow channel.

But just as the epoch produced "polite writers," so, on the other hand, it gave to the Philippines the first creative critic of the manners and morals of the period that gave him birth. Francisco Baltazár (1788–1862) witnessed with discreet silence the intolerable condition of Philippine society at a time in Europe when revolutions were rocking the throne of monarchy and social order was undergoing a vital transformation. While at the Colegio de San José, he fell under the influence of the learned Filipino cleric, the Reverend Mariano Pilapil. By this time he had already read much and had written some facile verses. His poverty led him to exploit his poetic gifts: he commercialized his talent and turned ghostwriter for the dull students of San José and the San Juan de Letran College. Learned not only in his native tongue, but also in Spanish and Latin, his fame as a versifier spread far into the districts of Binondo, San Nicolas, and Tondo. About 1836, he moved to Pandakan. Here he met the comely Maria Asunción Rivera, with whom he fell in love. The intrigues of his rival led to his imprisonment.

Perhaps it was this searing experience which shocked him into a realization of the grave injustice that characterized the period. It sharpened his social consciousness and gave him the material for a work that would embody his longings, and those of his people, time and place. He worked passionately, to epitomize in verse form the mute cries of his sensitive soul which was crying for justice and freedom. The epoch, it must be noted, was contemporaneous with the Middle Ages in Europe and hence fertile for the metrical romance and the allegory. Balagtás, learned in medieval lore, found the art of dissimulation a convenient vehicle to achieve his purpose. Hence the allegorical *Plorante at Laura,* an *awit* intended to be sung, which came off the University of Santo Tomas Press in 1838.

The story opens in a gloomy wilderness. We see the young Plorante, struggling to free himself where he is tied to a tree, lamenting his fate and invoking Heaven to right the wrongs done to him by his enemy, Count Adolfo. He remembers the days when Laura was his beloved. He falls into a swoon. At almost the same time a Moorish prince, Aladin, enters the forest and, finding Plorante about to be devoured by hungry lions, kills the beasts and sets the young man free. The latter comes to and tells the story of his life.

He was the son of Duke Briseo, the adviser of King Linceo of Albania. At an early age his father sent him to Athens to study. Here he became the idol of all his classmates except Count Adolfo who harbored ill feelings against him. Staging Aeschylus's *Seven Against Thebes,* Count Adolfo actually slashed at Plorante with his sword. Menandro saved Plorante from death. Upon his return to his country, he was commissioned by King Linceo to lead the Albanian forces against the Persians who were besieging the kingdom of Crotona. While plotting his strategy with the king and his father, Plorante met Princess Laura, the king's daughter, with whom he fell in love.

Plorante was victorious over the Persian invaders. Learning of another Persian horde that was attacking Albania, Plorante returned to his country and routed the Persians. Now he took the offensive against the infidels, and seventeen kingdoms fell into his hands. In the midst of the campaign against Etolia, he received a letter from

King Linceo asking him to return to Albania posthaste. Leaving his army to Menandro, Plorante returned to Albania only to find his father and the king murdered in cold blood by Count Adolfo, who had usurped the throne. Adolfo had him arrested and tied to a tree in the wilderness. The usurper also announced that Laura had already accepted his love.

Upon the conclusion of Plorante's story, Aladin introduced himself as the very Persian prince Plorante spoke of. Returning to Persia after the Albanian campaigns, he found himself condemned to death by his father, Sultan Ali Adab, apparently because of his defeat in Albania. The death sentence was changed to life imprisonment upon the promise of Flerida, Aladin's betrothed, to accept the sultan's love. Flerida, however, escaped and wandered in the forest of Albania. Learning of Flerida's escape, Aladin, too, escaped from Persia and journeyed far and wide in search of his loved one. It was during his search for Flerida that he chanced upon Plorante.

The two have just concluded their stories when they hear voices drifting their way. The voices are those of Laura and Flerida. Laura tells the story of how Flerida saved her from Count Adolfo who fled to the forest when Menandro arrived from Etolia. Adolfo tried to dishonor Laura, but Flerida, who had lost herself in the forest after her escape from the sultan, shot Adolfo with an arrow.

At this moment, Menandro and his army arrive. The two couples are brought to Albania. Plorante is proclaimed king, and Flerida and Aladin are baptized. Not long after, Sultan Ali Adab dies, and Aladin ascends the throne of Persia.

If *Plorante at Laura* has led some people to believe it is impossible and chimerical, it is because Balagtás made use of symbolism to veil his real purpose and intent. Thus, he succeeded in criticizing the hypocrisy, the immorality, the injustice and degradation of those that had made society destitute and without hope. In the guise of Plorante, bound to a tree, Balagtás voiced his bitterness and his criticism of the social evils of his time:

> There, hapless land! and even 'yond,
> Treason has flung his tyrant bond;
> Virtue the while lies moribund,
> Stifled in sloughs of deep despond.
>
> All noble deeds are hurled amain
> Amidst indignity and disdain!

> The wise, when to the gravehole ta'en,
> Must coffinless therein remain;
>
> Whereas the wicked and the mean
> On thrones of honor sit serene
> And before those of bestial mien,
> Incense is burnt, sweet-scented, clean.
>
> Wickedness struts by, proud and sleek;
> Virtue moves on, forlorn and meek;
> Reason impotent lies, so weak,
> She merely weeps, nor wipes her cheek.
>
> What lips yet venture to uphold
> The cause of Truth, of Wisdom bold,
> Straightway are struck, and stricken cold,
> By swords that reap death in their fold.

The bluntness of the criticism, cushioned by the allegorical nature of the poem, was not immediately felt, for the Spanish authorities were enthralled by the more obvious import of the narrative. It was enough to them that the finale, in a manner of speaking, was attuned to the best interest of the state religion, and the external message in keeping with the hoary tradition of the age—tradition, that is, of upholding Christendom, rightly or wrongly, to the discomfiture of the barbarous heathens. Nothing gave them more narcissistic gratification than to see their images reflected in the *awit,* unaware that Balagtás, while projecting the obvious to hide his inner message, had in fact exposed them and ridiculed their pretensions to superiority.

What more pungent, though indirect, criticism of the parochial mind and the religious hypocrite than the words he put in the lips of Aladin who, after nurturing Plorante back to consciousness, spoke in this wise:

> If on my lap, most loath art thou,
> Noxious the creed that I avow,
> I feel it mean to disallow
> All help to thee, ill fated now.
>
> Myself a Persian, I cognize
> You are Albanian, from your guise—

> In faith, my foe; in race, likewise;
> But common fate weaves friendly ties.

> This breast may be a Moor's indeed,
> But subject still to Heaven's creed;
> And in my heart, its Law I read:
> Commiserate with those in need.

The Moorish prince's oblique rebuke of Plorante who, as a Christian of his time, shunned those who did not belong to the faith of his fathers, was in reality Balagtás's plea for religious tolerance. The piecing together of the incidents in the *awit,* told in almost faultless verse, deliberately emasculated in order to dissimulate his hidden thoughts on the social, moral, and religious problems of his day, is masterly and testifies to the creative power of the bard whose awareness of the evils around him had led him to use the power of the written word to reform society. He was thus not only the interpreter of his age but also the first critic of a regime that, originally intended to be humanely paternalistic, had degenerated into despotism. Not the least significant because it touches, though tangentially, the problem of worship, is the connotative meaning of Aladin's words. Spoken with compassion and understanding of Plorante's mental state, they represent a valid plea for a universal faith not ruled by prejudice and bigotry but by a feeling akin to the divine. Balagtás, one might say, was a "freethinker" in an age of conformity.

There are sparks of folk wisdom in *Plorante at Laura* sufficiently recognizable and potent to illuminate the dimly lighted mind of the humble folks. Thanks to the friars who discouraged the teaching of Spanish to the multitude, the simple-minded masses turned to their native languages and so became the important factor in the survival of their speech forms. And Balagtás's *awit,* written in the language of the layman, fired the imagination of the common people and gave them something to think about. These little gems in the *awit* sank into their consciousness and became, in time, a part of their folk wisdom.

> I took your word, not once surmising
> That looks deceive which are enticing.

This holds more truth than the famous Shakespearean "Love is blind":

> O Love! Thou all-omnipotent one,
> Who sporteth ev'n with sire and son;

> Once sworn to thee, a heart then on
> Defies all else: thy will be done.

Homilies, imparted with the common touch, became the favorite quotations even of writers like Rizal:

> Love doth reveal to me it is
> Wrong to bring up a child in bliss;
> If happiness be always his,
> In age true comfort will he miss.

> Who grows in ease is often bare
> Of virtue, sense, and judgment fair—
> Sour fruit of misdirected care—
> His loving parents' deep despair.

The bard's unhappy experience in his courtship and the deceit and treachery that were common in society made him see life through the glass, darkly:

> If upon meeting you, he shows
> A beaming face, whence friendship flows,
> The more beware! Beneath the pose,
> Time might his enmity disclose.

And to those who, basking in superficial glory, think only of their fleeting present, Balagtás has these succinct reminders:

> As high the heights one doth attain,
> So low the downward fall again.
> For each one joy, a chain there is
> Of grief for man, till death be his.

Balagtás saw clearly the reason for the sad state of affairs in his country and told the people that they deserved their unscrupulous rulers:

> A king with grasping, greedy hand
> Is Heaven's scourge upon the land!

One pauses reading these lines, and smiles inwardly as one takes stock of one's age. How much truth there is in those lines and how contemporaneous they are! For Balagtás not only lived in and spoke for his age but for all epochs. He was the first truly modern Filipino in a medieval society who sought, through literature, the reforms necessary to make society a worthy place to live in and to die for. He was neither an escapist nor an ivory towerist who would create of beauty nothing but a sheer "joy forever." He was a poet who knew the true writer's function: to interpret life with the temperament of the artist and to bring his art to bear upon the social milieu. This, Balagtás knew, was the responsibility of the writer to society.

Balagtás was not a great poet, but he was a significant one. As the spokesman of the dumb majority in an age that did not know freedom, he evoked a resounding echo in the novels of José Rizal who, leaving the Philippines in 1882, brought with him a later edition (1870) of the *awit* and incorporated in his *Noli* some passages from the work of the Bard of Panginay. The poet's love of freedom is more openly expressed in his *Mahomet at Constanza,* a less known *comedia* based on the Greek struggle for emancipation. So "seditious" was the play that Balagtás, fearing for his safety, never allowed its presentation during his lifetime. Balagtás may be regarded as the precursor of the Propaganda Movement (1882–96) which culminated in the armed struggle for freedom and independence. Then, the medieval period in Philippine history was abruptly terminated by Commodore George Dewey's naval guns. The long night was over.

Balagtás is a Filipino classic in the sense that he still speaks to us through the voice of experience mellowed by folk wisdom. He will always be contemporaneous with all ages so long as social evils exist and so long as human nature remains the same. Well may we think of him as one of those who, in the words of Sainte-Beuve, "know all that we know, and we have found nothing new by bringing experience up to date."

[This essay first appeared in *The Philippine Quarterly*, June 1952, pp. 20–23.]

Notes

1. A comparative study of the languages of Malaysia and the Philippines shows that many words from their vocabularies have the same or similar meanings and so points to the conclusion that they belong to one parent stock. To my knowledge, the first linguistic scholar to use the term Malay-Polynesian and to classify the languages of Malaysia and the Philippines as agglutinative languages was Wihelm von Humboldt in his work *Über die Kawi-Sprache auf der Insel Java*... (Berlin, 1836–39), 3 vols. Renward Brandstetter, perhaps the foremost authority on Austronesian linguistics, in his *An Introduction to Indonesian Linguistics* (translated by C. O. Blagden, London, 1916), reconstructed what he termed original Indonesian roots. Otto Dempwolff, in his monumental *Vergleichende Lautlehre des Austronesischen Wortschatzes* (Hamburg, 1934–38), followed similar lines. Brandstetter also formulated what he termed "laws" governing the phonetic peculiarities of the languages of Malaysia and the Philippines, for example, the Hamzah law, the Pepet law, the R-law, the law of length, and the law of brevity. I should like to express here the opinion that both Brandstetter and Dempwolff had no sound basis for their so-called reconstruction of the original Indonesian or Austronesian roots. In the absence of sufficient proofs to fortify their claim, I prefer to call those roots Old or Primitive Indonesian or Austronesian. Again, it seems to me that "laws" have been labeled indiscriminately to certain phonetic characteristics, forgetting—or ignoring—that these so-called laws, whether in the Germanic or in the Austronesian languages, admit of many exceptions. These so-called laws, I believe, should be changed to sound shifts, for example, the R-G-H law to R-G-H sound shift, R-D-L law to R-D-L sound shift, etc.

For comparative purposes, the following books are of great help: Juan de Noceda and Pedro de Sanlucar, *Vocabulario de la Lengua Tagala,* 2nd ed., Manila, 1860; Andrés Carro, *Vocabulario Iloco-Español,* Manila, 1854; Juan Felix de la Encarnación. *Diccionario Bisaya-Espagñol,* 3rd ed., Manila, 1885; Diego Bergaño, *Vocabulario de la Lengua Pampanga,* Manila, 1860; J. C. G. Jonker, *Rottineesch-Nederlandsch Woordenboek,* Leiden, 1908; H. N. van Hazeu, *Gajosch-Nederlandsch Woordenboek,* Batavia, 1907; H. N. van der Tuuk, *Bataksch-Nederduitsch Woordenboek,* Amsterdam, 1861; H. N. van der Tuuk, *Kawi-Balineesch-Nederlandsch Woordenboek,* 's-Gravenhage, 1897; Aug. Hardeland, *Dajacksch-Deutsches Worterbuch*, Amsterdam, 1861.

2. Pedro Chirino, *Relación de las Islas Filipinas*, Rome, 1604; 2nd ed.: Manila, Imp. de Esteban Balbas, 1890, p. 52.

3. *Ibid.*, Chapter XV. Other descriptions of the Old Tagalog script may be found in Francisco Colin's *Labor Evangélica*, Madrid, 1663; Pastells's edition: Barcelona, 1900–1902 and Antonio de Morga's *Sucesos de las Islas Filipinas*, Mexico, 1609; Retana's edition: Madrid, 1909.

4. Many studies have been written about the ancient Filipino syllabaries, but the most important are Cipriano Marcilla's *Estudios de los Antiguos Alfabetos Filipinos*, Malabon, Tipo-Litografía del Asilo de Huérfanos, 1894; Trinidad H. Pardo de Tavera's *Consideración para el Estudio de los Antiguos Alfabetos Filipinos*, Losana, Imprenta de Jaunin Hermanos, 1884; and Ignacio Villamor's *La Antigua Escritura Filipina*, Manila, Tip, Pontificia del Colegio de Santo Tomás, 1922. Chirino believed that the Tagalogs wrote from top to bottom and from left to right, while Colin surmised that the direction was from bottom upward and from left to right. Morga, however, thought that the direction was from right to left. On the other hand, the Spanish scholar Sinibaldo de Mas (*Informe Sobre el Estado de Filipinas en 1842*, Madrid, 1843, Vol. I), Pardo de Tavera, and Marcilla thought that the direction was as it is today—horizontally from left to right. I share Chirino's conclusion.

5. Chirino relates how the early missionaries, including himself, destroyed about three hundred Tagalog manuscripts in the town of Balayan, Batangas.

6. W. E. Retana, *Orígenes de la Imprenta Filipina*, Madrid, Librería General de Victoriano Suarez, 1911, p. 67. See also the same author's *La Imprenta en Filipinas* (1593–1810). Madrid, Imprenta de la Viuda de M. Minuesa de los Ríos, col. 9 and 19; and Fr. Angel Perez and Fr. Cecelio Guemes, *Adiciones y Continuación de La Imprenta en Manila de D. J. T. Medina*, Manila, Imprenta de Santos y Bernal, 1904, XXV *et seq.*

7. A short description of the outdoor theater of the Filipinos during the Spanish regime may be found in W. Gifford Palgrave's *Country Life in the Philippines Fifty Years Ago*, London, 1887; reprinted in Manila, National Book Company, 1929, pp. 69 *et seq.*

8. W. E. Retana, *El Teatro en Filipinas*, Madrid, Librería General de Victoriano Suarez, 1910, pp. 62 *et seq., passim.* Retana's monograph deals mainly with the Spanish theater in the Philippines and omits the Tagalog theater. A brief description of the Tagalog *comedias* and theater may be found in Father Joaquín Martinez de Zúñiga's *Estadismo de las Islas Filipinas*, Retana's edition, Madrid, Imprenta de la Viuda de M. Minuesa de los Ríos, 1893, Vol. I, Chap. III, pp. 59 *et seq.* A vituperative work allegedly on the Tagalog theater—which, unfortunately, does not discuss the Tagalog theater but merely lambasts it—may be found in Vicente Barrantes's *El Teatro Tagalo*, Madrid 1889. José Rizal, reading this illiterate work, wrote a satirical rejoinder, in epistolary form, entitled *Barrantes y el Teatro Tagalo*, which was published in *La Solidaridad*, June 15 and 30, 1889. Incomplete and rather superficial treat-

ment of the Tagalog *karagatan, duplo,* and *awit* is found in Epifanio de los Santos's *El Teatro Tagalo,* published in *Cultura Filipina,* Vol. II, No. 1, April, 1911. The late Ignacio Manlapaz, using Epifanio de los Santos's article, wrote, a la Mencken, his "Filipino Drama: A Sketch," published in *Philippine Magazine,* Vol. XXVIII, No. 6, November, 1931. Other articles on the Filipino theater, more or less critical but not factual or historical, are Felipe G. Calderon's "*El Teatro Tagalog,*" in *El Renacimiento,* Vol. II, No. 347, November 4, 1902; and José Ma. Romero Salas's "*El Teatro en Filipinas,*" in *Cultura Filipina,* Vol. II, No. 9, December, 1911. A factual report on some dramatists and dramas of the early years of the American occupation is found in Raymundo C. Bañas's *The Music and Theater of the Filipino People,* Manila, 1924. The author is short on the drama, but long on the music of the Filipinos, which is his forte.

9. Retana, *El Teatro en Filipinas,* p. 155.

10. Henry Thomas Buckle, *History of Civilization in England,* New York, Hearst's International Library Co., 1913, Vol. II, Part I, pp. 34 *et seq., passim.* See also J. B. Trend, *The Civilization of Spain,* Oxford University Press, 1944, Chap. VI. The great Spanish historian, Rafael Altamira, avoided mentioning the brutal expulsion of the Moriscos and contented himself with mentioning, in passing, the dire effects of the expulsion on the Spanish economy, cf. *A History of Spain,* New York, D. Van Nostrand Company Inc., 1949.

11. W. E. Retana, *La Censura de Imprenta en Filipinas.* Madrid, Librería General de Victoriano Suarez, 1908, p. 3.

12. A. S. Riggs, "Seditious Drama in the Philippines," in *Current History,* Vol. XX, No. 116, April, 1951. The article as a whole is biased, uninformed, and badly written. Its only saving grace is its mention of some of the "seditious" plays written during the first five years of the American rule in the Philippines.

13. For other dramatic societies and the list of actors and actresses, *vide* José Ma. Rivera, "*Ang Kahapon at Ngayón ng Dulang Tagalog,*" in *Taliba,* June 13 and 20, 1925.

14. The Dramatic Philippines, composed mostly of graduates of the Ateneo de Manila—such as Narciso Pimentel, Jr., Alberto Cancio, Francisco Rodrígo, Jesús Paredes, Jr., Horacio Tagle, and others—was founded in 1943. The society staged Tagalog translations or adaptations of plays in English for example, *Passion Play, Applesauce, Seven Keys to Baldpate, Cyrano de Bergerac, The Husband of Mrs. Cruz, Julius Caesar,* and *Golden Boy.*

15. July, 1952.

16. Published daily in *Muling Pagsilang* from June 10, 1905 to August 31, 1906. It was later published in book form by the McCullough Press, 1906.

17. Teodoro A. Agoncillo, "*Ang Maikling Kuwentong Tagalog: Pasulyáp na Tingín sa mga Tao at Kilusán*" (being a historico-critical study of the Tagalog short story) in the author's *Ang Maikling Kuwentong Tagalog: 1886–1948,* Manila, Ináng Wikà Publishing Co., 1949, vi–xlvi.

Glossary

abá: an exclamation indicating surprise, admiration, wonder, etc.
abilidad: cleverness; phenomenal shrewdness especially in business affairs.
alagaw: a kind of medicinal plant.
Apò: term used as sign of respect and reverence for the aged; *apó: grandchild.*
atis: a tree that bears aromatic, very sweet fruits (*Anona squamosa,* L.).
Ave Maria Purissima: (Spanish loan phrase) O Mary Most Pure, usually uttered in surprise, fright, or sometimes in jests.

balato (from Spanish, *barato*): money given away by winning gamblers.
balut: boiled duck's egg with grown-up embryo; a native delicacy, extremely nourishing.
barong Malabon: long-sleeved shirt, a national costume, made of native cloth —either *piña, rami,* or other fibers—tailored in Malabon.
barrio: a district of a provincial town.
batalan: bamboo platform at the rear of the house which serves at the same time as kitchen, bathroom, washroom, etc., found in provincial houses.
bayong: a cylindrical sack about a meter high made of woven buri palm.
Bonifacio, Andres (1863–97): the popular organizer and leader of the proletarian revolution against Spain. He founded the *Katipunan,* League of the Sons of the People, which began the armed struggle in 1896 and became the driving force of the revolution. Fearful of the peasant forces gathered around the *Katipunan* banner, the Aguinaldo clique had Bonifacio executed.

cabesa: town chief, from the Spanish designation for the heads of the tribe-unit of the early Filipinos, the *barangay.*
calamansi: tree bearing acidic fruits (*Citrus mitis,* L.).
calesa: two-wheeled horse-drawn rig.
camotes: sweet potato (*Ipomoea batates,* L.).
carabao: water buffalo (*Bubalus buffalus,* L.).
chico: a sweet dark-brown fleshy fruit in the Philippines.

delicado: fastidious, finicky; discriminating.
Doña (Spanish loan word): Lady, Mrs.

duhat: a species of blackberries.

dulang: low dining table at which one squats on the floor to take his meal.

El Filibusterismo: a book published in Ghent, Belgium, sequel to *Noli Me Tangere* (Berlin, 1887), both written by José Rizal in order to expose and attack in satirical, realistic fashion the corruptions and abuses of the Spanish colonial system.

Plorante and Laura (1853): an *awit* or versified romance by Francisco Baltazar (1788–1862), otherwise known as Balagtás, the "prince of Tagalog poets." This work is considered as the greatest Tagalog poem ever written. Its romantic plot is in fact an allegory of the bleak Philippine condition throughout the Spanish regime.

ha?: okay?

hane?: mild coaxing tag after requests or commands; understand? all right?

hijo: son.

hoy, tsiko: a call in comradely, often bantering, terms.

Ilocos: northwestern coastal regions of Luzon, the largest island of the Philippines.

impong: grandmother.

inunan: placenta.

kakawate: a common shady tree in the Philippines (*Gliricida maculata,* L.).

kamagong: a tree with reddish sapwood and black or streaky heartwood.

kamatsile: tropical fruit with bland taste.

kapitan: captain, customary title for the town chief or *barrio* lieutenant, not necessarily connected with a military career.

karitela: native two-wheeled vehicle drawn by a horse, usually used for transport of goods; whereas the *calesa* is often used for passengers.

Katipunan: secret subversive league organized by Bonifacio and his compatriots to unite the Filipinos against Spanish tyranny.

kimona: a woman's loose dress with short wide sleeves.

kumare: the parents' term for the godmother of their child; the godmother's term for the parents of the child.

kutsero: rig driver.

kuya: term for eldest brother.

lolo, lola ('la): grandfather, grandmother, respectively.

laki sa nuno: popular expression meaning, literally, "reared by grandparents." Idiomatic meaning is "pampered grandchild."

Mabuhay, Herald, Foto News: Manila newspapers before the war.

mama: general appellation for man.

Maria Santissima: Mary Most Holy; exclamation of surprise, awe, etc.
merienda: light repast, usually in between lunch and supper.
Mindanao: the second biggest island of the Philippines, located in the southern-most part.
municipio: center of provincial town.

naku!: interjection conveying surprise, pain, wonder, etc.
nana, tata: familiar terms for mother and father, respectively.
novena: nine days' devotion and worship for a saint.
'Nyora (contraction of Señora): Mrs.

palay: rice plant; unhusked rice grain.
presidente: president, loosely used for any high official.
puto: a kind of native rice cake.

Rizal, Dr. José (1861–96): the national hero, great patriot and martyr, inter-nationally recognized as a genius and a Renaissance man who symbolizes the Malayan potentialities for self-development. Son of tenants on estates owned by the Church, he was educated in Catholic universities in Manila, and after study in Europe became an optical surgeon of note. In Europe, he joined with exiled Filipinos to denounce the tyranny of Spanish rule. His novels on the evils of the friar tenant system, such as *Noli Me Tangere,* had a profound influence on the independence movement. In 1892, he returned to his native land to form the *Liga Filipina* to petition for reforms. Forced to leave again, he was lured back to the islands on promises by the Spaniards that he would be unmolested, but he was arrested, and after a farcical trial was executed by a firing squad. His martyrdom touched off the revolt against Spain.

sago: a species of palm out of which fermented sap, starch, etc., are made.
Señorita: Miss, Lady.
sapang-putol: literally, "cut brook"; a stream whose route of flow has been suddenly aborted.
santol: a species of tree-bearing edible fruits (*Sandoricum indicum,* L.).
sari-sari: diverse, various; a type of "general merchandise store" where a potpourri of goods are sold.
sawali: interwoven splits of flattened bamboo used for walling, etc.
sitsaron: fried bacon rinds, a native delicacy.

Tandang: old
Tibag: eroded. It may also refer to the hill in which the Cross is supposed to be buried; the term "Tibag" refers to the hill that marks the end of the May procession.
The Twelve Peers (written circa 1750): a popular romance in verse narrating the fate of Charlemagne's twelve knights in their fight against the Saracens

in medieval Europe; probably adapted from a Spanish version, *Doce Pares*.

tse!: interjection signifying disapproval, usually accompanied with a tone of haughty contempt.

tio, tia (tiyo, tiya): uncle, aunt, respectively.

Tutuban Station: the central railroad station in Manila.

upo: a species of large tendril-bearing climber cultivated for its large edible club-shaped fruit; white gourd.

Visayas: the group of islands between Luzon and Mindanao, comprising Panay, Negros, Samar, Leyte, etc.